PERSONAL COMPUTING
DEMYSTIFIED

PERSONAL COMPUTING DEMYSTIFIED

LARRY LONG

McGraw-Hill/Osborne

New York   Chicago   San Francisco   Lisbon   London
Madrid   Mexico City   Milan   New Delhi   San Juan
Seoul   Singapore   Sydney   Toronto

McGraw-Hill/Osborne
2100 Powell Street, 10th Floor
Emeryville, California 94608
U.S.A.

To arrange bulk purchase discounts for sales promotions, premiums, or fund-raisers, please contact **McGraw-Hill**/Osborne at the above address. For information on translations or book distributors outside the U.S.A., please see the International Contact Information page immediately following the index of this book.

Personal Computing Demystified

1234567890 CUS CUS 01987654

ISBN 0-07-225514-5

Publisher
Brandon A. Nordin

Vice President & Associate Publisher
Scott Rogers

Editorial Director
Wendy Rinaldi

Project Editor
Janet Walden

Acquisitions Coordinator
Athena Honore

Technical Editor
Craig Zacker

Copy Editor
William McManus

Proofreader
Karen Mead

Indexer
Nancy Long

Composition
Kelly Stanton-Scott, John Patrus

Illustrators
Kathleen Edwards, Melinda Lytle

Cover Series Design
Margaret Webster-Shapiro

Cover Illustration
Lance Lekander

This book was composed with Corel VENTURA™ Publisher.

To Jon and Phyllis Kennedy, my life-long friends

ABOUT THE AUTHOR

Dr. Larry Long began his personal computing adventure at the dawn of the personal computer era, when crude PCs cost as much as luxury automobiles. He wrote his first book on his first PC in 1978. Twenty five PCs and 50-plus books later, he is still writing computer books, which are widely distributed in many languages throughout the world. One of his books, *Computers: Information Technology in Perspective*, is now in its twelfth edition.

Larry's goal is same for every book: say something that will be of value to the reader and say it in an interesting, succinct, and easily understood manner. His words are crafted from many years of experience with both personal computers and the people who use them.

Larry has served as a strategic-level consultant in over 100 organizations in the United States and abroad. He was a pioneer in the development of computer-based multimedia and Internet-based educational resources. He has over two decades of experience as a professor at the University of Oklahoma and Lehigh University. Larry's Ph.D. is in Industrial Engineering from the University of Oklahoma.

Larry lives in Arkansas with his wife, Nancy, and teenage sons, Troy and Brady, where they enjoy exploring the great outdoors. Larry plays tournament tennis, coaches the high school tennis team, and is an NCAA tennis umpire.

CONTENTS AT A GLANCE

CONTENTS

PART SIX

AT HOME: NETWORKING AND TELECOMMUTING

CHAPTER 18

CONTENTS

ACKNOWLEDGMENTS

The book you hold is the culmination of the efforts of many talented people. My friends and colleagues at McGraw-Hill/Osborne did an amazing job blending my manuscript and rough art into a very effective book. These professionals should be very proud of *Personal Computing Demystified,* for it is their book, too.

Wendy Rinaldi, editorial director, demonstrated her in-depth knowledge of the field during insightful content discussions. Athena Honore, acquisitions coordinator, and Janet Walden, executive project editor, kept the project rolling at full steam in the right direction from start to finish. Craig Zacker, technical editor and author of numerous books, was a fountain of ideas. Bill McManus, copy editor, and Karen Mead, proofreader, smoothed out all the rough edges. In addition, I'm grateful to Osborne's production and illustration departments for their diligence in the production process.

I would like to thank my friends Jim Kelly, vice president eLearning, and Bob Woodbury, editor-in-chief, both of McGraw-Hill, for their confidence in me and for encouraging me to join the McGraw-Hill family of authors. Also, kudos to marketing manager LeeAnn Bezazian who provides that final element so important to a successful book—sales.

Special appreciation is in order for my teenage son, Troy, whose considerable knowledge and insight were invaluable during the writing of the gaming chapter. Finally, I am perpetually indebted to my wife and many-time coauthor, Nancy, for keeping me focused and for editing every word of the draft manuscript.

INTRODUCTION

Welcome to the personal computing adventure—and it *is* an adventure. You might be surprised to learn that few people, even the word wizards who write dictionaries and encyclopedias, attempt to define personal computing. It's one of the phrases we just accept, thinking it has something to do with personal computers (PCs). And, it does. But, personal computing also encompasses PC software, the Internet, and an endless number of activities and applications. Personal computing is more an experience than an activity and is best defined by your imagination and your will to explore.

Because personal computing has its own language and humbling array of capabilities, it has an air of mystique. The primary objective of this book is to clear the air and demystify personal computing. I do this by familiarizing you with its terminology and introducing you to its seemingly endless possibilities. A secondary objective is to set the stage for accelerated learning so that you can keep up with your curiosity as it continues to push your personal computing horizons. Once you get to that point, you had better hold on because personal computing can be quite a ride.

My personal computing adventure began when I purchased my first PC in 1978. By today's standards it was a minimal system with a couple of now-obsolete eight-inch floppy disks for storage of programs and data, a tiny hard-on-your-eyes black-and-white monitor, a six-minute-per-page text-only printer, and a very slow processor. For what I paid for that PC, $12,000, I could have purchased a shiny new 1978 BMW. Since then, I've upgraded to a new PC every year. My current PC is 100,000 faster than my first one, and what I paid for it would not even buy the onboard computer in a new BMW.

Today's personal computing technologies offer tremendous value, one of many good reasons why most homes in the United States have at least one PC. Surprisingly, however, a large number of people barely tap the potential of personal computing.

This book is designed for people who want to live the breadth and depth of the personal computing adventure, namely:

- People who are in the market for a personal computer, whether first timers or PC veterans.
- People who want to get the absolute most for their personal computing dollar.
- People who want to expand their personal computing horizons.
- People who want to explore the wonders of cyberspace—the Internet and beyond.
- People who would like to set up a home network and/or a home office.

What Can You Do with Personal Computing?

My family is typical of a family actively involved in personal computing. My wife, Nancy, and I have been doing personal computing since Jimmy Carter was president. Our teenage boys, Troy and Brady, have had their own PCs since preschool. The Long family PCs are networked so we can share files and other resources, such as Internet access and printers. The cost of these four systems is easily justified when you consider how integral they are to our lives.

My PC, a desktop, is the foundation tool for my work, but I use it for much more than work. I use it to maintain the family photo album, to design all kinds of things (for example, a two-car garage/shop, a minigolf course), to stay abreast of the technology, to check the weather, to send e-cards on birthdays and anniversaries, to maintain the rosters for my youth sports teams, to listen to 1960s folk music on Internet radio, to create legal documents, and much more. My wife prefers the mobility of a notebook PC. She uses it to help her handle the family and business finances, to keep the records for a Boy Scout troop, to shop the Internet, to communicate with family and friends around the world, to prepare the school newsletter, and many other tasks. Troy and Brady use their PCs as homework/research aids, to prepare in-class presentations, and, of course, for PC-based gaming. Educational software and the resources on the Internet have made a significant difference in their learning experiences. The boys' PCs are their companion assistants for so many activities, including music composition, creating custom audio CDs, video editing, making posters and banners, watching DVD movies, keeping up with their tennis tournaments and rankings, buying and selling items at online auctions, interacting with their friends via instant messaging, and much, much more. These PC activities are just the tip of the personal computing iceberg at the Long household—more on this later.

As you can see, personal computing is personal and, therefore, a unique experience for each of us. Personal computing has four elements: *you,* the *hardware,* the *software,* and the *Internet.* These elements are like LEGO™ or Tinkertoy™ pieces in that they comprise a box of interlocking parts of various shapes, sizes, and functions. You can use these parts to build your personal computing experience to become whatever you wish it to be. You can build an amazing productivity tool, an entertainment center, a communications center, an online business, a classroom without walls, an investment management system, a home security control center, a personal web site on the Internet—the possibilities boggle the imagination.

Our New Digital Lifestyle

We are witness to a remarkable transformation in our society. Look around you. For better or worse, we are adopting a digital lifestyle. Anything in the physical and communications world that can be represented as binary ones and zeros in a computer is a candidate for digital conversion. Even newscasters are being digitized. Ananova, a popular virtual news anchor on the Internet, reads the news in four different languages.

Digital convergence has made our world more integrated and accessible, but in so doing, it has made our world look very different. Electronic books (e-books), tiny MP3 players with thousands of songs, electronic mail (even via cell phones), instant messaging, digicams, wireless palm PCs, PC networks on-the-fly, and videoconferencing are not only part of a new technology lexicon, they are part of our lives, too. Personal computing is the glue for an emerging digital lifestyle that is changing the way we live, work, and play.

At home, personal computing allows us to browse the Internet for a good deal on a new car, order tickets to the theater, get the best mortgage rates, and prepare the family's annual holiday newsletter. In our new digital lifestyle, personal computing has emerged as one of the most popular leisure activities. It's not uncommon for people of all ages to spend many hours each week doing instant messaging, "chatting" with people from around the world, or playing the electronic versions of golf, tennis, football, or hockey. Virtual malls continue to expand in numbers and variety of products to accommodate the ever-growing legion of people who prefer the convenience of shopping in cyberspace. Shortly, we will be able to watch any movie, hear any song, or read any book—anytime or anywhere we have the urge to watch, listen, or read.

At work, personal computing has emerged as an essential office activity. PCs actually outnumber telephones in many companies. Videoconferencing via PCs is now a routine business activity. Mobile workers with their portable PCs can be on the job with access to corporate information wherever they may be. Personal computing is actually changing the demographic landscape as millions of people are choosing to live where they want and work at home via telework.

At school, the fastest-growing classroom is the one without walls. Students, teachers, and administrators have embraced personal computing because it offers self-paced, interactive courses that can link students, instructors, and Internet-based content. The largest university in the United States, University of Phoenix, has no classrooms.

The Elements of Personal Computing

Part of any demystification process is to break the topic down into its basic elements. As eluded to earlier, the elements of personal computing are you, the hardware, the software, and the Internet (see Figure I-1).

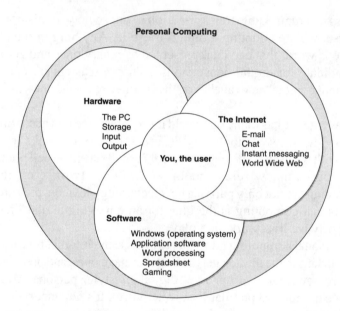

Figure I-1   The four elements of personal computing

You, the User

The most important element of personal computing is you, the user—the only nondigital element. After all, you put the "personal" in personal computing. It is your experiences, interests, and willingness to discover that add color and purpose to your personal computing sessions.

The Hardware

No matter where you go or which way you turn, you're going to see personal computers. PCs have only four basic hardware components:

- A *processor* to do the thinking
- *Input devices* that allow you to enter information into the system
- *Output devices* that present the results of processing to you
- *Storage devices* that allow permanent storage of digitized information

I use "information" in its broadest sense—that is, anything that can be entered into or extracted from a PC. Information can be textual material, data, still images, video images, audio, or anything else that can be digitized, such as sensor data from a home security system.

Personal computers come in a variety of shapes and sizes, including wearable PCs, handheld PCs, tablet PCs, notebook PCs, and desktop PCs. Our focus will be on the most popular and capable of the bunch, the desktop PC and notebook PC (see Figure I-2). Desktop PCs outsold notebook PCs until early in 2003. Now, notebook PCs (or laptop PCs) outsell desktop PCs. Modern notebook PCs offer desktop-level performance, so expect this trend to continue. We will always pay a premium for the portability of a notebook PC because it's simply more expensive to manufacture miniature components that are capable of withstanding mobile abuse. A variety of the input/output hardware devices can be attached to either of these types of PCs, including printers, scanners, digital video cameras, and others that will be introduced later in the book.

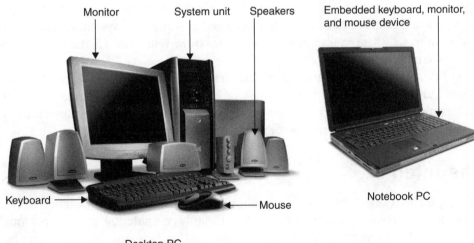

Figure I-2 Desktop PC and notebook PC

(Photos courtesy of Gateway, Inc.)

Hardware can be exceedingly complex, but unless you plan to build or repair hardware, you can bypass these complexities and go directly to personal computing.

You don't have to be a hardware wizard to be a sophisticated user, so our focus in this demystification process will be on the function and use of the various hardware devices.

An army of engineers and designers has worked tirelessly for 25 years to make hardware devices relatively easy to use. In honor of their efforts, I pledge to avoid unnecessary complexity in this book. After all, few of us understand our car's fuel injection system, but we know what happens when we push on the accelerator.

The Software

Software refers to a set of instructions, called programs, that tell your computer what to do. Programs allow you to do such activities as word processing, search the Internet, or participate in multiplayer games. All software activity revolves around the operating system program, usually a Microsoft Windows operating system, such as Windows XP. Earlier versions include Windows 95, 98, Me, NT, and 2000. With over 90 percent of all PCs running some version of Microsoft Windows, it's not surprising that Bill Gates has so many billions of dollars. There are other operating systems, such as those for the Apple line of computers, but our focus will be on Windows.

Windows and its graphical user interface (GUI) let us use a mouse to point and click our way around the desktop to open and close programs. Windows also manages computer resources, such as the processor and disk storage, to optimize system performance. Because of its overview function, the operating system is considered *system software.* The examples in the book are from Windows XP, the current version of Windows.

Application software refers to programs that address a particular user application. It's not unusual for four applications—word processing, e-mail, Internet browser, and gaming—to dominate a personal computing session. These four applications, however, represent less than 1 percent of available application software.

The Internet

During the first few decades of computing, computers operated in isolation of one another while spewing out reams of paper. Today's computers, including personal computers, have emerged as tools for communication between each other and between people. Most personal computers are linked to millions of computers via the *Internet,* also called the *Net.* The Internet is a worldwide collection of *inter*connected computer *net*works. The networks are in government agencies, commercial businesses, colleges, and every other type of organization. Literally billions of pages of information, images, songs, videos, and so on are readily accessible to anyone with a personal computer and Internet access.

Most people connect to the Internet via an Internet service provider (ISP). Internet access is a subscription service like telephone or cable TV service; in fact, most Internet access is delivered over telephone or cable TV lines.

Five Things to Remember about Personal Computing

Before you jump into Chapter 1, there are five things you should know about personal computing:

- *Hardware and software are relatively intuitive.* Hardware and software designers get lots of user feedback, much of which is unprintable, but the printable comment they hear most often is, "Make it easier to use." Although some may disagree, I sincerely believe that hardware and software companies have finally made user-friendliness a priority. Now, most PC products are relatively intuitive. For example, to grab images from a digital camera, simply plug it into the system unit and follow the on-screen directions.
- *Help is everywhere.* Eventually, you'll need help. Everyone does—even veteran power users. Even if you were able to learn every feature of every device or application, you would probably forget most of what you learned before you used it. Most of us learn the common features, and then we learn about features as we need them. Fortunately, help is readily available and easily accessible. All software packages offer a help feature that explains the function and use of every feature. At any time during a personal computing session, simply tap the F1 function key to get help, usually *context-sensitive help* (help about what you're doing at that time). Hardware manufacturers and software vendors frequently have online tutorials and helpful hints at their web sites.
- *PCs are amazingly durable.* One of the novice PC user's greatest fears is doing serious damage to an expensive PC. The reality is that you're not going to destroy anything, unless, of course, your frustration level drives you to whacking it with a sledgehammer (a recurring thought of veteran PC users). Under normal conditions and commonsense treatment, your PC will be obsolete before you face any serious hardware failures. The typical PC will work fine for a decade, but its useful life is only four to five years. PCs, especially notebooks, are designed with the assumption that they could be used in harsh conditions, even a kindergarten classroom.

- *Personal computing can be frustrating.* Just about everyone has heard PC horror stories or experienced them firsthand. Generally, stories about the dreaded blue screen and other horrific happenings are true, although some might embellish them a bit for effect. PCs just do things—strange and unexplainable things. You can solve most problems by restarting the system. These maddening moments are the price we pay to enjoy the wonders of personal computing.
- *Personal computing is fun and amazingly helpful.* Never forget that personal computing is and should be a lot of fun. Moreover, it can be incredibly helpful with so many of life's little chores.

Where to Begin

Chapter 1 is a good place to begin. However, feel free to jump directly into any chapter. The chapters are relatively independent, so you can hopscotch about the book depending on your specific information needs. Throughout the book, information is presented in small chunks to make it easy for you to skim content in search of specific material. If you read ahead and get hung up on a specific term, the index is always there to help you out.

This user-friendly book is a resource that can help you expand your personal computing horizons. It contains hundreds of experience-driven recommendations regarding personal computing capabilities and options. In addition, it has numerous tips that will help you save money and time, increase your productivity, have loads of fun, and make the absolute most of your personal computing adventure.

PART ONE

Personal
Computers

1

Processing Information: Inside the PC

You can live a long, fruitful life even if you don't know much about what happens inside your computer. However, if you want to be a savvy consumer of PC products and reach your personal computing potential, there are a few things you should know. Consider this excerpt from the "system requirements" printed on the box for Microsoft Office 2003:

- Pentium PC with Pentium 233 MHz or higher processor. Pentium III recommended.
- 128MB of RAM or above recommended.
- 400MB of available hard disk space.
- Super VGA (800×600) or higher resolution monitor.

If you don't understand what's on the box, you might have difficulty with what's in the box.

This chapter has more tech talk than any other chapter, but, trust me here—all of it is absolutely essential to demystifying personal computing. The personal computing world revolves around the personal computer, and to understand it, you will need a working knowledge of PC terminology and its parts. After reading these few pages, you'll be talking megahertz, DIMM slots, RAM, expansion cards, USB ports, AGP slots, motherboards, and so on. As you will soon see, the mysteries of the PC are not all that mysterious.

When talking about the inside of a PC, it's important to understand that each increment in speed and capacity will improve system performance, but it will cost extra. For each of us there is a trade-off between the level of system performance we want and what we are willing to spend. This chapter is about demystifying the guts of a PC so you can optimize performance and cost for your computing environment. If you get more PC than you need, you'll waste money and never use the excess capacity. If you purchase an overly slow system, the unnecessary wait periods can accumulate to an hour or two a day. That's as much as a workweek each month!

In this and the next three chapters, we'll look at the nuts and bolts of hardware, the things you need to know to become an informed consumer and an effective PC user. I offer specific suggestions on *what* to buy in Part Three, "Buying and Using a PC."

Going Digital: Bits and Bytes

That light switch on your wall is a good representation of the electronic nature of computers—*on* and *off*. Computers use these two digital states to represent letters, numbers, colors, sounds, images, shapes, and even odors—anything that can be digitized or converted to digital format. An "on" or "off" electronic state is represented by a *bit,* short for *binary digit.* In the binary numbering system (base 2), the *on bit* is a 1 and the *off bit* is a 0. That's why you see only 1's and 0's floating around computers in abstract technology images.

Computers don't actually store the color blue, the words "Beam me up," or a C chord on a piano. Everything entered into the computer, whether text, audio, graphics, or video, is converted to a combination of bits (1's and 0's) according to an *encoding system.* For example, *ANSI* (pronounced "AN-see") is a common 8-bit encoding system for converting text and special characters to the language of computers—1's and 0's. In ANSI, a string of eight 1's and 0's describes 256 (2^8) letters or characters. For example, an ANSI 01000011 represents a *C* inside a computer. ANSI evolved from its popular 7-bit cousin, *ASCII* ("AS-key").

The True Color 24-bit encoding system enables the display of 16,777,216 (2^{24}) different colors and brilliant photo-quality images. The typical display is made up of about a million dots, called *pixels* (picture elements). Each pixel displays one of the 16.7 million colors associated with its 24-bit code. For example, code consisting of all 0's is black, all 1's is white, and 001100110000000010011001 is a shade of blue.

In data storage lingo, 8 bits equates to a *byte*. Each 8-bit ANSI character requires a byte of storage, and the 24-bit True Color code for each pixel requires 3 bytes. The terms *kilobyte* (KB) and *megabyte* (MB), about 1000 and 1,000,000 bytes, respectively, are common measures of hardware capacities. *Kilobit* (Kb) and *megabit* (Mb) are used to express the rate at which data are transferred between devices and computers (for example, kilobits per second). Table 1-1 summarizes these and other higher-order measures. On output, these binary representations of written text, colorful images, and music are converted back to a form we humans can understand, such as a printed page, a graphic display, or played music.

Measure	Approximate No. of Bytes/Bits	Actual No. of Bytes/Bits	Compare to
Kilobyte (KB) Kilobit (Kb)	1000	$2^{10} = 1024$	Characters in the Gettysburg Address
Megabyte (MB) Megabit (Mb)	1,000,000	$2^{20} = 1,048,576$	Characters in this book
Gigabyte (GB) Gigabit (Gb)	1,000,000,000	$2^{30} = 1,073,741,424$	Population of China
Terabyte (TB) Terabit (Tb)	1,000,000,000,000	$2^{40} = 1,099,511,627,776$	Gallons of water consumed in North America per day

Table 1-1   Common Measures of PC Capacities

Physically, binary encoding is achieved in a variety of ways:

- In solid-state temporary storage, called *RAM* (random access memory), the two electronic states are represented by the presence or absence of an electrical charge in an integrated circuit.
- In disk storage (permanent storage), the two states are made possible by the magnetic arrangement of the surface coating.
- In CDs and CD-ROMs, digital data are stored permanently as microscopic pits.
- In fiber optic cable, binary data flow through as pulses of light.

Well, that's it for bits and bytes. And, no, proficiency in binary arithmetic is not a requirement for personal computing. It really doesn't matter whether you know that $1_2 + 1_2 = 10_2$ inside a computer. As long as you understand that computers operate by passing encoded 1's and 0's around the PC's components and that much of what the PC does is measured in terms of bits and bytes (for example, bits per second and megabytes), you are ready for any personal computing adventure. Binary arithmetic can remain a mystery.

The System Unit

The processing and storage components are installed in a metal or plastic case, usually a 1- to 2-foot tower, to create the *system unit* (see Figure 1-1). Figure 1-1 is intended to put the system unit and its component parts in perspective. We'll talk about all of them in this chapter or the next (on storage). Input/output (I/O) devices, such as the monitor and the printer, are connected to the system unit to complete the personal computer. The notebook PC's shell and the system unit are one in the same.

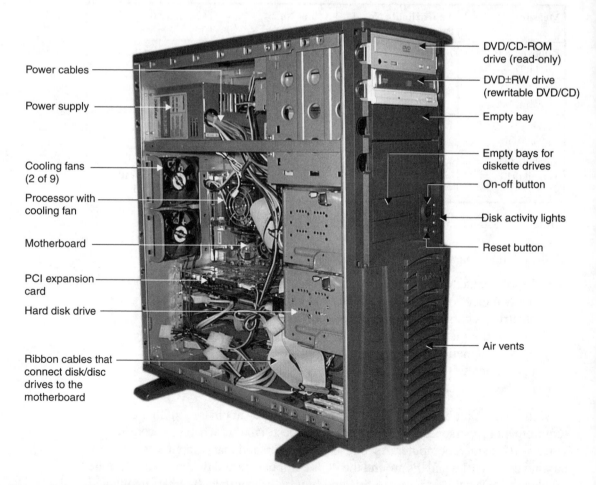

Figure 1-1   The desktop system unit, inside and out

The Motherboard

The primary circuit board in a PC is the *motherboard,* the mother of all boards. The motherboard (see Figure 1-2) contains the circuitry to handle all data flow within the system, including that for the I/O devices. Every once in a while, you'll hear PC veterans refer to the motherboard as the mobo or system board. The motherboard has a socket for the *processor* (the brains for the PC), several slots for *RAM* (memory chips for temporary storage of data and programs), and expansion slots for optional add-on capabilities in the form of *expansion cards* (add-on circuit boards).

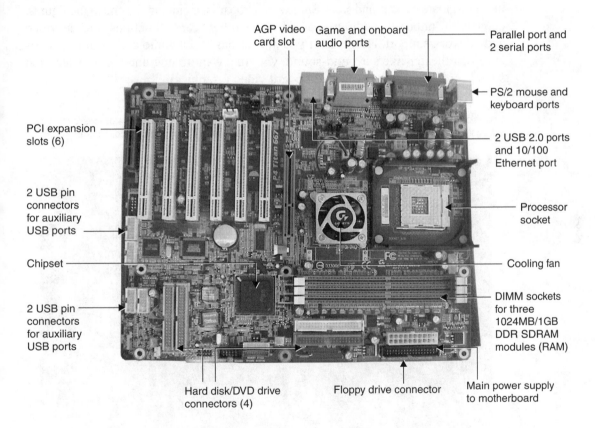

Figure 1-2 Motherboard

Input/output devices are linked to the motherboard via external electronic interfaces called *ports,* all those sockets on the back of a PC. The motherboard's *system bus* links all of the PC's components, inside and outside the system unit. The relationship between the processor and the system bus is much like that of the human brain and central nervous system. The brain sends and receives signals through the central nervous system, and the processor does the same through the system bus.

The motherboard includes a *chipset* to control the flow of information on the system bus. The chipset is important in that it determines what type of processor and type of RAM are supported by the motherboard. The motherboard's many ports permit links to I/O devices, and its sockets and slots accept add-on circuitry and functionality (see Figure 1-2).

In Figure 1-3 the motherboard is installed in the system unit. Notice that the *processor* (in this case a Pentium 4, 3 GHz), *RAM* (2GB), *AGP video card* (handles output to the monitor), and *sound card* (controls audio in and out) are inserted into the appropriate sockets and slots. Some motherboards, including the one in the figures, come with "onboard" audio functionality and other "card" functions, such as video and network support. However, if you are serious about audio and want to experience that theater-like surround-sound, you may want to upgrade to a full-featured sound card. The same is true of onboard video (graphics).

| Sound card in PCI expansion slot | Video card in AGP slot | RAM: Two 1GB DDR SDRAM modules in 2 DIMM slots | Pentium 4 processor 3 GHz (under cooling fan) |

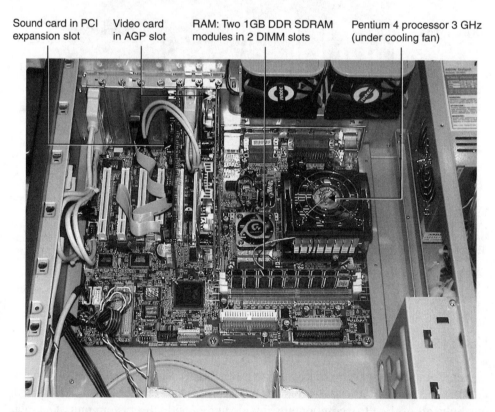

Figure 1-3 Motherboard in system unit with processor, expansion cards, and RAM installed

The Processor

When I assess a PC, I always look at the processor, first. The processor, an integrated circuit or "chip" about the size of a postage stamp, is the center of all activity on a PC. Under program control, the processor controls the flow of information and performs all computation and logic operations. Intel Corporation processors dominate the PC industry, but IBM, AMD, Texas Instruments, Hewlett-Packard, and Motorola manufacture comparable processors. When you shop for PCs, the first line you read or the first words spoken by the salesperson describe the processor. A good portion of the cost of a PC is its processor, so it's important that you know what you're buying. The next few paragraphs involve a little tech talk, but it's an important part of the demystification process. A little processor knowledge can save you plenty of headaches and bucks.

Processors are described in terms of *clock speed, bus width,* and *bus speed.* Inside a processor, a clock paces the execution of instructions. The clock speed is measured in terms of the number of clock cycles per second, which determines the number of program instructions that can be executed per second. Older PCs are measured in MHz (megahertz), or millions of cycles per second, and modern PCs in GHz (gigahertz), or billions of cycles per second. That's amazingly fast. If you walked across the United States 150 times and counted every step, you would be close to a billion steps.

Table 1-2 summarizes clock speeds for modern Intel processors. To give you an idea of the pace of evolution of processors, Table 1-2 includes the clock speed for the processor used in the first IBM PC. The introduction of the IBM PC in 1981 marked the beginning of the personal computing revolution. The Apple II computer made waves five years earlier, but primarily as a tool for education.

Processor	Clock Speed (Range)	Release Dates (First–Most Recent)
Pentium 4	1.4–3.20 GHz	Nov. 2000–Nov. 2003
Mobile Pentium 4	1.4–2.55 GHz	March 2002–April 2003
Pentium III	450 MHz–1 GHz	Feb. 1999–March 2000
Mobile Pentium III	400 MHz–1.33 GHz	Oct. 1999–Sep. 2002
Celeron	266 MHz–2.8 GHz	April 1998–Nov. 2003
Mobile Celeron	266 MHz–2.5 GHz	Jan. 1999–Nov. 2003
Intel 8088 (in 1981 IBM PC)	5–8 MHz	June 1979

Table 1-2   Intel Processors: Now and in the Original 1981 IBM PC

The *bus width* refers to the number of bits that can be handled as a unit. Most modern processors have a bus width of 32 bits, but some processors have made the jump to a 64-bit bus. Like processors, bus speed is rated in MHz and GHz. Modern PCs have processors with bus speeds ranging from 400 to 800 MHz. That's fast, but not fast enough. Bus speed has long been the bottleneck for PCs because processor clock speed continues to outpace bus speed. A typical processor might be described as a 32-bit 3.4 MHz processor with a bus speed of 800 MHz.

Memory

It's helpful to understand the various types of memory in a PC because every time you purchase or upgrade a PC, you have to deal with a memory trade-off: system performance versus cost. The amount of memory in a PC can have a dramatic effect on overall system performance and/or your bank account. A memory upgrade can add from $50 to $500 to the cost of a PC. Depending on your personal computing objectives, the extra cost could be well worth the money. Frequently, people buy a PC within their current budget and then add RAM later. It's an easy upgrade if you understand that all you have to do is slip a RAM module into a DIMM slot. Read on.

RAM: Random Access Memory

High-capacity disk/disc storage, such as the hard disk or DVD+RW (rewritable) disc, provides long-term storage of your programs, databases, and user files so that you can recall them as needed. (I go into detail on disk/disc storage in Chapter 2.) During processing, however, data and programs are stored in RAM, high-speed solid-state memory chips, so they can be accessed by the processor at electronic speeds. RAM access speed is about a million times faster than disk access speeds.

Prior to processing, all data and programs must be read from disk/disc storage and transferred to RAM for processing. RAM modules of various capacities are installed in DIMM (dual inline memory module) slots as shown earlier in Figure 1-3. RAM technologies change every couple of years and we are introduced to a new acronym. The two 1GB RAM modules in Figure 1-3 are DDR SDRAM, which, if you must know, stands for double data rate synchronous dynamic RAM. Most people just say "RAM" and omit the technology qualifier.

It's important to understand the trade-offs between the various high-speed solid-state storages (memory chips). RAM, which typically ranges from 128MB to 4GB in PCs, is the main holding area for the data and programs during processing. The processor rolls needed instructions and data to and from RAM at nanosecond speeds (around 30 billionths of a second). That, however, is slow relative to processor speeds.

Cache: High-Speed Memory

To increase processor throughput, computer designers use very high-speed memory, called *cache memory*. Cache is an important consideration when buying a PC; I always compare the amount of cache for the alternative PCs. Cache sits between RAM and the processor, either on the processor chip or on a separate cache chip. Cache capacity is relatively small, usually no more than 2MB. Typically, cache will hold instructions and data that are likely to be needed later as processing continues. This way, the processor can pull them from high-speed cache rather than the slower RAM.

You might ask, "If cache is so fast, why not just use it for all temporary storage?" Good question. Although cache can transfer information ten times as fast as RAM, it may also cost ten times as much as RAM. This is your classic trade-off between speed, capacity, and cost. The more cache you have, the better the system's overall performance.

Flash Memory: Nonvolatile Memory

Flash memory is nonvolatile; that is, its contents remain intact if the electricity is turned off. With RAM and cache, everything is lost when the power is interrupted. The memory stick in your digital camera is flash memory. All current PCs, I/O devices, and storage devices have flash memory. In fact, scores of common things we use every day have flash memory, such as cars, dishwashers, cellular phones, TVs, and digital watches.

With flash memory, the logic of PC devices can be upgraded without having to change out chips and circuit boards. Yes, we used to do that. When you turn on your PC, the *BIOS* (pronounced "BYE-oss") *software* is loaded from flash memory to RAM to enable system startup.

Adding Peripheral Devices: Ports and Jacks

Look at the back of any desktop PC and you will see an ugly jumble of wires and cables that link the various I/O devices and an occasional storage device to the system unit. Collectively, these external devices are called *peripheral devices*. Many people, including me, have attempted to tidy up this clutter, but the task is hopeless. The stringy mess may include wires to the printer, speakers, microphone, monitor(s), mouse, keyboard, game controller, computer network, telephone or TV cable access, and so on.

Every PC has a variety of *ports* into which you plug wires and cables from the peripheral devices, from Internet access providers, and/or a computer network. The motherboard comes with a group of closely clustered ports that are accessible from the rear of the PC (see Figures 1-2 and 1-4). With the exception of an occasional built-in sound card (as is the case in Figure 1-4), motherboards provide a similar mix of onboard ports. The other ports are on expansion cards and are accessible from the back side of the PC (see Figure 1-5). Some PCs have USB ports on the front or side of the system unit. Each port provides a direct connection to the system bus and, ultimately, RAM and the processor.

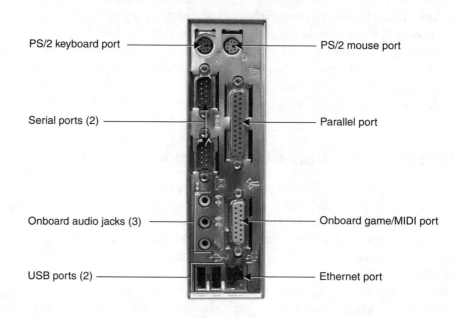

Figure 1-4   Ports built into the motherboard

The USB Port

The most popular standard for connecting peripheral (I/O) devices to a PC is the *USB (Universal Serial Bus)* port. A modern PC will have from four to eight USB ports (see Figures 1-4 and 1-5). If that's not enough, you can expand that number with a *USB hub,* a device that connects to a USB port and offers three to five additional USB ports. And if that's not enough (and it probably will be), hubs can be connected in a "tree" to provide up to 127 USB ports in all for each USB port. If you need more, you are spending way too much money on I/O devices.

All new PCs and I/O devices support USB 2.0, a standard that permits data transfer at 480 Mbps (megabits per second). USB 2.0 is 40 times faster than the original USB standard and is 4000 times faster than the serial port, which is now an antique.

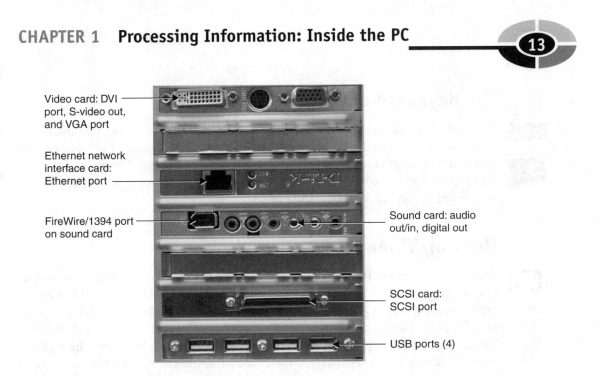

Video card: DVI
port, S-video out,
and VGA port

Ethernet network
interface card:
Ethernet port

FireWire/1394 port
on sound card

Sound card: audio
out/in, digital out

SCSI card:
SCSI port

USB ports (4)

Figure 1-5   Ports on expansion cards

To put 480 Mbps in perspective, 50 copies of this book can be electronically transferred each second via a USB 2.0 port. USB 2.0 devices are compatible with regular USB ports, but, remember, if you plug a USB 2.0 device into a regular USB port, the data transfer rate is that of the slower port.

An incredibly helpful feature of USB is that it lets you *hot plug* I/O devices. That means devices can be connected to or removed from the USB port while the PC is running. Gamers love this feature because they can switch controllers so easily. Another helpful feature of USB is that it can provide power to USB devices with relatively low power requirements, such as force-feedback game controllers—those that vibrate.

FireWire or 1394 Port

FireWire or *1394* (the IEEE standard number) is an interface standard that offers 400 Mbps speed, which is comparable to USB 2.0 (see Figure 1-5). The new FireWire standard, FireWire 800 or 1394b, transfers data at 800 Mbps. USB is more popular for use with I/O devices, but FireWire is more popular for use with audio/video (A/V) appliances, such as digital video cameras. If you purchase a digicam and you want to do video editing, you may need a FireWire connector to pass video between your camera and your PC. Like USB devices, FireWire devices can be hot plugged and I/O devices can be daisy-chained to a single FireWire port. It's unlikely that you'll link more than one, though. Most modern PCs come with FireWire support, but I would recommend that you check anyway.

The Keyboard and Mouse Ports

The keyboard and mouse have their own special ports, a 6-pin connector called a *PS/2 port* (refer to Figure 1-4). Modern mice and keyboards, like other I/O devices, are outfitted with USB connectors, making the PS/2 port obsolete. However, if you run out of USB ports, you can use an inexpensive PS2-to-USB adapter to connect your mouse and/or keyboard via the PS/2 ports.

Monitor/Video Port

The monitor, the video display, plugs into a *monitor/video port.* Usually this connection is to a graphics expansion card that is inserted into a *PCI* or an *AGP* slot on the motherboard (refer to Figure 1-3). All newer graphics adapters use AGP (Accelerated Graphics Port) technology, which is four times faster than the PCI (Peripheral Component Interface). Sometimes the graphics function is built into the motherboard, in which case a separate graphics card isn't needed. When a function is built into the motherboard, it's said to be *onboard.* Most notebook PCs and some desktops have onboard video support.

The better graphics cards provide dual-monitor support (two video ports); that is, your viewable area is spread across two monitors so that you can have one application displayed on one monitor and another on the other monitor (refer to Figure 1-5). If you work with multiple applications, as I do, having a dual-monitor setup can save a lot of time. My productivity improved 20 percent when I went to two monitors. The mouse pointer moves between the two monitors as it does across a single screen. Typically, the graphics adapters with dual-monitor support have a standard VGA port and a DVI port. DVI is the next generation video interface, but most existing monitors have only a VGA connector. If your monitors are VGA, then you may need an inexpensive DVI-to-VGA adapter.

Notebook PCs have a built-in monitor, but they also have a standard video port so that you can connect to an external monitor or an LCD projector for presentations.

Many graphics cards and notebook PCs have an *S-video port* for linking video between other devices that support S-video, such as TVs and video camcorders (refer to Figure 1-5).

Game/MIDI Port

The 15-pin *game/MIDI port* (refer to Figure 1-4) usually is found on the sound expansion card. It has been around a long time and is called by several names: game port, MIDI (Musical Instrument Digital Interface) port, and, originally, A-D (analog to digital) port. Millions of old joysticks, game pads, and music synthesizers are still in use, so the game/MIDI port continues to get its share of bit traffic. However, new gaming and MIDI devices are equipped with USB 2.0 connectors.

Serial and Parallel Ports

Most modern PCs have at least one 9-pin *serial port* and one 25-pin *parallel port* (refer to Figure 1-4). These old, slow ports are provided as a convenience in case you have an old I/O device that isn't supported by USB. Many older-model printers, which use the parallel port, just refuse to die. The parallel port, which mostly supports printers, is called the *printer port*, too.

Ethernet Port

Network interface cards (NICs) enable computers to talk to one another, electronically, that is. The NIC or network adapter is an expansion card (refer to Figure 1-5) or an onboard motherboard function (refer to Figure 1-4) that provides the interface for the exchange of information, usually via an Ethernet cable or a wireless connection. *Ethernet* is a popular standard for computer networks.

There are lots of ways for network adapters to link computers in a network. For example, many home networks use existing twisted-pair telephone lines or A/C power lines to link PCs throughout the home. Home networking is the rage in personal computing. We'll talk about networks and networking in some detail in Chapter 18, "Building a Home Network."

Audio Jacks

On desktop PCs, standard audio in and out jacks are available on a separate sound expansion card to support headphones, microphones, and speakers (refer to Figure 1-5). Some desktop motherboards and all notebook PCs have an onboard sound function (refer to Figure 1-4). Some high-end sound cards come with sophisticated control modules that can be mounted in front of the system unit in an unused disk/disc bay. If you're an audio fanatic, it's handy to have the controls and ports/jacks readily accessible from the front of the system.

The motherboard for the PC in Figures 1-4 and 1-5 provides onboard sound; however, motherboard sound is disabled because a separate sound card with more sophisticated features is installed.

Internet Access Port

A *modem* permits a connection to the Internet via a telephone line, digital TV cable, or satellite. Modems, in the form of an internal expansion card or an external unit with a USB connector, will have at least one port for a link to an Internet access line, probably a telephone line or a or TV cable.

The Evolution of Interface Technology

Ports and jacks change with the technology. That's why we have so many ways to interface I/O devices with the processor. Motherboards must support obsolete interfaces, such as the serial and parallel ports, as long as users have workable printers, scanners, and so on based on these technologies.

At one time the SCSI (pronounced "skuzzy") port, the first port to support daisy-chaining of devices, ruled the high-speed peripheral world. Now, however, at 80 Mbps, it is being phased out to make way for the less expensive and faster USB 2.0 port. The SCSI card in Figure 1-5 supports an older scanner. I would expect that the next edition of this book will not even mention serial, parallel, and SCSI ports.

Expansion Cards: Add-on Capabilities

The typical PC gives you plenty of room for growth, primarily in the form of *expansion cards* for desktops and *PC cards* for notebooks (see Figure 1-6). On desktop PCs, special-function expansion cards (also called *expansion boards*) are inserted into a PCI slot on the motherboard to give the unit added functionality (refer to Figure 1-3). The graphics adapter goes in the AGP slot. On a notebook PC, a credit card–sized PC card is plugged into an external PC card slot whenever it is needed.

Much of what used to be exclusively on expansion cards or PC cards is being built into the motherboard, including graphics, sound, modem, and network support. However, if you prefer something more than basic onboard functionality, you will want to purchase an add-on expansion card.

These are among the most popular expansion cards or PC cards:

- **Data/voice/fax modem**   The data/voice/fax modem performs the same function as a regular modem, plus it turns your PC into a telephone or fax machine.
- **Network interface card**   Each PC in a computer network, including a home network, must be equipped with an NIC.

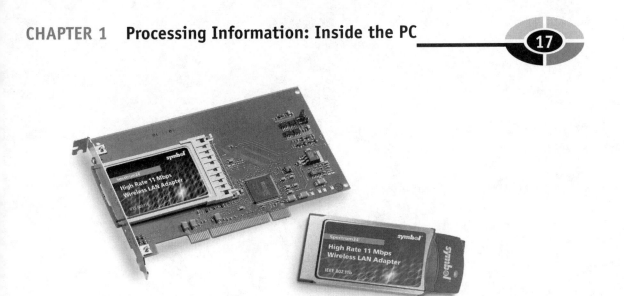

Figure 1-6   PCI Expansion Card and PC Card

(Photo courtesy of Symbol Technologies, Inc.)

These are the most common desktop-only expansion cards:

- **Graphics adapter**   The graphics adapter is the device controller for the monitor(s) and has its own onboard RAM, called *video RAM* or *VRAM*. It allows interfacing with one or more video monitors and normally is inserted into the AGP slot.
- **Sound**   The sound card permits sounds to be captured and stored on disk and allows sounds to be played through external speakers. The typical sound card has jacks for a microphone, a headset, and audio output and most have a port for a game controller and a MIDI port.

The features, and therefore the cost, of graphics adapters and sound cards can vary widely. Serious gamers, stereo buffs, and audio/video professionals may pay several hundred dollars extra to get dazzling graphics and/or 500 watts of seven-track audio.

Storing Information: Disks, Discs, and Flash

Of all the intriguing devices that comprise a PC, the ones that hold the greatest mystery for me are the permanent storage devices, such as the hard disk. Most of what's inside the system unit is electronic, but the hard disk is mechanical with moving parts. Data are transferred around the motherboard at electronic speeds, but something has to move when data are read or written to disk storage. I've been working with computers for a long time and I'm still amazed that a mechanical device with gears and motors can find and transfer data to RAM in only six milliseconds. That's considerably faster than a blink of an eye. And, it can do it a million times a day for years—without error. Remarkable! Oh, did I mention that the disk is spinning at 100 mph?

My disks are my most precious material possessions. I clean and pamper them more often than I do my dog. Those disks contain my family photo album, the source material for all of my books, my personal and business communications for years, my financial records, my medical records, my contacts list, and on and on. If lightning strikes and fries my motherboard, no problem, I can get another. Everything on a PC can be replaced, except the information on your disks. Even though disks are very hardy, you need to treat them with tender loving care in the unlikely event your disk crashes or a malicious virus attacks your PC.

Much of what we used to view and use in physical form has evolved to bits on permanent disk/disc storage. The Rolodex file has become the disk-based contacts list. The 20-volume set of encyclopedias is now a CD-ROM. As the trend to digital convergence rolls along, all of those bits begin to converge to disk/disc storage.

NOTE: *I spell disk with a "k" for references to magnetic disk media and with a "c" for references to optical disc media, such as CDs and DVDs. This is a common convention, but you may see it the other way around, too.*

This chapter introduces you to commonly used PC storage devices from a hardware perspective. I make specific recommendations on *what* disk/disc storage devices to buy in Part Three, "Buying and Using a PC." The care and maintenance of disk storage is covered in Chapter 10, "Installation, Maintenance, and Troubleshooting."

The File: The Basic Unit of Storage

Except for a few bytes here and there, all permanently stored information in a PC is in a *file,* an electronically accessible recording of information. In plain language, it's just a long string of digitized information (1s and 0s) that is stored and retrieved as a unit, that unit being a file. Files hold many different kinds of information—a letter to the editor, the Beatles' *Hey Jude,* the holiday mailing list, or a chess program.

When we create a word processing document, perhaps the minutes of a staff meeting, we give it a descriptive name and store it as a named file, for example, "June staff meeting.doc." If we wish to view or revise the document, we recall it from disk storage by its *filename*—June staff meeting.doc.

In the Windows world, filenames have two parts, separated by a period. To the left of the period is the user-assigned name for the file (June staff meeting) and to the right is an automatically assigned *extension* that identifies the type of file. For example, "doc" is the extension for Microsoft Word files. Files with a "jpg" extension identify a particular type of image file. For now, it's enough to know that all information is stored in files. Recent versions of Windows do not show the extension unless you request it.

Files can be any size. The smallest file on my PC is 1KB (kilobyte) and the largest is 412MB (megabytes). Chapter 6, "Working with Files," is devoted to files and file management—how you name, organize, store, retrieve, copy, move, and delete files.

Fixed and Removable Disk Storage

At a minimum, every PC has a hard disk and a CD-ROM drive. In casual conversations, the terms disk and disk drive are used interchangeably. Technically, however, the *disk drive* refers to the storage device and the *disk* to the medium, the actual surface on which information is stored. Disk drives are designed for either removable or fixed media.

You're probably familiar with the ubiquitous 3.5-inch *disk*—the *floppy*. It's called a floppy because its 5-inch predecessor was flexible and "floppy." The actual media is still flexible, but its enclosure is not. Typically, floppies and other removable media are used to transport user files between systems and for backup. The *fixed disk drive* is a permanently installed *hard disk* that contains the operating system, applications, programs, and your personal files. The terms *hard disk* and *fixed disk* are used interchangeably. It's also called the *C: drive*; disk drives are assigned letters.

Figure 2-1 shows *Windows Explorer,* an important file management tool that we talk about at length in Chapter 6. The PC in this example is somewhat typical in that it has four disks/discs, each indicated by a disk/disc drive icon and a letter:

- **A:**   Floppy
- **C:**   Hard disk
- **D:**   DVD-RW disc (rewritable CD and DVD)
- **E:**   DVD-ROM disc (read-only DVD-ROM and CD-ROM)

The pictographs in Figure 2-1, called *icons,* indicate the type of drive and whether or not it is empty. When a removable disk/disc drive is empty, the media is outside the icon (A: and D: in the example). The media, along with its name, is shown when loaded to the drive (in the example, PC Dem BU 1 in E:). Drive letters are written with a trailing colon.

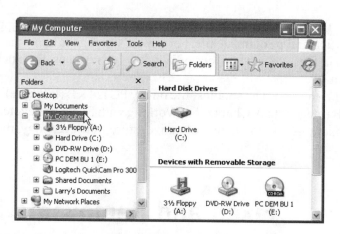

Figure 2-1 Disk drives: icons and letters

There is no typical PC. The example in Figure 2-1, however, includes the most popular storage devices. But where is B:? Chances are you'll never see a B: disk/disc. A: and B: were set up as floppy drives at the dawn of personal computing, but you don't need a second floppy now. In fact, you don't need a floppy at all—more on that later.

Today, the vast majority of PCs have only one hard disk and one optical storage drive, identified as C: and D:, respectively. If you have two hard disks, the second would be D: and the optical storage device would be E:.

The Hard Disk

Engineers who design hard disks have done their jobs well. Each year they put more information in less space and increase the speed at which information is transferred to RAM for processing. When I was a young IBMer in the late 1960s helping customers install systems in banks, universities, and other organizations, all disk drives had removable media. A bank might have 20 or more disk drives, each the size of a washing machine. The capacity of the removable "disk pack," which was about the size and weight of a PC's system unit, was 800MB. The total online capacity of 20 disk drives was 16GB (gigabytes, or billions of bytes). The total online capacity of the five hard disks on my family's home network is about 500GB and, together, they take up less space than this book.

The hard disk operates in a hermetically sealed case, but the 250MB disk in Figure 2-2 is exposed to show its inner workings. The arm extending over the surface of the disk has six read/write heads, one for each of the three disk platters. The heads literally float about 15 microns over the disk face surface as the disks spin at 7200 rpm; for comparison, a particle of smoke is 215 microns. The read-write heads for each surface move back and forth across the disk platters to access its files. Fortunately, the operating system keeps track of where files are located on the disk. All you have to do is request a file by its filename and the operating system does the rest. Occasionally, however, you will need to "clean" and reorganize your disk to ensure that it operates at peak performance. We talk about this in Chapter 10.

The hard disk will forever remain a mystery if you don't know the essentials of how information is organized on a disk. This brief 200-word explanation involves a little tech talk, but you'll appreciate having the disk mystery unveiled when you run the utility programs that keep your disk healthy.

The hard disk in Figure 2-2 has three disk platters and six access arms, one for each disk surface. The access arms with their read/write heads move together between concentric *tracks* to record bits by magnetizing the surface of the disk. Each set of similarly positioned tracks on the six disk recording surfaces comprises a *cylinder*. The disk in Figure 2-2 has 16,000 cylinders, each with six tracks (one for each surface).

1 of 6 access arms

1 of 6 read/write heads

1 of 6 disk recording surfaces

1 of 3 disk platters

Figure 2-2   250MB PC hard disk

The illustration in Figure 2-3 shows how a disk recording surface is organized. The example surface has 27 tracks that are divided into 9 wedge-shaped *sectors*. An actual disk may have hundreds of sectors. Typically, the storage capacity of each sector for a particular track is 512 bytes. Adjacent sectors form *clusters,* so the capacity of a cluster is always a multiple of 512 bytes. This brings us to the file. A cluster is the smallest unit of disk space that can be allocated to a file, so even the smallest file requires a full cluster, which can be up to 32KB depending on the disk (each KB is a thousand bytes).

When we store a file by a filename, the operating system associates the filename with its location; that is, the track(s) and sectors. You can't see tracks and sectors, even with a microscope, but the operating system knows where they are by their relative positions.

To determine the capacity of your hard disk (or any other disk) and the amount of disk space, move the mouse pointer over the hard disk icon in Windows Explorer. Then, click the right mouse button and select Properties to display disk properties, as shown in Figure 2-4.

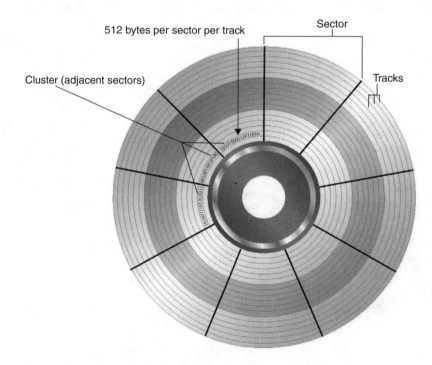

Figure 2-3   Hard disk organization

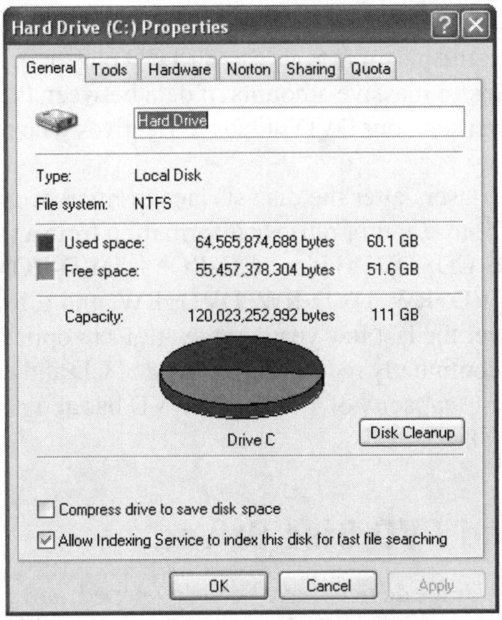

Hard Drive (C:) Properties

General | Tools | Hardware | Norton | Sharing | Quota

Hard Drive

Type:	Local Disk
File system:	NTFS

■ Used space:	64,565,874,688 bytes	60.1 GB
■ Free space:	55,457,378,304 bytes	51.6 GB
Capacity:	120,023,252,992 bytes	111 GB

Drive C   Disk Cleanup

☐ Compress drive to save disk space
☑ Allow Indexing Service to index this disk for fast file searching

OK   Cancel   Apply

Figure 2-4   Disk properties: capacity, used space, and free space

The Floppy Disk

Over the last four decades I've seen many computer technologies come and go, in- cluding the punched card and the amazing daisy-wheel printer. Now, the floppy drive and its higher-capacity cousin, the Zip drive, are poised to become historical artifacts. Sure, most PCs, including mine, have a floppy disk drive, but it's a special request on new machines. Inexpensive high-capacity rewritable optical storage (CD/DVD burners) and the ability to pass files over the Internet and networks have made floppies obsolete. They make great coasters, though.

CD and DVD Disc Drives and Media

Even if you haven't had much experience with personal computing, you're familiar with music CDs and DVD movies. The technology industries have taken these common audio/video media and retrofitted them to give personal computers a high-capacity, inexpensive, interchangeable alternative storage technology. You can burn a custom audio CD for pennies and play it in your car, on a CD player, or on your PC. You can use DVD+RW to transfer massive amounts of data between PCs or to back up your personal files. You can send out DVD videos to relatives who missed the family reunion.

In optical storage, lasers alter the disc surface in microscopic increments to record the 1's and 0's to store and/or retrieve information from a variety of storage media, including audio CD, DVD-video, CD-ROM, DVD-ROM, CD-R, DVD+R, DVD-R, CD-RW, DVD+RW, DVD-RW, DVD±RW, and a few others. I know; it confuses me, too. Over the last few years, innovations in optical storage have come in rapid succession, continually redefining the type of CD and DVD drives we put in our PCs. With a storage capacity of 4.7GB, the DVD has about seven times the digital capacity of the 700MB CD.

Popular CD and DVD Disc Drives

A number of optical storage devices have been developed, and you'll find all of them still spinning away in someone's PC. Our focus, however, will be on disc drives that are being installed in modern PCs. These are summarized, along with their capabilities, in Table 2-1 and discussed in the following list.

Capability	CD-ROM	DVD-ROM	CD-RW	CD-RW/DVD combination	DVD±RW/ CD-RW
Music CD	▓	▓	▓	▓	▓
CD read-only	▓	▓	▓	▓	▓
DVD movie		▓		▓	▓
DVD read-only		▓		▓	▓
CD burner (write)			▓	▓	▓
CD rewritable			▓	▓	▓
DVD rewritable					▓

Table 2-1   Capabilities of Popular Disc Drives
(CD format = 700MB, DVD format = 4.7GB)

- **CD-ROM drive**   The read-only CD-ROM drive plays audio CDs, loads commercial software packages to hard disk, and enables access to CD-ROM-based reference material, such as encyclopedias. This drive, however, will soon be history as it gives way to the DVD-ROM drive.
- **DVD-ROM drive**   The read-only DVD-ROM drive does everything that a CD-ROM drive will do, plus, it will play your DVD movies. Eventually, software will be distributed on the higher-density DVD-ROM rather than CD-ROM.
- **CD-RW drive**   Commonly known as the "CD burner," the CD-RW drive does everything that a CD-ROM drive will do, plus, it allows you to create your own custom music CDs and data CDs on read-only CD-R discs or rewritable CD-RW discs. This capability would have cost you $100,000 in 1990. The CD-RW drive provides a much needed and inexpensive way to store large amounts of data (for example, video files, digital images) and to back up user files.
- **CD-RW/DVD-ROM combination drive**   This combo drive overcomes a shortcoming of the CD-RW drive in that it also will read DVD-ROM.
- **DVD±RW/CD-RW drive**   This all-in-one drive accomplishes all optical disc functions, including rewritable DVD on DVD+RW and DVD-RW, the two main formats. The industry has yet to standardize on a format for rewritable DVD.

Measuring Disc Drive Performance

The yardstick for CD and DVD drive performance is *disc speed,* the number of bytes per second read or written to the disc. When you buy a PC, the disc drive's specifications are listed with other specs, such as processor speed. The disc spec might look something like this: 16X DVD-ROM and 8X DVD+RW. Disc speed is measured in multiples, "X," the data rate of the original audio CD or video DVD. For CD drives, the X is 153.6KB per second and for DVD drives, the X is 1.25MB per second. Notice that the DVD X is eight times faster than the CD X. They probably should have used another letter for DVDs to avoid confusion, but then there would be no mystery.

When only one speed is presented in the spec, that speed refers to the read speed for read-only devices (16X DVD-ROM) or the write speed for read/write devices (8X DVD+RW). A detailed set of drive specs could include read, write, and rewrite speeds for both CD and DVD.

When you buy a PC, it's always a good idea to do a little disc comparison shopping. Any DVD-ROM drive will play audio CDs and DVD movies because they run at the same speed, but if you plan to burn CDs and DVDs and use discs for data storage, there is a whole lot of difference between the capabilities of a 24X CD-RW/DVD-ROM combo drive and an 8X DVD+RW drive.

Flash Memory for Permanent Storage

Prior to the Internet, we had the "walknet." To transfer information from one place to another, we would store it on a floppy and then walk it to another computer. Today, we can do the same thing with interchangeable CD and DVD media, but there is another, more convenient alternative—the *USB flash drive.*

Called by several names, such as mini-USB drive and memory key, the USB flash drive is packaged within ballpoint pens, key chains, and other small personal items (see Figure 2-5). When plugged into a PC's USB port, a USB flash drive is recognized immediately as an active drive and is assigned an unused letter. Any type of files can be saved in or retrieved from the flash memory module, which can have capacities up to 1GB, a capacity equal to that of 700 floppies.

With the USB flash drive you can have your own personal storage drive on any PC—your home PC, your customer's, your boss's, your friend's—well, you get the idea. It certainly lends itself to innovative uses.

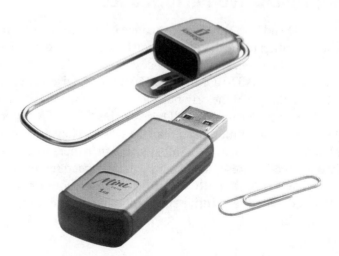

Figure 2-5   Iomega® Mini USB drive

(Photo courtesy of Iomega Corporation)

The Best Mix of Storage Options

Choosing the right mix of storage devices for your circumstances requires a little thought. Every PC will have a hard disk and one disc drive. Basically, you have to choose how much hard disk space you will need and your requirements for rewritable disc capabilities. PC hard drive capacities range from 40GB to 400GB. Keep in mind that a high-end hard drive can add several hundred dollars to the cost of a PC. Rewritable DVD is becoming standard equipment on mid- to high-end PCs. Budget PCs may have only a CD-RW drive. Some people, including me, like the convenience of having both a DVD-ROM drive and a rewritable DVD drive. All of these choices involve trade-offs between disk/disc capacity, budget, and application. I'll talk more about the storage mix and offer specific recommendations in Part Three, "Buying and Using a PC."

3

Getting Information In: Input

Remember all of those ports from Chapter 1—the USB, parallel, FireWire, and all the rest? Well, what do you do with them? You might use one or two of them to connect to a network or the Internet, but mostly you use them to hang peripheral devices on the system unit. These might include a storage device, such as a USB flash drive, but the typical peripheral is an input/output (I/O) device.

The variety of I/O devices available to enter and present information continues to grow, with at least one new innovative device being added each month. You can capture real-time video from your desktop digital camera or play DVD movies while enjoying theater-like surround sound. In this and the next chapter we talk about the input and output devices you will most likely encounter in your first few years of personal computing. As you gain experience, you may wish to explore other I/O devices. For example, some people use biometric fingerprint verification scanners to ensure the security of their PCs. Of course, we routinely use source data automation devices that aren't part of the personal computing world. For example, we swipe credit cards, scan grocery items, and "talk" with irritating automated telephone systems.

In this chapter, I'll run through common input devices; I will do the same for output devices in Chapter 4. In both chapters the emphasis is more on function than on mechanics, physics, or electronics. These devices are fascinating engineering marvels, but you really don't need to know how a cordless optical mouse works. However, if your curiosity gets the best of you and you just have to know how inkjet printers form the tiny ink droplets to create images, you're normal. That's why there are plenty of available explanations posted to the Internet. A good resource for explanations of the inner workings of I/O devices is the popular Internet site, *How Stuff Works*, at www.howstuffworks.com.

Before we get into I/O devices, it might be helpful if I describe a typical PC. Why not mine? With a couple of exceptions, it has the usual I/O devices. I continually switch between a mouse, keyboard, and headset microphone (for speech recognition) to enter text and commands to my PC. My other input devices are a flatbed scanner, which I use a few times each week, and a desktop video camera (one of the exceptions), the kind you would use for videophone conversations. I rarely use the camera. I have two open-ended cables in my front USB ports, one to download pictures from my still digital camera and the other for my digital camcorder. My output devices are dual monitors (one is more typical), an inkjet printer, and surround sound speakers. I probably print ten pages a week, on average, and listen to Internet or CD music every other day or so.

The Mouse

A PC's mouse is so named because it looks like a house mouse, although its tail is beginning to disappear as we enter the cordless era. The mouse, which changed the way we interact with PCs, allows us to "point" and "click" our way around the Windows interface. The mouse, though, is but one of many types of devices that do the same thing—controls the movement of the pointer.

Mouse Technologies

For its first decade, the mouse was a simple electromechanical device with a couple of buttons on top and a small recessed rubber ball on the bottom. You can still purchase a mouse with a mechanical ball, but for a little more money you can enjoy one of today's precision high-tech mice. These mice use optical technology to sense the movement of the mouse. With no moving parts, the optical mice tend to live longer, too. Although some mice are hand-neutral, most are designed for use by either a left or right hander.

Some mice are cordless, so you don't have to worry about an always-in-the-way tail on a busy desk. Cordless mice transmit movements to a transceiver that is plugged into a USB port.

Operating the Mouse

The operation of the mouse is intuitive. As you move it across the desktop, the pointer on the display moves in the same direction. As the pointer across the screen, it is constantly changing shapes to reflect its function as you move between applications and menus. Mostly it's an arrow you use to select options and navigate about the screen. In a word processing document, it's an *I* beam symbol that lets you click where you wish to begin text entry. In an Internet browser, it changes to a hand with a pointing finger when rolled over a link to another Internet destination. In a graphics program, a crosshair pointer indicates you are ready to draw.

Mice and other similar devices have two regular buttons (a primary and secondary), a wheel button, and possibly two or more additional buttons, as shown in Figure 3-1 and described here:

- **Primary button**   Because most of us are right-handers, the primary button typically is the left button under our forefinger. Use this button to select and choose items, to position the pointer within a document,

Figure 3-1   Wheel mouse

(Photo courtesy of Logitech)

and to move things. You tap, or *click,* the primary button to select items, such as a file, an application, or a menu option. You tap a button twice in rapid succession, or *double-click,* to choose an item. For example, you double-click on a file to open it. For *drag* operations, where you move items, press and hold the left button, then move the pointer to the desired location and release the button. For example, you can drag a window by its title bar to reposition it on the screen. Or, you can drag a block of text from one paragraph to another.

- **Secondary button**   The function of the right button varies between software packages, but often it is used to call up a menu of options related to the current activity. Right-click anywhere at any time to call up a menu of related operations.

- **Wheel button**   Roll the wheel with your forefinger to scroll up or down to view whatever is currently above or below the viewing area. The wheel comes in handy when doing word processing and surfing the Internet. Like the secondary button, the function of the wheel varies, depending on the position of the pointer and the application. On some mice the wheel can be clicked, too, giving the mouse additional functionality.

- **Additional buttons**   Some mice, such as the one in Figure 3-1, have two additional buttons on the side that can be operated with the thumb. Usually, these buttons are used to page forward and backward in a document or a web site; however, you can set user preferences such that they can perform different functions.

Mouse Properties

You can give your mouse its own unique personality. To customize the operation of your mouse, open the Mouse Properties dialog box shown in Figure 3-2 (click Start | Control Panel | Mouse) and change preferences to meet your needs (more on this in Chapter 5, "Working with Windows"). One out of ten people, the lefties, switch the primary and secondary buttons. You also can change the precision or the appearance of the mouse pointer, perhaps to the "conductor" theme in Figure 3-2.

Other Types of Mice

For now, the mouse is the most popular *point-and-draw device.* There are many other devices that perform the same function. The ones you see most often are the finger-operated *trackpad* and *trackpoint,* shown in Figure 3-3, and the *trackball.* All are common with notebook PCs.

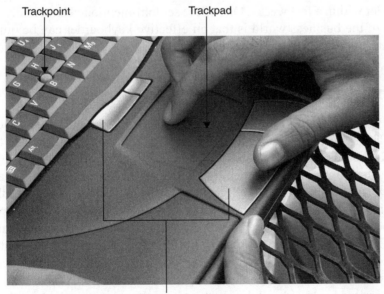

Figure 3-2   Customize the mouse using the various tabs in the Mouse Properties dialog box

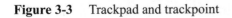

Figure 3-3   Trackpad and trackpoint

The Keyboard

Only in retrospect do I appreciate my high school typing class, arguably the most useful class I have ever taken. The keyboard has been my tactile friend for over 40,000 pages of books and three times that in other phases of my work and domestic life. And, I'm not unique. Countless people are knowledge workers and/or personal computing enthusiasts who interact frequently with PCs.

Anyone old enough to read this book has been exposed to the keyboard, so I'll just talk briefly about keyboard technology and expose you to the various parts of the standard 104-key PC keyboard. But first, I need to address an often asked question.

Do You Need to Learn Keyboarding Skills?

Not really. I've been around hundreds of amazingly effective hunt-and-peck keyboarders. For every successful hunt-and-peck person, though, there are a dozen who are seriously keyboard challenged. If you are one of them, I recommend that you purchase an inexpensive keyboarding software package. With a little diligence, these practice and drill tutorials can teach you to become a reasonably effective keyboarder within a few weeks. One of the seldom-mentioned but vividly apparent realities of the business world is that an effective keyboarder can be much more productive than an ineffective keyboarder.

Keyboard Technologies

Generally, keyboards fall into two categories, traditional and ergonomically designed. The keys on the traditional keyboard are aligned in neat rows in the same plane. Keyboards with the "ergonomic" label are designed to be more human-friendly. There are many types of ergonomic designs. The one my wife, Nancy, has used for years is split such that half the keys angle to one side and half to the other. This design enables better alignment with the wrist and forearm. My wife swears by her keyboard as it has eliminated any problems she has had with carpal tunnel syndrome. On other ergonomic keyboards, the keys are split widely and contoured to better accommodate the variation in finger length. I'm a reasonably proficient keyboarder who becomes a klutz on these ergonomic keyboards.

The standard keyboard and the ergonomic keyboard are available with a variety of extra features. The typical off-the-shelf keyboard might have a scroll wheel, which does much the same thing as the wheel button on a mouse. It might also have multimedia buttons for playing audio CDs or videos and a volume control knob.

Many have one-touch buttons that can be used to initiate common tasks, such as displaying your e-mail program or your home page on a browser. The mix of supplemental buttons and features varies between keyboards. And, like mice, keyboards can be cordless.

The Keyboard Layout

Figure 3-4 shows a representative keyboard with a standard 104-key layout. I know. Many of you will already have experienced a oneness with this layout; however, you may not have examined its parts from a personal computing perspective. To help give greater meaning to these keys, I've divided the standard keyboard into logical parts, each of which is identified in Figure 3-4 and described in Table 3-1. You might wish to look over this figure and table now and refer to them again when I talk about Windows-specific uses of the keyboard in Chapter 5, "Working with Windows."

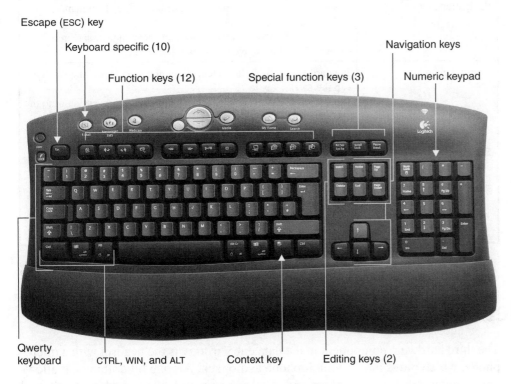

Figure 3-4   The standard 104-key keyboard and its parts

(Photo courtesy of Logitech)

Feature	Description
Escape (ESC) key	Tap to negate the current command or menu.
Keyboard specific (10)	Many modern keyboards have one-touch buttons for specific tasks (open e-mail, media players, or Internet home page).
Function keys (12)	Trigger the execution of software. F1 is Help. Others vary by application.
Editing keys (2)	INSERT: Tap to toggle between insert and typeover modes. DELETE: Delete character at cursor position.
Special function keys (3)	PRINT SCREEN: Captures screen image in Clipboard (ALT+PRT SCR to capture active window). SCROLL LOCK: Tap to toggle scroll feature on/off. PAUSE: Temporarily suspend current task.
Numeric keypad	Permits rapid numeric data entry and facilitates arithmetic computation.
Navigation keys	HOME/END: Move to beginning/end of line, page, document, and so on. PAGE UP/PAGE DOWN: Move to previous/next page or screen. Arrow keys: Move cursor up, down, left, and right.
Qwerty keyboard	Standard keyboard includes letters, numbers, and special characters. Tap the ENTER key to "Do." Tap TAB to advance to the next tab stop in word processing or to the next data entry area. Tap the BACKSPACE key to move the cursor one position to the left and delete that character.
Context key	Displays the shortcut menu for the selected item (same as right-click).
CTRL, WIN, and ALT	CTRL (Control), WIN (Windows), and ALT (Alternate) keys are used in conjunction with another key to give a key new meaning (for example, CTRL+S to save a document, WIN+E to start Windows Explorer).

Table 3-1   Keyboard Features and Descriptions

The Headset with Microphone

The third hardware component in the data entry trilogy is the headset with a microphone, which plugs into the microphone audio jack. Among other things, it allows you to enter words and numbers and to issue commands via *speech recognition*. I have talked to my computer since the early-1990s when I installed the first speech recognition software for PCs. At that time, PC technology clearly lagged that of so-phisticated speech recognition software, so I had to speak in discrete speech with a slight separation between each word. I did talk-stop-talk speech until MHz-level PCs came on the market with enough power to interpret continuous speech at rates up to 160 words a minute.

Speech Recognition

With speech recognition capability built into modern versions of Microsoft Office suites, speech recognition is gaining in popularity. For most people, the Office speech software will suffice. If you wish to have software with a larger dictionary (the words it can interpret) and/or an application-specific dictionary (law, medicine, engineering, and so on), these options can be purchased separately.

Headset Technology

As with all audio equipment, the biggest variable in headset microphone technology is quality. The better headset microphones have the frequency responses and micro-phone sensitivity that you must have for speech recognition and should have to enjoy static-free music and Internet-based conversations. A headset microphone can be purchased with one or two headphones, so you have the choice of monaural (mono) or stereo. If your primary application is speech recognition, interactive gaming (where players talk with one another), or Internet voice chats, then you might prefer one with a single headphone. If your primary application is listening to music, you would probably prefer a stereo headset.

The Scanner

The *image scanner* is making a major contribution to the trend toward digital con-vergence because millions of PC users routinely convert images to a digital format. Scanners work like copy machines, except the button is "scan" rather than "copy." Lift the cover, place the image on the glass, and scan it. Some scanners come with automatic photo feeders so you don't have to lift the cover and position the photo for each scan. Of course, there are scanners with automatic sheet feeders for high-vol-ume business applications.

Scanner Applications

Scanners are handy multifunction devices that service many applications:

- **Image scanner**   Use the scanner to create digital images of photos, any hardcopy document, or small items (watches, jewelry, keys, and so on). People love to scan their old photos and create well-organized electronic photo albums. I scan small valuables for insurance documentation.
- **Fax machine**   When used in conjunction with a fax/modem (a link to a telephone line), the scanner is a fax machine. When you push the Fax button on my scanner, a screen pops up and requests that you enter "fax to" information.
- **Copy machine**   When used in conjunction with a printer, the scanner is a duplicating machine. When you tap the scanner's Copy button, you're presented with traditional copy machine options, such as reduce/enlarge, darken/lighten, and number of copies.
- **OCR scanner**   When used in conjunction with *optical character recognition (OCR)* software, scanners can interpret alphanumeric characters on regular printed pages, like this one. The better OCR software can scan a document, such as a brochure, and place the printed characters along with images directly into a word processing document.
- **Slide scanner**   With the proper attachment, a scanner can scan in the images on your 35-mm negatives and slides.

Scanner Technology

The flatbed image scanner in Figure 3-5 is representative of a quality home scanner that can convert your treasured home photos into brilliant digital images. This scanner includes a lighted adapter for scanning 35-mm slides and an automatic photo feeder for 3×5 and 4×6 photos. There are many different types of special-purpose scanners, such as business card scanners, photo scanners, handheld scanners, and image processing scanners for business use. But we're talking personal computing here, so our discussion will focus on the typical flatbed consumer scanner.

When you examine the technical specifications for a flatbed scanner, you look at maximum resolution, maximum color depth, and maximum scan area:

- **Maximum resolution**   *Resolution,* the clarity of the scanned image, is measured in *dots per inch (dpi).* The dpi qualifier refers to the number of dots per linear inch in a scanned image, horizontally or vertically. That is, a 2400-dpi scanner, like the one in Figure 3-5, is capable of storing an image

Figure 3-5   Flatbed image scanner with photo feeder and 35-mm slide adapter
(Photo courtesy of Hewlett-Packard Company)

with 5,760,000 (2400 times 2400) dots per square inch. The typical home
scanner will have this photographic quality resolution, or "res."

- **Maximum color depth**   One of the scanner specs is the number of bits
  associated with each dot, its *color depth*. The color depth of the scanner in
  Figure 3-5 is 48 bits. That means that the scanner can detect and code many
  millions of colors for each dot (2^{48} or a lot of colors). I seldom scan at this
  color depth, though, because there is a trade-off between the color depth
  being used and the size of the scanned image. Huge images are cumbersome
  to work with and take up storage space. You can opt to scan at much lower
  color depths with relatively little loss in image quality, especially if your
  plans are to view images via a monitor.
- **Maximum scan area**   The typical area will be slightly larger than a
  standard sheet of letter paper (8.5×11). You can get a scanner with a larger
  scan area, but you pay for it and you probably won't need it.

Most scanners are sold with a variety of support software, including the basic
scan software, OCR software for interpreting text, and imaging software that allows
you to digitally modify images with special effects.

The scanning function is built into all-in-one multifunction devices, which are introduced in the next chapter on output.

The Desktop Video Camera

I would imagine that, in time, the *desktop video camera* will be as common as the keyboard. I'm not talking about a handheld digital camcorder that costs as much as a PC. This is a small video camera that sits on the desktop, a shelf, a monitor, or somewhere around your PC (see Figure 3-6). These incredible little devices, which can be purchased for as little as a good mouse, have a lot of applications and a bright future in personal computing. Here are just a few of the ways they can help animate your life:

- **Video with instant messaging** Add live video to Internet instant messaging. Your recipients can read your messages and see you, too.
- **Videophone calls** A growing number of people use the Internet to call people. Many of them use a desktop video camera to enjoy videophone conversations where they see and hear the party on the other end of the line.
- **Videoconferencing** Many companies save airfare and use these inexpensive cameras to have videoconferences, instead. They're also great for electronic family reunions.
- **Webcam** *Webcams* are digital video cameras that are continuously linked to the Internet so they can beam real-time still and video imagery into cyberspace from zoos, classrooms, living rooms, and so on.
- **Video monitoring** You can set up one or more wireless desktop video cameras to monitor the goings on around the house or yard.
- **Still camera** Point the desktop video camera and click to capture still images just as you would with a digital camera.

Figure 3-6   Desktop video camera

(Photo courtesy of Logitech)

The specifications that you look for in a digital video camera are its video capture resolution, still capture resolution, and frame rate. Even the inexpensive cameras offer capture resolutions of up to 640×480 pixels, the little picture elements (colored dots) that make up the display. This is a reasonably clear display for desktop video applications, such as a videophone or Webcam. The frame rate has to do with the number of images presented per second during a video display, usually 30 frames per second. Expect to pay a premium for specs that exceed 640×480 resolution and 30 frames per second; however, you probably wouldn't use any extra capacity for Internet applications. Any higher resolutions or frame rates would bog down during Internet transmission and be shown as spurts of video.

Cameras can come with a variety of extra features, including a built-in microphone, wireless remote-control operation, a zoom lens, and the ability to track you as you move around a room.

4

Getting Information Out: Output

We communicate with our PCs via input devices and our PCs communicate with us through output devices, primarily those that produce hard copy (printed material), video, and audio output. The number and variety of features you get with a particular device has a lot to do with its price tag. You can purchase a reasonable printer for less than a pair of sneakers or you can pay as much for one as you would a side-by-side refrigerator. It's good to have a working knowledge of an output device's options and features because, ultimately, it is you who decides how big, fast, clear, or loud you want these devices to be.

The Monitor

It's always fun to see my monitor transform itself from black nothingness to a vivid window into personal computing and cyberspace. Fortunately, that window offers some wonderful vistas, because many of us will spend a good portion of our working day and our leisure time looking through it. At work, our monitors let us interact with the tools and information of business. At home, it's a drawing board, a movie/slide-show screen, a calendar, a painter's canvas, a game board, a TV, a security monitor, and much more.

Types of Monitors

The two basic types of monitors, also called *displays,* are the traditional *CRT (cathode ray tube)* and the *flat panel* (see Figure 4-1). Today, more CRTs are in use than flat panels, but that is changing. A thin flat panel display is built into every notebook PC, and the majority of all new desktop PCs are being sold with flat panel displays. The heavy, boxy CRT monitor uses the same basic TV-type technology that has been around since the 1940s. Nevertheless, CRTs offer excellent resolution at affordable prices. Their footprint, however, can overwhelm a desk. When I traded my 65-pound, 21-inch CRT for a flat panel monitor, it was as if I had purchased a bigger desk, too. That extra space, though, comes with a cost. A flat panel display can cost twice that of a CRT with a similar viewing area. Even though a flat panel display can increase the cost of a PC by several hundred dollars, the trend is clearly to these space-saving displays for PCs at work and at home.

Figure 4-1   A CRT monitor (left) and an LCD flat panel monitor (right)

(Photos courtesy of ViewSonic)

Monitor Technology

Everyone is familiar with the cathode ray tube—affectionately known as "the tube." The trend, however, is away from the tube to flat panel displays. The most popular technology used in flat panel displays is TFT (thin film transistor) active matrix *LCD (liquid crystal display)* technology. Millions of transistors are needed for TFT LCD monitors because three transistors are required for each pixel (picture element): one each for red, green, and blue. The pixels, each with its own color, are the tiny dots that make up the image. The typical LCD display has 1280 ×1024 resolution, that is, 1024 rows of 1280 pixels, or about 1.3 million little colored dots.

The most visible monitor specification is the VIS (viewable image size), the diagonal measure (to an opposite corner) of the image. Typical sizes for personal computing applications are 15-, 17-, 18-, 19-, and 20-inch monitors. CRT monitors are available up to around 22 inches and flat panel monitors can be up to 50 inches. You may need to mortgage your home to buy a flat panel in excess of 22 inches, though.

A decade ago, I could get very technical, very quickly when talking about monitors. I was concerned about acceptable color depth, dot pitch, refresh rate, resolution, and other specs. Anymore, the typical PC will have "unlimited" color depth (number of possible colors) and the dot pitch (distance between pixels) is excellent for all commercial units. The refresh rate is no longer mentioned. I still look at the resolution, but the maximum resolution for flat panel monitors is the same (1280×1024) for all but the small 15- and 17-inch monitors, which can be 1024×768 resolution. CRTs can have higher maximum resolutions, such as 1600×1200 up to 1920×1440, but personal computing at these resolutions can be cumbersome because everything is downsized to fit on the screen. A maximum resolution of 1280×1024 is just about right for normal personal computing applications.

If you decide to spend the extra dollars and purchase a flat panel display, then you should consider the *viewing angle* and the *contrast ratio*. The viewing angle is just that, the total angle at which the screen can be viewed. It's not a big deal when one person is sitting in front of the screen, but the viewing angle is important when several people are looking at the same screen, possibly watching a DVD movie. Consider anything less than 150 degrees as unacceptable. The contrast ratio refers to the measure of the difference in light intensity between bright white and black. A good contrast ratio is 400:1 (400 to 1). 700:1 is better.

Graphics Adapters

A monitor works with a *graphics adapter,* which is installed in the AGP slot on the motherboard. You will also hear it called a *graphics card* or a *video card.* The graphics adapter, with its own processor and memory, is the brains of the PC's video system (see Figure 4-2). Graphics cards that support one monitor normally have a standard VGA port and an S-Video port that allows you to send signals to a TV or screen image projector. Graphics cards that support two monitors (dual monitors) have the S-Video port plus two VGA ports or one VGA port and one DVI port, the next-generation video interface. If your dual monitor cables are both VGA, then you may need a DVI-to-VGA adapter. All output video signals from the computer's processor pass through the graphics adapter, where they are converted to signals that the monitor can interpret and display.

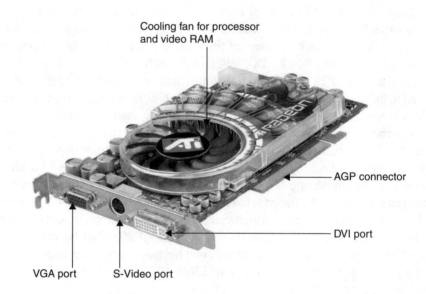

Figure 4-2   AGP graphics card with onboard processor and 256MB video RAM
(Photo courtesy of ATI Technologies)

Graphics adapters have *video RAM,* which is actually the same type of RAM used by processors. Monitor-bound images are composed in video RAM before being sent to the display. The amount of video RAM determines the number of possible colors, the resolution of the display, and the speed at which signals can be sent to the monitor. Typical video RAM capacities will be 64MB, 128MB, and 256MB. Gamers, video editors, and others with heavy-duty graphics demands will want to spend the extra money to get a high-end graphics card with plenty of video RAM.

Monitor Operation

Monitors are among the easiest I/O devices to use. Connect the cable to the monitor port, plug in the power cord, and it is ready to go. Typically, no further adjustment is needed, but every monitor has built-in controls that let you make adjustments to the display via the on-screen display (OSD). On most monitors, press the leftmost button on the front of the monitor to display the OSD main menu over whatever is on the screen. Use the + (up) and − (down) buttons to make adjustments. This is not a Windows program so you can't use the keyboard or mouse. Monitor controls are not standardized, so you may need to refer to your manufacturer's manual to make these adjustments to the viewing area: reset to factory specifications, move display horizontally or vertically, stretch/squeeze display horizontally or vertically, increase/decrease brightness or contrast, and adjust color.

Dual Monitors

Until recently, most of us tacitly assumed that PCs have one monitor, one keyboard, and one mouse. That's beginning to change now that modern hardware and software support two monitors. I suppose it's a natural progression to want more viewing area as our personal computing experiences expand. I routinely use and view three or more programs simultaneously on dual monitors. For their school projects, my children do Internet research in one display and take notes in the other. Of course, they enjoy the panoramic multiscreen view while gaming.

On a dual monitor system, the mouse pointer and application windows are moved seamlessly between the displays. A spreadsheet window can be stretched between the two viewing screens so we can see the whole of an extra-wide spreadsheet. The use of dual monitors is catching on with people who require extra viewing area or switch frequently between open applications. Personal finance, gaming, video editing, graphics, and surfing the Internet are a few of the many applications that benefit from a dual monitor setup.

The Multimedia Monitor

Occasionally, you will hear the term *multimedia monitor*. All that means is that a couple of tiny speakers and, possibly, a mike like those in notebook PCs are embedded in the monitor housing. These are more for the office environment where excessive sound is discouraged. On a home system, you probably will want to wrap yourself in more sound than these can produce.

The Projector

Until recently, screen image projectors were considered business-oriented hardware, but their price has dropped so dramatically that they are beginning to creep into the home. Projectors (see Figure 4-3) can display what you normally see on your monitor onto a large screen that can be viewed by the whole family or a group of friends.

A ceiling-mounted projector is the basis for our home theater. The projector is linked to several sources, including a DVD/CD player, a VHS player, a TV signal, and an Internet-linked PC so that we can watch movies and television, view family photos, and surf the Internet on an amazingly vivid 7-foot screen. We use a cordless keyboard and mouse with the PC, so we can sit anywhere in the "theater." The price and quality of projectors are now at a point that we may see an explosion of PC-enabled front-projection home theaters.

Figure 4-3   Screen image projector

(Photo courtesy of ViewSonic)

The Printer

Prognosticators have been predicting an evolution to a paperless society for the last 30 years. We are moving in that direction, but the paperless society will have to wait until we tire of putting pictures on refrigerators, until teachers ask for e-term papers, until tax accountants accept bits and bytes for receipts, and until holiday newsletters arrive as electronic documents. Until that happens, we will need printers.

Printers are available to meet any printing requirements. Business printers print everthing from cash register receipts for customers to office building blueprints for architects. In the personal computing world, though, print volume, print speed, and size of the document are not as much of an issue. Personal computing printing is low-volume, low-speed color printing on various sizes of documents up to legal size (8.5×14 inches) and on various types of documents, including photo paper and envelopes. Scores of relatively inexpensive printers in the $40 to $300 range are available to meet the most demanding personal computing print needs.

Types of Printers

The price and performance of *inkjet printers* have made them the overwhelming choice for personal computing (see Figure 4-4). It's rare, but some people with dual home offices buy the more expensive *laser printer.* Both inkjet and laser printers are capable of printing crystal-clear photo images. Inkjet printers are designed for low volume printing (500–1000 pages per month) and laser printers are designed to serve many office workers. The cost per printed page for laser printers is considerably less than for inkjet printers, but their upfront cost makes them too expensive for most home users.

Figure 4-4   Inkjet printer

(Photo courtesy of Hewlett-Packard Company)

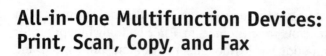

All-in-One Multifunction Devices: Print, Scan, Copy, and Fax

Until recently, most people purchased separate machines to handle print, scan, copy, and fax jobs. It turns out that these machines use similar technologies, so innovative manufacturers created the *all-in-one multifunction device* (see Figure 4-5) to do it all. The all-in-one printer, as it is often called, uses inkjet technology. It is very popular in personal computing because you can get all these capabilities for about a third the cost of all three or four machines. Some multifunction devices do not have a fax capability. It's an easy choice when you consider that there is relatively little loss of functionality when compared to separate devices. You just can't print and scan at the same time.

If you go the all-in-one route for your printing, scanning, copying, and faxing needs, you will need to decide on what type of scan/copy/fax capabilities you want—flatbed, document feed, or both. Both methods have advantages. You will pay a little more for all-in-ones that offer both capabilities.

Figure 4-5   All-in-one multifunction printer: print, scan, fax, and copy

(Photo courtesy of Hewlett-Packard Company)

Printer Technology and Features

The inkjet printer's print heads move back and forth across the paper as small injection chambers squirt tiny ink droplets on the paper. The droplets, which dry instantly as dots, form the letters and images. Maximum resolutions for the typical inkjet printer are about 1200 dpi (dots per inch) for regular black and white printing and up to 4800 dpi for color printing on premium photo paper. The higher the resolution, the more ink you use. Prior to printing, you can view the print Properties dialog box to choose a print resolution that fits the job—Best, Normal, or Draft (see Figure 4-6).

All inkjet printers, even portable ones, offer quality color printing on paper up to legal size. You can find printers that offer all or a mix of these features:

- Two-sided printing
- Built-in Ethernet (network) printing
- Paper-type sensor
- Direct camera-to-printer printing
- 11×17 printing

Keep in mind that additional features and each increment in speed and quality of output add to the cost of the printer. Once the printer has been installed, load the feed tray with paper, turn it on, and you are ready to print.

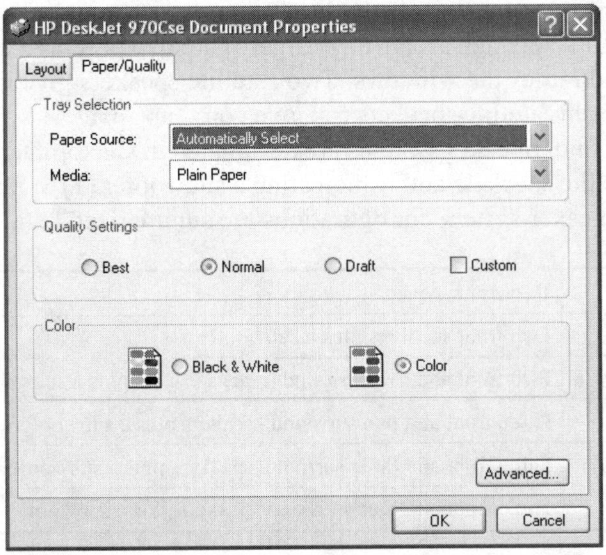

Figure 4-6   Printing options in the Properties dialog box

The Audio System

My first PC had a tiny tinny-sounding speaker that "beeped" me when an operation was completed or when I did something wrong. PC audio systems have evolved to wall-shaking surround sound for DVD movies and gaming sound effects. Anymore, audio is as much a part of the PC I/O mix as the printer. Listening to streaming music/video over the Internet, playing CDs, and making multimedia presentations are common personal computing activities.

The PC's audio system, which can have a big impact on your personal computing experience, has two pieces—the *speaker system* and the *sound card*. As with any audio system, the component quality and capabilities vary with price. Generally, if you buy a high-end sound card, you will want a high-end speaker system that takes advantages of its capabilities. If your PC is in an office setting with coworkers nearby, then a couple of inexpensive speakers will suffice. However, if you want the rich, vibrant sounds that PCs are capable of producing, you will want a speaker system that includes at least a subwoofer and between two (stereo) and seven satellite speakers (multichannel sound).

Speaker System

Speaker systems have a *subwoofer* for bass output and external speakers, called *satellites,* for the mid- and high-frequency ranges. The subwoofer is the big one that sits on the floor and rattles the windows. Two satellite speakers give you stereo. Four, five, six, and seven satellite speakers can give you four-, five-, six-, and seven-channel surround sound. Speaker systems are designated in *s.w* format, with *s* being the number of satellite speakers and *w* indicating a subwoofer (1) or no subwoofer (0). Common PC speaker system configurations are summarized here:

2.0 audio	Two front speakers
2.1 audio	Two front speakers plus a subwoofer
4.1 audio	Two front and two surround (rear) speakers plus a subwoofer
5.1 audio	Three front and two surround speakers plus a subwoofer (see Figure 4-7)
6.1 audio	Three front and three surround speakers plus a subwoofer
7.1 audio	Three front and four surround speakers plus a subwoofer

Figure 4-7   5.1 speaker system: five satellites and a subwoofer

(Photo courtesy Altec Lansing)

To enjoy cinematic surround sound, you must have a sound card that supports 4.1, 5.1, 6.1, and/or 7.1 audio and a source that provides multichannel audio. The standard for surround sound is Dolby Digital 5.1, which is available with DVD movies, Super Audio CD (SACD), DVD-Audio, and PC games. Occasionally, you will find a movie, SACD, or DVD-Audio with 6.1 audio. There is no end to the gamer's demand for better audio, so some games offer 7.1 audio. And yes, you can actually hear the difference that an additional channel/speaker will make.

Sound Card Technology

The sound card is the voice of your PC. Sound card circuitry is built into some motherboards, but if you're serious about audio with your movies, games, and music, you may wish to invest in a feature-rich sound card. The sound card (or motherboard sound) splits the audio signal into channels, amplifies the signals, and sends the signals to the speakers. Besides the playback function, the typical sound card supports speech recognition and digital audio recording applications. It also provides an interface for MIDI (Musical Instrument Digital Interface) and game controllers and provides jacks for speakers and microphones.

Sound cards are 16 bit or 24 bit, the latter offering the highest audio quality. Most sound cards will support Dolby Digital 5.1, the standard for multichannel audio. The better sound cards support 6.1 and 7.1 audio and they have a variety of features for audio enthusiasts, such as an equalizer that enables adjustments to volume and frequency for each channel.

It's easy to get excited about PC-based Dolby Digital 5.1 sound. I find it fascinating to hear a racing car move across the room as I see it move across my screen. When I listen to 5.1 music, I feel like I am sitting in the middle of the band. Innovations in the audio output capabilities of a PC have opened a new chapter in personal computing.

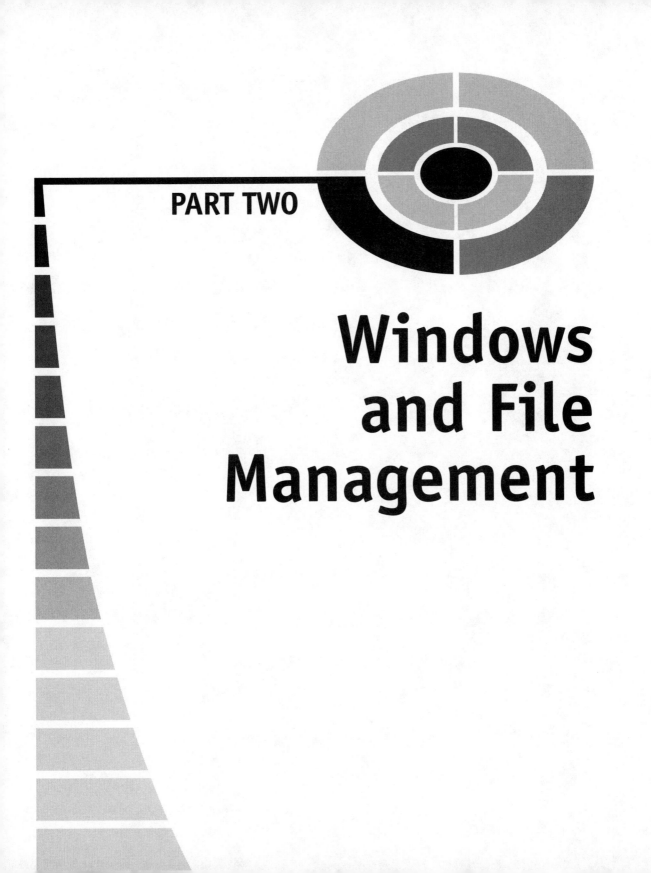

PART TWO

Windows and File Management

5

Working with Windows

Just as the processor is the center of all hardware activity, the operating system is the center of all software activity. *Microsoft Windows,* the operating system on most PCs, lets us interact with our PC, enables communication among PC components, optimizes the use of the processor and disk, keeps track of our files, and alerts us when problems occur.

In personal computing, we are constantly working with the Windows point-and-click *graphical user interface (GUI).* To truly enjoy personal computing, you need to achieve a certain level of comfort with Windows. This chapter and the next present the basics of Windows terminology, navigation (getting around), and file management. All of the examples in this book are based on Windows XP—the XP stands for "experience." The concepts are the same for older versions of Windows; however, there are slight differences in appearance and the naming of features and buttons.

Windows is a massive program with hundreds of user options and procedures. Few PC veterans really "know" Windows. What we know are its principles, the rules of interaction, what it can do, and most importantly, how to find step-by-step instructions on how to accomplish a particular task. As you gain confidence and

experience, you will begin to explore the finer points of Windows. The place to start, however, is with the basics.

Startup/Shut Down

There is nothing more basic than turning the PC on and off. However, there's more to it than pressing the on/off button on the system unit.

System Startup: The Boot Procedure

You turn on a PC just like you do a TV. However, when you press the power switch on a PC, you begin a process called *system startup* or the *boot procedure*. It's a good idea to turn on I/O devices prior to system startup.

A startup program in flash memory checks to see if memory, other electronic components, and I/O devices are working properly. If everything is OK, the program pulls the operating system into RAM from the hard disk. Once in RAM, Windows takes control of the system, at which time you may be asked to choose a *user account* and enter a *password*. The *logon procedure* identifies you to the computer system, and possibly a computer network, and verifies that you are an authorized user.

The boot procedure ends when you see the Windows desktop (see Figure 5-1), which can be personalized with background images of your choice. I like taking pictures with my digital camera, so I am continually changing my desktop background image to enjoy my kids' latest soccer victory, a high school reunion, a great vista in the Ozark Mountains, or whatever I want to relive for a few days.

System Shut Down

You don't just turn a PC off. Well, you can, but you might get into all kinds of trouble, including loss of important data, if you don't exit programs normally. This means you will need to close all active applications so that all windows are removed from the desktop. To close an application, click File | Exit in the application program's menu bar. Once all applications are closed, click Start | Turn Off Computer in the Start menu, shown in Figure 5-2.

Windows Overview

One very important step on the ladder to personal computing happiness is having a good understanding of Windows-specific terminology and concepts. The good news is that the Windows terminology and concepts that you learn in this chapter—such as minimized, shortcut key, toolbar, wizard, and dialog box—are applicable to all

Figure 5-1 The Windows desktop at startup

Windows programs. This gives all Windows programs, whether Excel, Quicken, or any other, the same look and feel. Once the Windows lingo is demystified, you'll have no trouble moving about Windows or any of its applications.

Many Windows terms have slipped into the realm of cultural literacy, so you're probably familiar with such terms as windows, icons, desktop, and others.

Figure 5-2 The Start menu

The Window

A *window* is a rectangular section of a display screen that is dedicated to a specific application, such as Microsoft Word or Paint. Windows can run multiple applications at the same time, with each *open application* in its own window. Several applications can be open or running at the same time, but there is only one *active window* and your commands apply to the application in that window. The active window's *title bar* (at the top of each application) is brighter than the others. Other open applications, which are dimmed, are running but are said to be inactive.

For all of us who endured the one-application-at-time era of personal computing, running multiple applications is a big deal. I keep four programs open whenever I'm at the computer: speech recognition (Dragon NaturallySpeaking), word processing (Word), e-mail (Outlook), and an Internet browser (Internet Explorer). On top of these, I routinely run other software. Also, your PC will have a number of programs, called *processes,* running to handle a variety of ongoing functions, such as virus protection. The number of applications and processes your PC can have running at any given time depends on the size of the programs and your PC's performance capabilities (for example, amount of RAM and processor speed).

Help

Arguably, the most important Windows feature is *Help*. Help is there for the desperate—"I'm drowning, HELP ME!!" And, it's there for the curious—"What is a device driver?" Windows is designed so that help is no more than a click away:

- **Help for Windows**   Click Start | Help and Support to get help with any Windows feature or procedure (see Figure 5-3). Windows Help includes step-by-step instructions for most common Windows activities, from how to use a mouse to how to set up a home network. You can "Pick a Help topic" and drill down to a specific need, use a keyword search, or work from an index by clicking the Index icon in the toolbar. If you wish, you can click on the Add to Favorites button to add a topic or search result to your Help and Support Favorites list so that it is easy to find in the future.
- **Help for a Microsoft Office application**   Within an Office application, such as Word or PowerPoint, click Help in the menu bar to view help options, one of which is to Show or Hide the *Office Assistant* in Microsoft Office applications. Merlin, one of several Office Assistants, is happy to answer your written questions (see Figure 5-4). Or, in some recent applications, you can "Type in a question for help" in the search box located in the menu bar. It's a good idea to be linked to the Internet when you request help, because many of Help's resources are online.

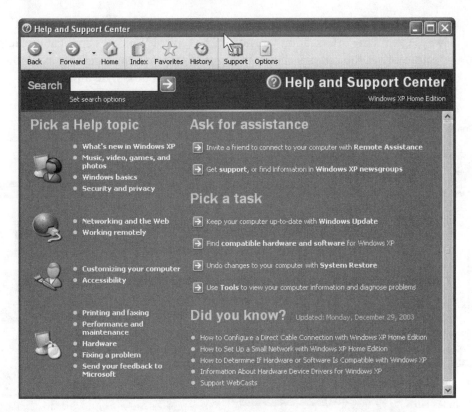

Figure 5-3   Help and Support Center for Windows

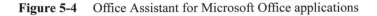

Figure 5-4   Office Assistant for Microsoft Office applications

- **Help for a non-Office application** Most applications offer you several ways to find the information you need. The typical Windows application Help feature offers the options shown in Figure 5-5: Contents (presents available help in categories), Index (enables scanning of a book-style alphabetical index), and Search (enables keyword searches of help content).

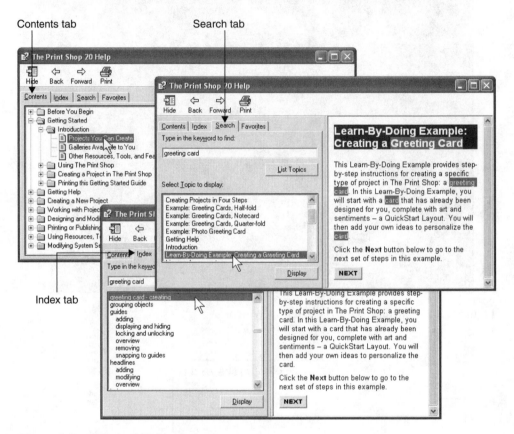

Figure 5-5   Standard Help window

- **F1: context-sensitive help** Tap the F1 key at any time to get help that relates to whatever is active.
- **? in the title bar** Most user preference boxes will have a circled ? in the title bar. To get help on any portion of the box, click the ? and the pointer becomes an arrow and a question mark. Point to the item in question, and then click again. Or, you can right-click on the item and then click the What's This? button.

So, what if you don't find what you want from the software's Help feature? Most software vendors have a variety of user support capabilities at their Internet site, including *online tutorials,* helpful *hints,* answers to *frequently asked questions (FAQs),* and, possibly, a *newsgroup* that gives their users an opportunity to interact with one another. When I have a really tough problem, I post it to the software's newsgroup, kind of an electronic bulletin board. Without exception, a friendly user somewhere in cyberspace responds with a solution.

The Desktop

The first thing you see after startup is the Windows *desktop* (see Figure 5-1). The desktop can be anything from a white screen, which would be really boring, to something that is colorful, interesting, and informative. Common elements of a desktop are identified in Figure 5-6 and explained in the following list. Figure 5-7 illustrates what the same desktop might look like for a dual monitor setup that spreads applications across the screens of two adjacent monitors.

- **Windows**   Most applications run in the traditional rectangular window. The active window displays the current application (weather). Other windows are running but are said to be inactive windows.
- **Skins**   Some applications are given unique *skins* and a different look and feel, such as the audio play center and weather applications. Most multimedia applications that play audio and video, such as Windows Media Player, can be run within a unique skin.
- **Active online content**   The desktop can display real-time Internet content, such as the weather (shown in Figure 5-1) or stock prices.
- **Taskbar**   The *taskbar* includes the Start button, the Quick Launch bar, taskbar buttons, the Notification Area, and the clock. The taskbar can be displayed all the time or it can be hidden to give you just a little more viewing area for applications. When hidden, the taskbar shows when the mouse is moved to the area of the taskbar. To reposition the taskbar to either side or to the top of the screen, just drag it (point to it, press the left mouse button, then drag it).
- **Clock**   This area shows the time of day.
- **Notification Area**   This part of the taskbar displays icons of programs loaded on system startup.
- **Taskbar buttons**   The taskbar area shows buttons that correspond to open applications.
- **Quick Launch bar**   This area holds icons for single-click access to user-selected programs.
- **Start button**   Click this button to access the Start menu. Use the Start menu to call up recent documents, change user options (Control Panel), or find help and support.

- **Background** This can be anything from a single-color screen to an elaborate image.
- **Recycle Bin** Deleted items remain here until you empty it.
- **Icons and shortcuts** Small pictographs, called icons, represent programs and other Windows elements. Click the My Computer icon to gain access to all system and network resources. An icon with a tiny arrow is a *shortcut* or a pointer to a program or file.

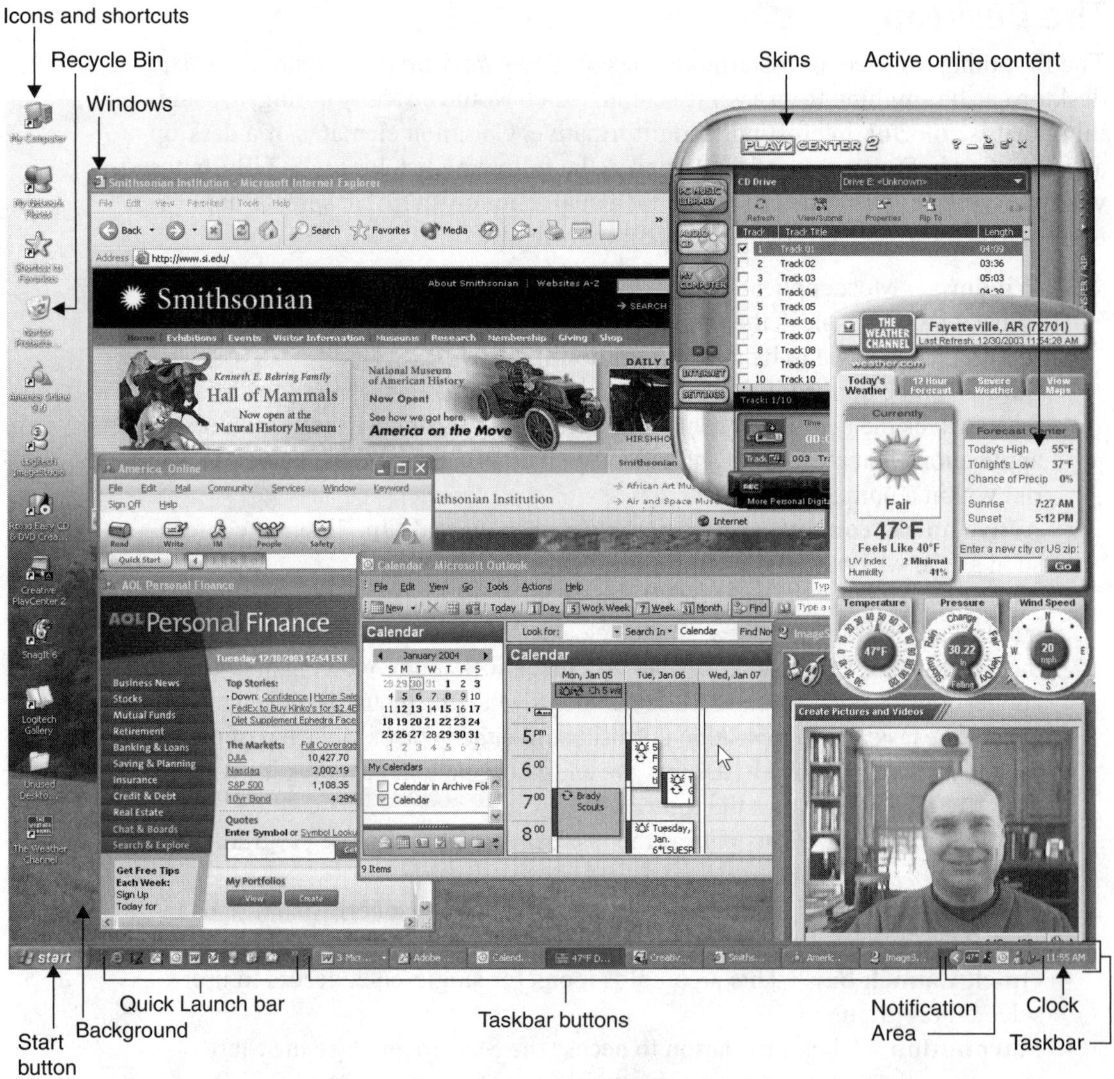

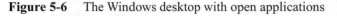

Figure 5-6 The Windows desktop with open applications

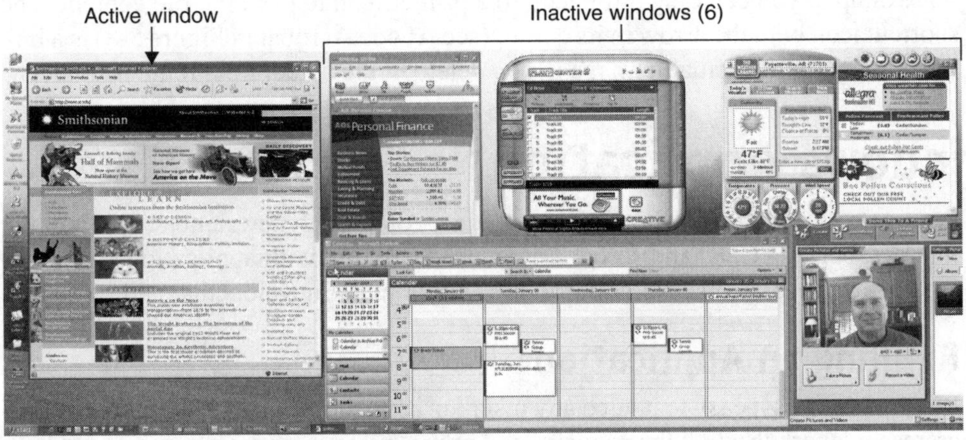

Active window   Inactive windows (6)

Figure 5-7 The Windows desktop with open applications (dual monitor setup)

Most people customize their desktop to reflect their personality, as well as their processing and information needs. I like variety, so I am constantly changing the appearance of my desktop.

Icons

Icons, the small graphical representations of Windows elements, play an important role in the Windows interface. They provide a link to any item on your PC or network, including a program, file, folder, disk drive, web page, printer, or another computer on the network. Figure 5-8 shows a sampling of commonly used icons. An icon can be positioned on the desktop, in a folder, in the Start menu, or in several other places. Click (or double-click) the icon to open an application, view an image file, call up a web page, or do whatever the icon represents. Icons have many uses.

 Application icon
(Movie Maker)

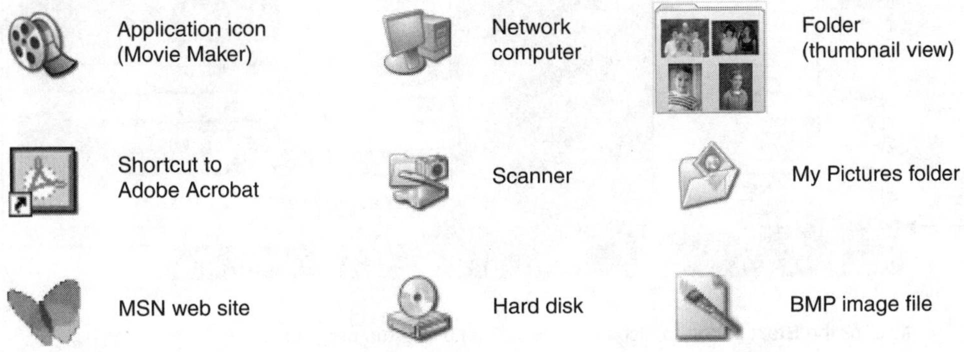

 Network
computer

 Folder
(thumbnail view)

Shortcut to
Adobe Acrobat

 Scanner

 My Pictures folder

MSN web site

Hard disk

 BMP image file

Figure 5-8 Sampling of Windows icons

For example, you can drag a file icon to a printer icon to print the file content. The shortcut icon with the arrow in its corner (see Abode Acrobat in Figure 5-8) is a link to an item, not the actual item, so if you delete it, the actual item remains intact.

The Windows Application

Personal computing is about doing things—preparing newsletters, surfing the Internet, burning CDs, and so on. That means working with application programs, such as Microsoft PowerPoint, Grolier's Multimedia Encyclopedia, and so on.

Running an Application

Windows makes it easy to launch any installed application. Just click Start | All Programs and work through the program and program group options to run an application. The steps shown in Figure 5-9 illustrate the procedure for opening an existing document. We run, launch, open, and start programs—the terms are interchangeable. When you run an application, you load the program into RAM and execute it, the result being an open application window (Paint in the example of Figure 5-9). To begin a new document, select File | New to open a clean workspace.

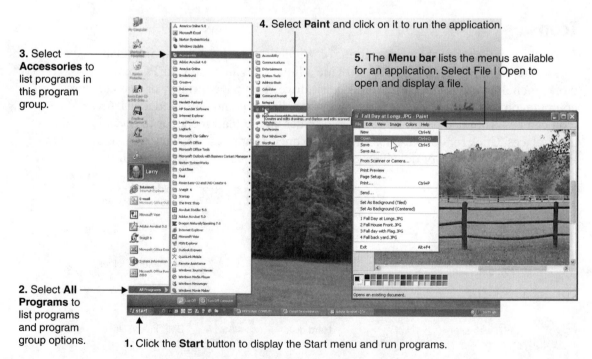

Figure 5-9   Run an application from the Start menu

Parts of an Application Window

Figure 5-10 shows Microsoft Excel running in an application window. The Excel program has two spreadsheet documents open in the application *workspace.* The workspace and other elements of the application window are shown in Figure 5-10 and explained in the following sections.

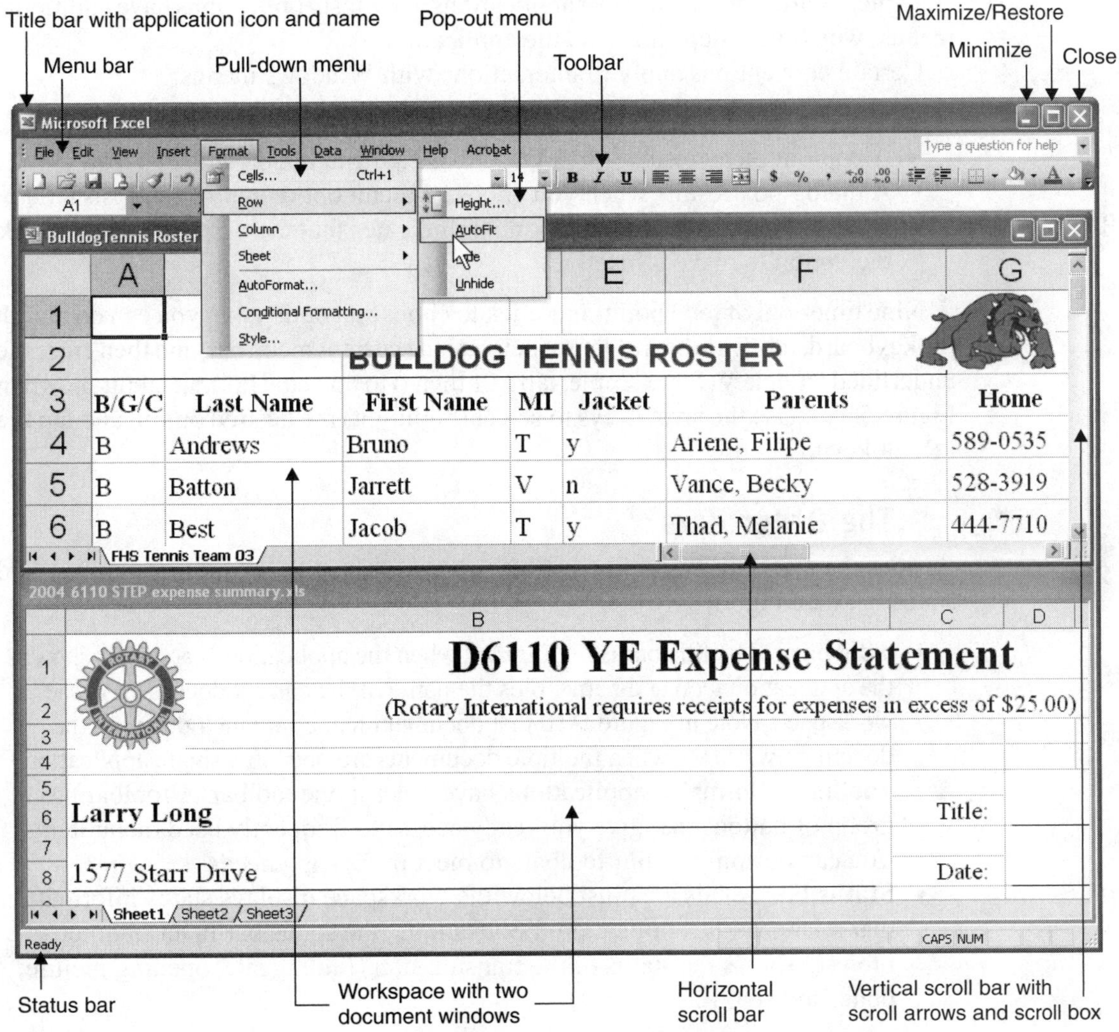

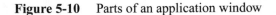

Figure 5-10   Parts of an application window

The Menu Bar and Other Menus

In personal computing you'll see a menu bar with every application, plus you'll see pull-down menus, pop-out menus, floating menus, and some others, too. All are just a list of options. The main menu for an application is the *menu bar* that runs the width of the window just below the title bar (see Figure 5-10). A *pull-down menu* is presented when you choose an option from the menu bar. The File, Edit, View, and Help menus are common to most applications and most applications have additional menus, which vary depending on the application.

Certain conventions apply to interactions with Windows menus:

- You can select only the boldface options (dimmed options are not available).
- A pop-out menu results when you choose a menu option with an arrow (▶).
- A dialog box results when you choose a menu option with an ellipsis (…).
- A check mark (✓) by a menu option indicates that the option is active (click the option to make it inactive).

Nine times out of ten I point-and-click to choose an option, but you can do it with the keyboard, too. Tap the ALT key to activate the current menu bar, and then enter the underlined letter key (for example, tap ALT then O to open the Format menu shown in Figure 5-10). Use the arrow keys to select (highlight) the desired option and tap the ENTER key to choose it.

The Other Bars

Besides the menu bar, most application windows also have a title bar, toolbar, and status bar (see Figure 5-10):

- **Title bar**   The title bar is highlighted when the application is active. It shows the application icon and name, plus the name of the current document in the workspace. Note in Figure 5-10 that document names are included with the document windows when multiple documents are open in a single application.
- **Toolbar**   Normally, applications have at least one toolbar. A toolbar has a group of buttons that give you ready access to frequently used menu items. You can customize your toolbars to meet processing needs.
- **Status bar**   This area just below the workspace displays status information that relates to the application. For example, the status bar in an Internet browser shows the status of the transmission (finding site, opening picture, done, and so on).

The Workspace

In Figure 5-10, two *document windows* are displayed in the application window's workspace. Both are Excel spreadsheets.

Resizing and Repositioning an Application Window

I am always resizing and moving multiple applications around the screen for optimal viewing. To do this, I use the three buttons on the title bar and the drag capabilities of the mouse. Every application title bar has these three buttons.

▬	Minimize button	Click this button to "shrink" the active window to an application button in the taskbar. Click the application button to expand the program to be the active window.
▢ ▢	Maximize/ Restore button	Click this button to fill the screen or restore the window to its previous size. To resize an application window, it must be a window on the desktop (not maximized).
☒	Close button	Click this button to close (exit) the application.

To resize a window, position the mouse pointer over one of the window's sides or corners. The pointer changes to a double arrow, indicating the directions you can drag the sides or corners to the desired shape. To reposition a window, position the mouse pointer over the title bar and drag the window to the desired position.

Viewing an Application Window

Many applications, such as Microsoft Excel, allow multiple document windows, each of which can be sized, shrunk, and arranged by the user within the workspace. As an alternative, the user can request that the document windows be automatically presented as *tiled windows,* as shown in Figure 5-10, or as *cascading windows* where the Windows overlap such that all title bars are visible. To tile or cascade multiple document windows, click Window | Arrange All, Tile, or Cascade. Right-click on the taskbar to tile or cascade all windows on the desktop.

Note that some applications, such as Microsoft Word, open separate application windows complete with their own set of menus and toolbars. In these applications, the Compare Side-by-Side With command, also in the Window menu, places two documents adjacent to each other.

What happens when the document is bigger than the window? Vertical and/or horizontal *scroll bars* appear to the right and/or bottom of the document window (see Figure 5-10). Drag the scroll box and/or click the scroll arrows to view other parts of the document.

Switching Between Windows

The active window is always highlighted and all parts of the window are visible. Other open windows are to the side or behind the active window. To switch between open applications, point-and-click anywhere on the desired inactive window or on its button in the taskbar.

The Dialog Box

Dialog boxes are secondary windows that appear when Windows or an application asks you to enter further information. There are a lot of dialog boxes, including the Mouse Properties, Font, Find, Print, and Folder Options dialog boxes. I keep seeing dialog boxes for the first time and I've worked with Windows since 1985.

You use the *Display Properties* dialog box, shown in Figure 5-11, to customize the desktop. Right-click anywhere on the desktop's background image and choose Properties to display this dialog box. Elements that you might find in a dialog box are explained in the following list and most are illustrated in Figure 5-11:

- **Tab**   Similar properties are grouped within tabs.
- **Text box**   Enter text information here.
- **Spin box**   Click up/down arrows to "spin" through options.
- **Command buttons**   Click these buttons as needed.
- **List box**   Shows a list of available choices.
- **Drop-down list box**   Used when the dialog box is too small for a list box.
- **Drop-down color palette**   Displays a matrix of available font, line, and fill colors.
- **Radio button**   Click this circular button to insert a dot and activate the option and deactivate the other options.
- **Scroll bar adjustment**   Drag the indicator to change options, such as the speed at which the cursor blinks or the speaker volume.
- **Check box**   Click a box to activate the associated feature.

You'll see these same user-choice tools in Windows applications, too.

Wizards

Windows and its applications have many interactive *wizards* that guide you through a process or task, such as creating a newsletter (see Figure 5-12). A Microsoft Word wizard does this by stepping you through a series of dialog boxes, each of which asks you to choose options or enter information. There are wizards that help you with sending a fax

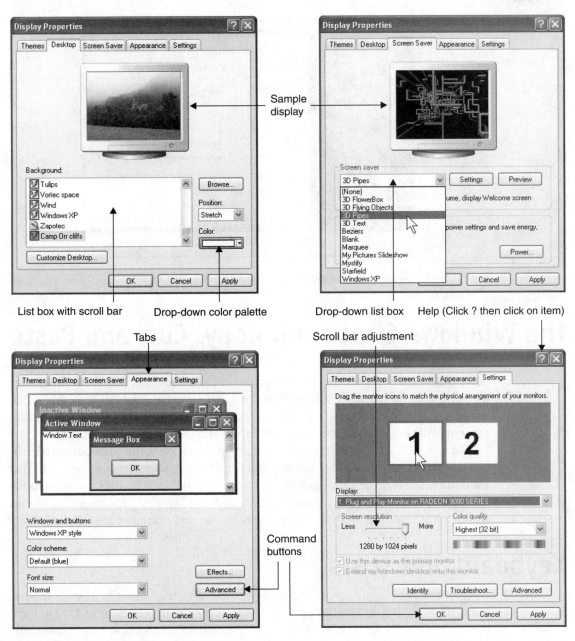

Figure 5-11 Elements of a dialog box

(via your PC), installing software, creating a database, preparing a web site, producing a resume, and completing many other day-to-day personal computing tasks.

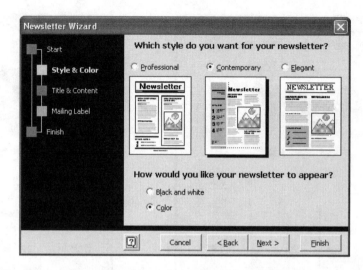

Figure 5-12 Wizard for creating a newsletter in Microsoft Word

The Windows Clipboard: Copy, Cut, and Paste

The easiest way to share information within and among applications is to use the Windows *Clipboard* in conjunction with the Edit option in the menu bar. The Clipboard is a holding area for whatever you move or copy to it—files of any kind, text, images, or whatever can be highlighted. The information in the Clipboard can be on its way to another application, or it can be moved or copied within the current document.

The Edit menu lets you Cut, Copy, or Paste information in the Clipboard. The procedure for copying information using the Clipboard is shown in Figure 5-13. This example illustrates the Copy procedure where selected information is copied to the Clipboard and it remains in the source application. When you Cut something, the information is removed from the source application and placed in the Clipboard.

Keyboard Shortcuts

Many menu options are associated with *keyboard shortcuts,* usually a key combination with the CTRL, ALT, SHIFT, or Windows key. For example, enter ALT+F4 to Exit; that is, press and hold ALT, then tap F4. Use keyboard shortcuts to issue commands without activating a menu.

There are scores of general Windows keyboard shortcuts and hundreds more application-specific shortcuts. Microsoft Word has over 200. Rather than devote the next 40 pages to listings of keyboard shortcuts, I'll show you the ones I use on a regular basis and tell you how to find complete lists of keyboard shortcuts.

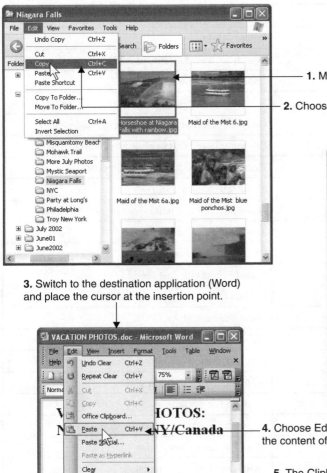

1. Mark (select) the information to be copied.

2. Choose Edit | Copy to place the image in the Clipboard.

3. Switch to the destination application (Word) and place the cursor at the insertion point.

4. Choose Edit | Paste to copy the content of the Clipboard.

5. The Clipboard content is pasted to the cursor position.

Figure 5-13   Copy and paste using the Clipboard

Table 5-1 has some handy keyboard shortcuts that are applicable to Windows and most applications and can be issued from any keyboard. The shortcuts with the Windows key are in Table 5-2 because some people have the older keyboards that don't have this key.

Key and Key Combinations	Action
F1	Display Help
F3	Search for a phrase, file, or folder
ESC	Cancel the current task
CTRL+A	Select all (everything in document)
CTRL+C	Copy the selected text or object to Clipboard
CTRL+X	Cut the selected text or object to Clipboard
CTRL+V	Paste text or object from the Clipboard
CTRL+B	Make selected text bold
CTRL+I	Make selected text italic
CTRL+U	Make selected text underlined
CTRL+Z	Undo the last action
CTRL+Y	Redo or repeat the last action
CTRL+F	Find text, formatting, and special items
CTRL+O	Open a document
CTRL+W	Close a document
CTRL+S	Save a document
CTRL+HOME	Go to beginning of document
CTRL+END	Go to end of document
ALT+ESC	Show Start menu
ALT+F4	Close the active application
ALT+TAB	Switch between open items
ALT+Underlined letter in a menu name	Display the corresponding menu
CTRL+ALT+DELETE	Display Windows Task Manager
PRINT SCREEN	Captures image of screen in Clipboard
ALT+PRINT SCREEN	Captures image of active window in Clipboard
TAB	Move forward through options in a dialog box
SHIFT+TAB	Move backward through options in a dialog box

Table 5-1 Commonly Used Keyboard Shortcuts

Key and Key Combinations	Action
WIN	Display or hide the Start menu
WIN+BREAK	Display the System Properties dialog box
WIN+D	Show desktop
WIN+M	Minimize all open windows
WIN+SHIFT+M	Restore minimized windows
WIN+E	Open My Computer
WIN+F	Search for a file or folder
WIN+F1	Display Windows Help

Table 5-2   Keyboard Shortcuts with the Windows Key

To view a list of keyboard shortcuts and other information about shortcuts, enter **keyboard shortcut** in the Help search box for Windows or an application. Used judiciously, shortcuts can speed up whatever you are doing.

Customizing Windows

Your home is you, as is your car/truck and your clothing. In time, personal computing becomes very much a part of who you are, too. Windows gives you the flexibility to tailor your personal computing environment to fit both your processing needs and your personality.

When you purchase a PC, you get the default settings for Windows and its applications. For example, the Windows default desktop background is Bliss, a landscape with blue sky. I prefer a family picture or a landscape of my own.

Much of what can be customized is accessed from Control Panel (Start | Control Panel). You can toggle between the Classic View of Control Panel items and the Category View, shown in Figure 5-14, which has nine categories. Clicking on an item or "change" task displays the applicable Properties dialog box (see Figure 5-14) or a wizard.

Most icons and many program elements are associated with a Properties or Customize dialog box. To see if an icon or element within a program can be revised, point to it and right-click. If the shortcut menu appears with a Properties or Customize option, click that option to display the dialog box. For example, right-click anywhere on the desktop and select Properties to display its Properties dialog box or right-click anywhere on an application program's toolbar and select Customize to display its Customize dialog box.

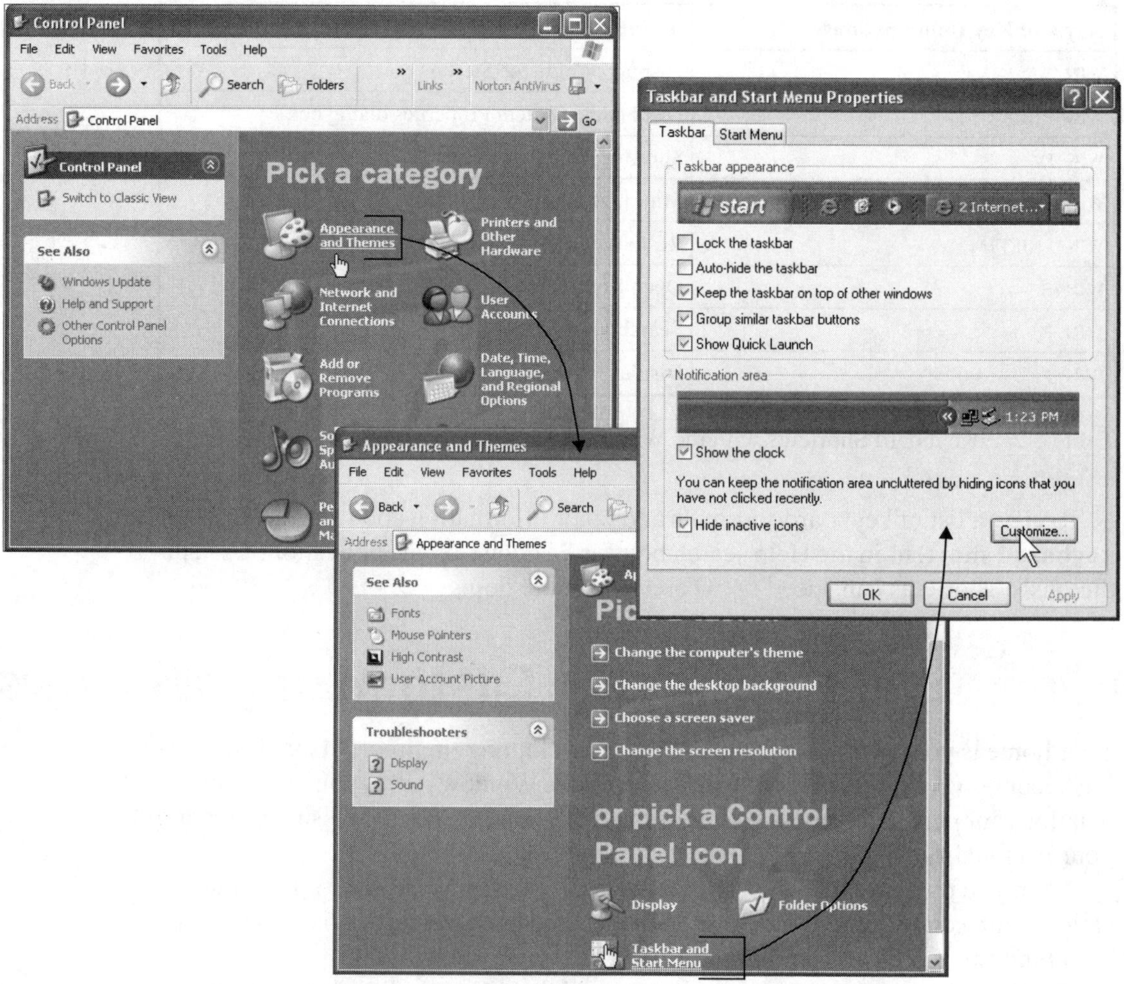

Figure 5-14   Customizing the taskbar and Start menu

The following examples should give you a feel for the many ways you can customize your personal computing environment. At this point, it's more important to know what you can do to customize your PC than how to do it. The Windows Help and Support Center (Start | Help and Support) has easily accessible step-by-step procedures that walk you through the use of the appropriate dialog box or wizard.

- **User accounts**   Windows can be personalized for each person sharing a PC, so if everyone in the family uses the same PC, user accounts can be set up such that when you or a family member logs in, the desktop and all other aspects of Windows reflect that user's choices.

- **The display**   The display properties give your PC a visually unique appearance. You can select a *theme* that determines your background, the fonts and colors used in the windows, the three-dimensional effects, the appearance of the icons and mouse pointers, and what sounds are used. Or, you can create your own theme by customizing the elements.
- **Accessibility**   If you have difficulty keying or using the mouse or have impaired vision or hearing, you can use the Accessibility Options dialog box to choose to be given visual warnings for sound, to increase the display contrast, to alter the keyboard, and so on.
- **Toolbars**   Right-click on any toolbar to change the mix of buttons or the placement of the toolbar.
- **Taskbar and Start menu**   Right-click on the taskbar to display a dialog box that lets you customize the appearance of the taskbar and the Start menu (content, placement, and so on).
- **Keyboard**   Set up your own keyboard shortcuts and choose the speed at which the cursor blinks.
- **Sound**   Adjust volumes for the audio in and out.
- **Date and time**   You can opt to synchronize your PC's clock with an extraordinarily precise clock at an Internet Time server.
- **Dual monitors**   Adjust your dual monitor setup such that the primary unit is left, right, top, or bottom.
- **Printer**   Your printer's dialog box offers a number of options, including whether a document is printed in sequence or in reverse sequence (last page, first).
- **Power management**   You can save power by opting to turn off your monitor or disk after a certain period of time.

Each application can be customized, as well. To customize an application, such as Word, Outlook, or Internet Explorer, click Tools in the menu bar then select Options or Customize. For example, Outlook, the e-mail program, gives you the flexibility to choose how closely you filter junk mail.

I can assure you that the time you spend exploring the Options and Customize dialog boxes for Windows and your applications will enhance your personal computing experience. You adjust the seat and mirrors in your car, don't you? It's the same with personal computing, except you have a whole lot more to adjust.

6

Working with Files

Every PC has a lot of files—songs, reports, images, programs, and so on. A *file* is any electronically accessible recording of information. When my virus protection software scans my hard disk for infected files, it reports the number of files checked—now over 700,000 files. Your PC may have fewer or more files, but the number will astound you. These files are yours to care for and manage.

Windows uses the folder metaphor to refer to a named group of files, so files are placed in *folders*. The Windows folder icon looks like the file folder we use to store hard copy documents in a metal file cabinet.

Not counting my backup files, I have slightly over 50,000 user files, which are organized into about 2500 folders. Windows software has 12,390 files in 638 folders. The folder for the material used to compile this book has over 500 files in 38 folders. You will be surprised how quickly the number of files can grow for any major project at home or work, so managing files is always an issue in personal computing.

Considering the numbers involved, it's easy to see why it's important that files be organized into logical folders and *subfolders* (folders within folders or subfolders). If your files are well-organized, you will be able to navigate right to the file you need.

Types of Files

Files are defined by the software that creates them. For example, Microsoft Excel, a spreadsheet program, creates a type of file designed to be read and processed by Excel software. When we create an Excel file, we must give it a name and Excel stores it to disk with an .xls extension. If you'll remember from Chapter 2, the user-designated portion of the Windows filename is to the left of the rightmost period and the program's unique extension is to the right of that period (for example, World Population.xls). Windows filenames can have up to 255 upper- or lowercase characters, but the following special characters are not permitted— " " / \ : * < > |. Windows filenames are not case sensitive, so "MY FILE.doc" and "My File.DOC" are the same file as far as Windows is concerned.

There are many types of applications and, consequently, many types of files. Some of these popular types of files are illustrated in Figure 6-1 and described in the following list:

- **ASCII file (TXT)** The ASCII or TXT file is a text-only file created with and displayed by any word processing program or text editor (Readme.txt is 41KB).
- **Document file (DOC)** Word processing document files contain text and, often, embedded images (Intel Processor Timeline.doc is 41KB).
- **Excel Spreadsheet file (XLS)** A spreadsheet file contains rows and columns of data (World Population.xls is 190KB.)
- **Audio file (WAV, MP3, and others)** An audio file contains digitized sound, such as the sound you hear when Windows begins (Windows XP Startup.wav is 415KB at 4 seconds).
- **Video file (WMV, AVI, and others)** A video file contains digitized video frames that when played produce motion video (Home movie.wmv is 361KB at 12 seconds).
- **Graphics file (BMP, JPG, TIF, and others)** A graphics file contains digitized images (Earth at night.bmp is 8438KB).

Most applications read and/or produce files in their *native file format*. For example, Microsoft PowerPoint, a presentation program, creates PPT files. However, some applications can work with several types of file formats. Graphics programs can read

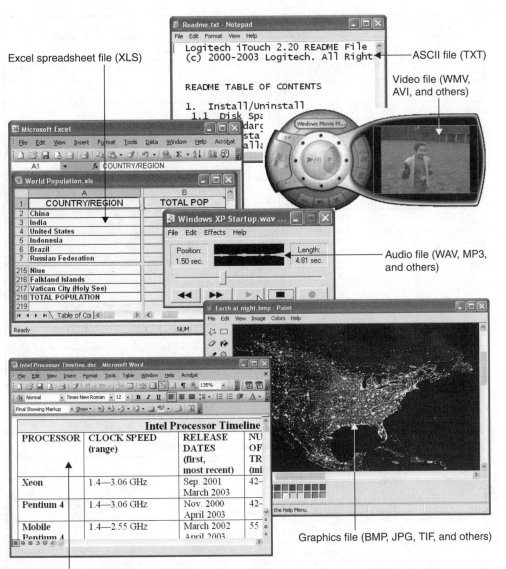

Excel spreadsheet file (XLS)

ASCII file (TXT)

Video file (WMV, AVI, and others)

Audio file (WAV, MP3, and others)

Graphics file (BMP, JPG, TIF, and others)

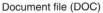

Document file (DOC)

Figure 6-1   Types of files

and create many types of images, including JPG, GIF, and TIF. Table 6-1 provides a summary of common file types. The file extensions in the table are only a sampling of the hundreds of extensions you might see in personal computing. For a complete list of extensions, enter **file extensions** into the search box for any Internet search engine.

WORD PROCESSING AND TEXT DOCUMENTS	
.doc	Microsoft Word and WordPad
.wpd	WordPerfect
.wks	Microsoft Works
.txt	Plain ASCII text/unformatted
.pdf	Adobe Acrobat/Reader (Portable Document Format)
.pub	Microsoft Publisher
.rtf	WordPad (minimally formatted text)
SPREADSHEETS	
.xls	Microsoft Excel
.wq1	Corel Quattro Pro
.wk1 .wk3 .wk4	Lotus 1-2-3
DATABASES	
.mdb	Microsoft Access
.db	Paradox
PRESENTATION	
.ppt	Microsoft PowerPoint
GRAPHICS	
.gif	CompuServe graphics interchange format
.jpg	JPEG compressed graphics format
.bmp	Windows bitmap
.tif	Tagged image file format
.eps	Encapsulated PostScript
.vsd	Microsoft Visio
.ai	Adobe Illustrator
.pds	Adobe Photoshop

Table 6-1   Popular File Extensions

SOUND	
.wav	Windows WAV
.aif	Macintosh AIFF
.ra	RealAudio
.mp3	Compressed audio
.mid	MIDI file
VIDEO	
.avi	Windows Video
.mov	Macintosh QuickTime video
.mpg	MPEG video format
COMPRESSED FORMATS	
.zip	Compressed file format
.hqx .bhx	BinHex compression (Apple computers)
WINDOWS FILES	
.eml	Microsoft Outlook message
.pab	Outlook personal address book
.ini	Windows initialization file
.sys	System file
.exe .com	Executable file
.bat .pif	MS-DOS batch file (information to run programs)
MISCELLANEOUS FILES	
.htm .html	HTML code (web pages)
.shtml	HTML secure web site
.vbp	Visual Basic program file
.cpp	C++ program file

Table 6-1   Popular File Extensions *(continued)*

What to Do with a File

Just about everything you do on a PC involves a file. Here are some of the things you can do with a file:

- *Create, name, and save files.* You create files when you name and save a drawing, a spreadsheet, or an audio clip to disk storage.
- *Copy, move, and delete files.* You copy files from CD-ROM to hard disk during software installation. You move files when reorganizing them. When you no longer need files, you delete them.
- *Retrieve and update files.* You can retrieve and update your files as often as you wish (for example, Daily diary.doc).
- *Display, print, or play files.* Files that involve text and/or graphics can be displayed and printed. Audio and video files are played.
- *Execute files.* You can run program files (those that end in .exe, .com, .bat, and .pif).
- *Download and upload files.* You can *download* useful files from the Internet to your PC. You can also *upload* files from your PC to another computer, usually an Internet server computer.
- *Export/import files.* When you *import* a file, you convert it from its foreign format (perhaps an Excel spreadsheet) to a format that is compatible with the current program (perhaps to a table in Word). You can *export* files when you want to convert a file in the current program (a Word table) to a format needed by another program (an Excel spreadsheet).
- *Protect files.* You can protect files by limiting access to authorized persons. For example, you might wish to protect a Word file that contains your passwords.
- *Encrypt files.* You can encrypt sensitive files being sent over computer networks or the Internet so that only those recipients with the key can decrypt and open the digitally scrambled file.
- *Back up files.* You can create and keep backup files as protection against the loss of valuable information.
- *Compress files.* You can compress files (make them smaller) so that they use disk space more efficiently or can be transmitted over the Internet in less time.

Compression may need a little more explanation. File compression is like squeezing the air out of a sponge. The sponge gets smaller, but it returns to its original shape when you release it. *File compression* works in the same way in that it takes the dead space out of inefficient files. For example, one compression technique used with graphics files involves replacing those portions of an image that are the same color with a brief descriptor that identifies the color only once and the area to be colored. On average, a compressed file takes up 50 percent less space. In Windows, we *zip* and *unzip* files to compress and uncompress them—more on this later.

Windows Explorer: File Management

The Windows file management tool is *Windows Explorer,* a multifunction tool that can double as an Internet browser. In fact, Windows Explorer and Internet Explorer are one in the same. Windows Explorer toolbars are oriented to file management and those in Internet Explorer are oriented to cruising the Internet. They are "different" applications so that you can customize Explorer for file tasks and Internet Explorer for Internet-based tasks.

There are three ways to display Windows Explorer:

- Select Start | All Programs | Accessories, then click Windows Explorer.
- Double-click My Documents, My Computer, or My Network Places on the desktop.
- Right-click any file or folder icon, and then select Explore.
- Use the shortcut key, WIN+E.

Windows Explorer is one of the most active programs on my computer as I am always manipulating files. The face of my Explorer is never the same because I change the way it looks to meet my immediate personal computing needs.

The Explorer Command Interface

At the top of Windows Explorer are up to four bars that you can use to issue commands in file management tasks or to link to an Internet site:

- **Menu bar**   Always at the top, the menu bar lets you select file options (Print, New, Save, Delete, and so on), select edit options (including Copy, Cut, and Paste), and change the way you view files.
- **Toolbar**   Because Windows Explorer is based on Internet Explorer, the buttons in the toolbar are designed primarily for Internet navigation and will be discussed in Chapter 12, "Internet Applications: Cruising the Internet."
- **Address bar**   The Address bar shows the folder path to the current (highlighted) folder.
- **Links bar**   This bar shows Internet links to frequently visited web sites.

Windows Explorer and every other aspect of Windows gives us a variety of ways to accomplish the same task. With a little practice, patience, and experimentation you will home in on the interactive methods that suit your personal computing style.

Viewing Files and Folders

Explorer includes a *folders pane* to the left that shows the hierarchical file structure. Each folder in the Folders pane either has nothing to its left or has a + or a – symbol. Those folders with nothing to the left contain no subfolders, but they might contain files. Those with a + have at least one subfolder and are said to be *collapsed*. Click the + to *expand* the folder and show its subfolders. When the folder is expanded, the + changes to a –. Click the – to *collapse* the folder and hide its subfolders.

The following list describes the file viewing options for each folder, which are also shown in Figure 6-2. To select a particular view, click View in the menu bar, then select the desired view.

- **Thumbnails**   This view shows a thumbnail (an image reduced to thumbnail size) of the file or an icon that represents the type of file. This view is particularly helpful when viewing image files.
- **Icons**   In this view, all files and folders are presented as icons with the filename under the icon.
- **Tiles**   This view is like the Icons view, except the filename is presented to the right.
- **Details**   This view provides detailed information for each file. Typically this information will be the filename, file type, file size, and the date the file was last modified.
- **List**   This view presents a list of files and folders, each of which is preceded by its associated program icon. This view is handy when the folder has many folders/files.

- **Filmstrip**   This view is best suited for picture folders. In this view, the images are presented as thumbnails in a horizontal filmstrip, which can be scrolled left and right. Select an image to view an enlarged version of the image.

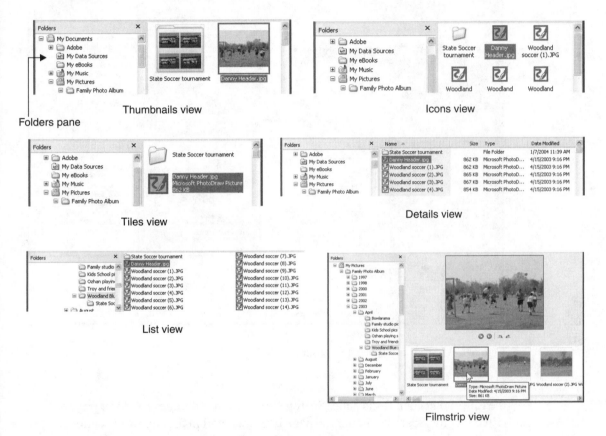

Figure 6-2   Folders pane with various ways to view files

Other Explorer options are shown in Figure 6-3. The files group option lets you show files in groups by file detail (name, type, size, and date modified). To display groups, select View | Arrange Icons By, and then select the desired grouping.

The Explorer pane, the left panel, has several views, too. Select the Folders button in the toolbar to toggle back and forth between the Folders pane shown in Figure 6-2 and the Tasks pane shown in Figure 6-3. The Tasks pane changes depending on what tasks are applicable. For example, Figure 6-3 illustrates the System Tasks pane and

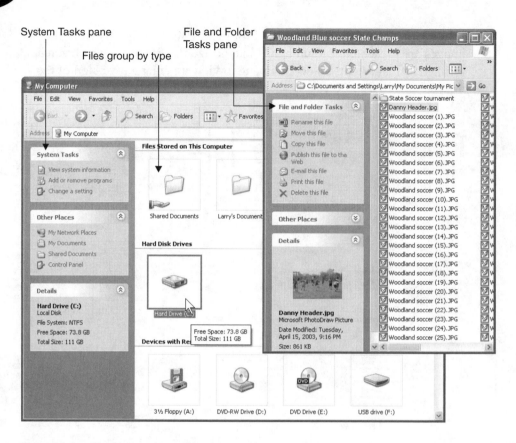

Figure 6-3 Explorer pane and groups

the File and Folder Tasks pane. Search Companion is another Explorer pane option. (I'll cover the Search Companion pane in more detail in the "Search" section later in the chapter.)

You might ask, "Why so many views?" Surprisingly, each view serves a purpose; however, I must admit that I seldom use the Icons or Tiles views. Mostly, I use the List view along with the Folders pane, except when I need file details (Details view) or when I am working with a group of images (Thumbnails view). Occasionally, I toggle the Explorer pane from Folders to Tasks when I want to view a thumbnail and/ or file details for a specific image. Generally, the tasks listed in the Tasks pane are readily available elsewhere. For example, select an image and right-click it to view a menu with these and other choices.

Organizing Files into Folders

We store files in a tree structure, with folders being the limbs and branches, and the files being the leaves. The trunk of the tree is a disk drive. My computer has a floppy disk (A:), a hard disk (C:), a DVD-RW drive (D:), a DVD-ROM drive (E:), and a removable USB flash drive (F:). Each of these drives is assigned a letter and is the *root folder* from which other folders and subfolders grow. My computer has five trees when removable media are in their drives and the USB flash drive is in a USB port. Ninety percent of the time, though, it's just one tree, the hard disk (C:).

Often, you hear people use the parent/child metaphor to describe the hierarchical file structure of PCs. A parent is any folder that contains subfolders (children). Children become parents when they have subfolders. The root can only be a parent.

Personal Folders: My Documents

Windows creates a special folder called *My Documents* to be your personal folder for all user files. Windows gives you several ways to navigate to My Documents. You can display this folder by clicking its icon on the desktop. You can click it at the top of the Folders pane in Explorer. Or you can select Start | My Documents. To further encourage you to store your user files in My Documents, Windows creates a *My Pictures* folder and a *My Music* folder to get you started. As you install programs, they may create subfolders in My Documents. Also, some programs, especially digital imaging programs, store files in My Pictures by default. Of course, you will create folders, as well, perhaps one for files that pertain to your work and a catch-all miscellaneous folder. Creating a new folder is a three-step process:

1. Use the Folders pane to navigate to the folder in which you wish to place the new folder.
2. Select File | New | Folder.
3. Enter a name for the new folder.

Microsoft would prefer that all user files be in the My Documents folder. Even the Windows backup routines are designed to look for user files in this folder. The main reason Microsoft does this is to discourage you from creating folders that are children of C:, the root folder. This keeps you away from the Windows and Program Files folders, the location of Windows and applications programs. If a few of these files are accidentally moved or deleted, your PC might get very upset and refuse to function. Yes, there are times that you will believe your PC has a personality.

Shared Documents

If more than one person will be using a PC, you should set up a separate *user account* for each person. Each person with a user account has his or her own personal My Documents folders. Other users do not have access to your My Documents files and vice versa. If you wish to share files with other users on your PC, highlight the file/folder you wish to share. Drag it to Shared Documents (it might say Shared Pictures or Shared Music, too), which is located in the Explorer Tasks pane under Other Places.

To add users to a PC, select Start | Control Panel | User Accounts. If three people in the house use the PC, it's a good idea to give each person his or her own account so they can enjoy the benefits of a personalized PC.

The Path

We create a logical hierarchy of folders to hold our songs, word processing documents, family photos, and other user files. The operating system stores and retrieves files based on their *path,* the hierarchy of folders that leads to their location on disk storage. If you stay within the GUI and Windows Explorer, you probably won't have to deal with the written paths of files. But if you do, the path for the highlighted image in Figure 6-4 (River friends 1.jpg), for example, is as follows:

C:\Documents and Settings\Larry\My Documents\
  My Pictures\Family Photo Album\2003\April\Troy and friends on Buffalo River

This Windows path is shown in the Address bar in Figure 6-4.

The folders within My Documents are portrayed within Explorer as if My Documents were the root folder. Actually, it's not. As you can see from the preceding path, it is three levels down from the root folder, C:. A Beethovens 5th.mp3 file that is in the Classical subfolder to My Music within the My Documents folder would have the following path within the Explorer workspace:

My Documents\My Music\Classical\Beethovens 5th.mp3

However, the actual path recognized by the operating system and shown in the Address bar would be this:

C:\Documents and Settings\Larry\My Documents\My Music\Classical\Beethovens 5th.mp3

For the most part, Windows users rely on the graphical hierarchy in Windows Explorer to deal with files. However, on occasion, you may be asked to confirm or create a path presented in text format. Just remember, the folders in a path are separated by a backslash (\), not a forward slash (/).

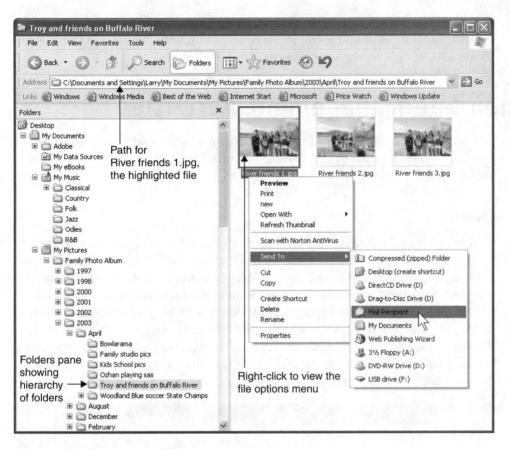

Figure 6-4 The path and file options

Right-click any folder to display a menu of file management options. The menu in Figure 6-4 includes Preview, Print, Open With (select a program to use), Send To (a disk or e-mail recipient), Cut (to Clipboard), Copy, Create Shortcut, Delete, Rename, and Properties.

Folder Options

By now you're probably thinking that you've seen all the options for Windows Explorer—wrong. To see more, select Tools | Folder Options. The Folder Options dialog box has about 20 more ways to further customize Windows Explorer. Generally, the Windows defaults work well for most people, but I like to display file extensions with the filename, so I uncheck Hide Extensions for Known File Types in the View tab. The File Types tab lists all of the extensions on the PC and their program association. If you click a JPG file and it opens up in Microsoft PhotoDraw and you would prefer that it open in Windows Picture and Fax Viewer, then this is where you change that association.

Common File Management Activities

The most frequently completed file management activities are open, save/save as, copy, cut, rename, paste, delete, restore, zip, unzip, search, and undo. Let's look at each of them.

Open

To open a file in Explorer, find the file by navigating through its path in the Folders pane, then double-click the filename to open the file. The file opens in its associated application program or, if it's a program file, opens and runs. As an alternative, you can right-click the file and choose Open With in the options menu.

If you open a file within any application, such as Paint, you select File | Open to display the Open dialog box (see Figure 6-5). Entering CTRL+O, the shortcut key, does the same thing. Use the shortcut icons in the panel to the left or the drop-down box at top to navigate to the desired folder. Select a file, then click the Open button or double-click the file to open it into an application program's workspace.

Figure 6-5   Open dialog box for applications

Save/Save As

Choose the Save or Save As option in an application's File menu to create and save files to a folder. In either case, you give the file a name and save it to a folder on a particular disk. Choose Save As if you wish to store the current document, which has already been saved, as a new file with a new filename and, possibly, to a different folder and/or disk. The Save dialog box looks like the Open dialog box in Figure 6-5 except that the button reads Save rather than Open.

Copy and Cut

Choose the Copy option in Explorer to create a duplicate of one or more files or folders. Highlight what you wish to duplicate and choose the Copy command from the Edit menu or from the right-click options menu. This sends a copy of the file to the Clipboard.

You can highlight multiple files by pressing the CTRL key and clicking on the desired files or folders. Click Copy to place the files on the Clipboard. To complete the copy operation, navigate to where you wish to save the copy (the path), then choose Edit | Paste. Or, if you prefer, you can use the mouse to drag the highlighted file(s)/folder(s) to another folder in either the Folders pane or the file viewing area. Press and hold the CTRL key during copy drag operations (CTRL+drag operation). Drag the item(s) over the icon of the desired folder or into the folder's file area.

The Cut command works like the Copy command except that a cut operation deletes the highlighted item(s) from its original folder. To move a file with a mouse drag, just drag the item(s) to its new location. To move a file to another disk, you need to press and hold the SHIFT key while dragging.

If you plan to copy/move several files to different locations, I would suggest that you open two Explorer windows. You can eliminate the Clipboard and save time by dragging the items between the two windows.

Rename

To rename a file or folder, highlight the desired file or folder, then choose Rename from the File menu or the right-click options menu. A third option, which I prefer, is to click the actual filename (not the icon), wait a second, and then click it again. Each approach converts the filename area to a text box in which you can edit the old name or enter a new name.

Paste

The Copy and Cut operations place the content on the Clipboard. Once on the Clipboard it can be pasted to another folder or directly into an application. For example, an image can be pasted (inserted) into a Word document. A Cut/Paste combination effectively "moves" a file from one place to another. Paste the file as many times as you wish.

Delete and Restore

Delete is easy. Highlight the files/folders and then tap the DELETE key. Or, you can use the Edit or right-click menus. Restore is a little more involved. When you delete a file, it isn't actually deleted from your hard disk. It's moved to the *Recycle Bin*. The Recycle Bin is an icon on your desktop that looks like a trash can. If you accidentally delete a file, there's no reason to panic. Simply open (double-click) the Recycle Bin, find and select your file, and choose Restore This Item in the Tasks pane. Occasionally, you'll want to empty the Recycle Bin. To do this, simply right-click the desktop icon and choose Empty Recycle Bin.

Zip and Unzip

It seems like I'm always zipping or unzipping files. *Zipped files* are compressed so they take up less disk space and they take less time to download/upload over the Internet. A zipped file must be unzipped before it can be used. And, what's the icon for a zipped file? You guessed it—a folder with a zipper.

If you want to send a dozen recent shots of your new baby or some other group of files over the Internet, you can zip them all into a single convenient zip file. The unzip process restores the individual files.

To zip a file or files, you must first create a zip folder. To do this, select the files in Explorer, select File | New | Compressed (Zipped) Folder. Move or copy as many files as you want to the zip folder just as you would any other folder. To unzip a zipped folder, right-click it and choose Extract All, which displays the Compressed Folders Extraction Wizard. Follow the directions to unzip its files.

Search

The Windows search capability is the quickest way to find a file, a folder, and information on the Internet, too. To begin a search, click the Search button in the Explorer toolbar to display the Search Companion pane. Or, if Explorer is not open, select Start | Search.

The Search Companion is the launch pad for finding files and folders on your computer or a network. The Search Companion allows you to search for folders and files using a variety of search criteria, including name, part of a name, file type, or file size. You can also search for a file or folder based on the approximate dates you created it. If you know a phrase in the document, such as "know thyself," you can search for specific text in the file, too.

The best way to search for a file is to give the Search Companion as much information as you can. If you know the file is somewhere in My Documents, then use the Address drop-down list box to narrow the search to My Documents. Figure 6-6 illustrates how a search for a file with the word "Flyer" in its filename might proceed. If you don't know what type of file it is, select All Files and Folders, then enter the search word, "Flyer," in the All or Part of the File Name box. Click Search to get the results.

The Search Companion offers very sophisticated tools for searching your computer, a network, or the Internet. It's relatively intuitive and easy to use, but you need to spend a few minutes exploring its many options. For example, you can choose to search the files in the highlighted folder or you can choose to search its subfolders, too. You also can use wildcard characters in the search criteria. For example, the asterisk is a substitute for zero or more characters. Enter ***.jpg** to find all graphics JPG files in a folder.

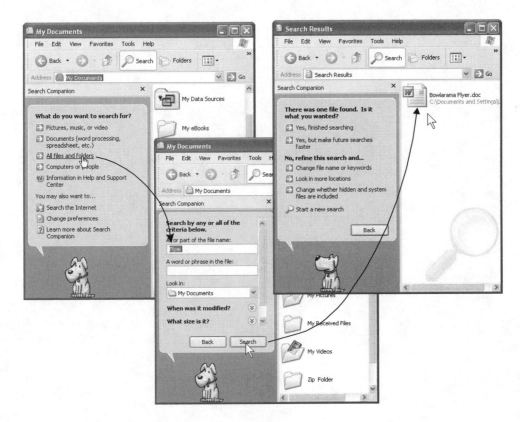

Figure 6-6   The Search Companion

Undo

 I've saved the best for last. It's the best because it saves us from our self-destructive ways. It's inevitable that you will do something in Windows Explorer that you did not want to do. If you move files to the wrong place, delete your homework assignment, or do something else silly with your files, all you have to do is click Edit in the menu bar and then select Undo. I use Undo so often that I customized my Explorer toolbar to include an Undo button (see Figure 6-4). The great thing about Undo is that you can enjoy a freewheeling attitude about personal computing. Every Edit menu in every application has an Undo option. Wouldn't it be great if life had an Undo button?

PART THREE

Buying and Using a PC

CHAPTER

7

Buying Issues and Considerations

This chapter and the next present a disciplined approach to buying PC hardware and software. Hopefully this approach will demystify an often confusing process so that when you make purchases, you are confident you have spent money wisely. The emphases in this chapter are what you need to consider and the issues you need to resolve before any money changes hands. Chapter 8, "What and Where to Buy," answers the questions "What PC do I buy?" and "Where do I buy it?" Hints, tips, and recommendations are sprinkled liberally throughout these two chapters in hopes that they can help you avoid the purchasing pitfalls and buy the right system at the best price.

When to Buy?

If you don't have a PC, now is a good time to buy one. It's been a buyer's market for personal computers for a number of years. That's not expected to change in the foreseeable future.

If you own a PC and it is more than three or four years old, you're a candidate for a new one. If you work at home and share your work computer with your family, you really should consider buying another PC that would be 100 percent yours during the workday (but you probably already know this). If your PC balks when your kids attempt to run the latest games, that's a clear sign that you need a better PC. "When are you going to be finished with the PC?" If this phrase is heard over and over at your house, you may be ready to become a multiple-PC home. Having two or more PCs in a family is becoming commonplace and many of these families have linked their PCs in a home network.

"Wait a few months and the price will drop." It's true, but this is hollow advice. You can always wait two, four, or six months and get today's $1000 PC for a few hundred dollars less. But what about opportunity cost? In today's connected society there is a price to pay if you don't have this amazing tool at your beck and call. You may pay $800 six months from now for the same system, but that system is only worth $800 because it is six months closer to the recycle bin.

A good PC can help you improve your productivity at work and at home; give you much needed information; expand your intellectual and cultural horizons; amaze you, your family, and your friends; and give you endless hours of enjoyment. Why give this up for any length of time?

The PC Investment

The process of buying a PC is an adventure, whether you're a first-time buyer, buying a replacement system, or buying a second or third system. Let's put this purchase into perspective. The typical home PC is used 10 to 50 hours a week. It's not passive like a TV. We interact with it to have fun, be informed, and do the chores of life. As any PC owner will tell you, the PC quickly becomes a major part of what you do and, even, who you are.

The price tag for an entry-level personal computer system from a name-brand manufacturer begins around $1000. Sure, you can get a PC for $499, but this is a minimal system. Once you add the car equivalent of turn signals and a paint job, the final cost can be easily double the "come-on" price. Count on the cost of a PC system to be into four figures when you add a quality printer, upgrade a few components (monitor size and disk capacity), add a DVD+RW drive, and purchase essential supplies/accessories (DVD+RW discs and a surge suppressor) and critical software (for example, antivirus software). A high-end notebook PC and a full complement of peripheral devices, software, and mobile accessories can cost in excess of $6000.

PC supplies, routine maintenance, additional software, software upgrades, and Internet access charges can easily add $1000 a year to the total cost of ownership. As you can see, living the personal computing adventure can run into serious money—quickly. However, any PC purchased with purpose and invigorated with imagination is well worth its cost—and then some.

Things to Think about Before Buying a PC

Prior to embarking on a quest for a new PC, I would recommend that you formulate a good answer to each of the following questions.

How Much to Spend?

Ultimately, how much you spend is dictated by three considerations: your financial circumstances, your family's spending priorities, and your personal computing needs. The good news is that there's a PC for every family budget.

If funds are scarce, you may have no choice but to go with a low-end or used PC system. My first car was riddled with rust but it did its job quite well. A low-end PC will do its job, too. However, if you have discretionary funds that you can devote to this purchase, you'll be better off in the long run with a midrange PC. Here's why. It's inevitable that your personal computing needs will grow. It's quite possible that you will grow out of a budget PC much sooner than you think. If you can afford it, you're better off buying a system that can grow with your needs rather than having to upgrade a low-end system one component at a time.

So, what if cost is no object? This is a great situation, but it doesn't necessarily mean that you should walk out the door with a high-end professional graphics workstation. "Faster is better" doesn't always apply to personal computing. The PC industry has given us a great opportunity to balance performance with cost. If all you want to do is buzz around town and take short cross-country trips, you don't need a Ferrari. A Jeep Cherokee will do fine.

How much PC do you need? If all you want to do is do word processing, surf the Internet, and send/receive e-mail, an inexpensive entry-level system will suffice. A midrange PC will do just about anything the typical user can dream up, unless you like to do these things at the same time. I'm forced into high-end PCs because my PC is routinely filled with numerous applications, at least one of which likes to eat up processor capacity.

Which PC: Desktop or Notebook?

Although the extended personal computer family includes *wearable PCs, tablet PCs, pocket PCs, handheld PCs,* and others, the choice for the primary PC usually is between a desktop PC and a notebook PC (see Figure 7-1). That choice depends primarily on your *need for portability* and how *much you want to spend.*

- **Portability** If your lifestyle demands portability in personal computing, then you should seriously consider a notebook PC.
- **Cost** Mobile computing with a notebook PC can be costly—as much as double that of a desktop PC with similar capabilities. If your budget is tight and/or portability isn't important, the desktop PC may be the answer.

Apparently portability is an issue with most PC buyers, because notebook PCs now outsell desktop PCs. Notebook PCs are expected to comprise an increasingly larger share of the PC market each year.

Figure 7-1   Desktop PC (system unit not shown) and notebook PC
(Photos courtesy of Microsoft Corporation, left, and Hewlett-Packard Company, right)

Desktop PCs

People may have purchased more notebooks than desktops last year, but the desktop still reigns in terms of numbers of PCs in use, especially in the home. The desktop's system unit may be placed in any convenient location (on a nearby shelf, on the desk, or on the floor). Expect the size of the desktop's footprint to be just a little smaller with each passing year. It could be much smaller already, as most of the space in the modern tower PC is occupied by air.

Notebook PCs

Only a few years ago, many businesspeople would purchase two PCs—a notebook PC for its portability and a desktop PC for its power, ease of use, and extended features. Today, the situation is much different. Modern notebook PCs offer near desktop-level performance. Their long-lasting batteries give you the portability to operate on an airplane or a wilderness trail for up to 20 hours. Today, the notebook PC is the "main," and often the only, computer for millions of people. They take it with them wherever they are—at work, at home, or on vacation. Forecasters tell us that notebooks will begin to outnumber desktops sometime in 2007.

Notebook PC owners sacrifice some conveniences to achieve portability. For instance, input devices such as the keyboard and point-and-draw device are given less space in portable PCs and may be more cumbersome to use. Generally, notebook PCs take up less space and, therefore, have a little less of everything, including USB ports, disk space, RAM, and processor speed.

Types of Notebook PCs

People in the market for a notebook PC look at the same specifications as they would for a desktop PC, such as processor speed, size of display, and storage capacity. However, they also look at variables that have to do with portability, such as overall dimensions and weight. The dimensions of a notebook PC can range from $1\times9\times11$ inches to $2\times11\times15$ inches. The weight can be as little as three pounds and as much as eight pounds. Because of the limited space, the number and variety of ports is an important consideration, as well.

There are no generally accepted categories for notebook PCs; however, for the purpose of discussion, they can be conceptualized in four distinct groups:

- **Affordable notebook PC**   Any notebook that sells for less than $1000 would be considered "affordable." Any modern notebook, including those in this group, have powerful processors and can run virtually all applications. These notebook PCs tend to weigh more and have fewer features, and the

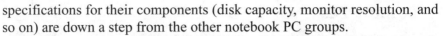

specifications for their components (disk capacity, monitor resolution, and so on) are down a step from the other notebook PC groups.

- **Business-class notebook PC**   This full-featured notebook PC is designed to handle the needs of mobile professionals. Generally, the speeds, capacities, and qualities associated with this group of notebook PCs surpass those of the affordable notebooks. Costs and dimensions are in the middle of the notebook PC road.
- **Ultra-thin notebook PC**   This high-end notebook PC is sleek and slim, sometimes less than an inch thick. Although the ultra-slim notebook may have similar features to a business-class notebook, you can expect to pay a premium for carrying from two to five fewer pounds.
- **Workstation notebook PC**   This class of notebook PCs is so named because it has similar capabilities to a high-end desktop PC. By notebook standards, workstation notebooks are bulky and heavy. High-capacity disk drives, multiple optical drives, a larger display, a high-end graphics card, and other "workstation" capabilities add weight and size to this hefty notebook PC.

The Upside for Notebook PCs

There is great value in mobile computing. Knowledge workers like to have their PCs and their capabilities with them wherever they are—in the conference room, at home, or on a business trip. Many companies are installing wireless networks so employees and their notebooks can be online anywhere they may be within reach of the company's wireless network (usually the company offices and grounds). For many, a wireless home network gives them the same mobility in and around the house.

At home, most people are still opting for desktop PCs. However, the sale of notebooks in the home is beginning to gain momentum as the price of notebooks tumbles. Our two boys and I have desktop PCs; however, my wife's lifestyle is more compatible with a notebook PC. Whenever any of us needs mobile computing, she kindly consents to use one of our PCs. Nancy serves on a variety of committees and frequently takes her PC to meetings. We always take it with us when the family travels, whether by car or air. We take pictures along the way, and then we store and view our digital photos on the notebook. All of us like to keep up with our e-mail when away from home. The PC's GPS (global positioning system) helps us navigate between and within cities. Her notebook has plenty of games to keep the boys occupied during long trips. We frequently play DVD movies on the notebook while in the car (or airplane) or through the TV in the hotel room. I take the notebook on business trips several times a year and the boys will occasionally take it to school to make a multimedia presentation.

The Downside for Notebook PCs

I see two big downsides with notebook PCs. First, with their reduced-size I/O devices, they are more cumbersome to use than desktops; however, that downside can be overcome with a *port replicator* that lets you use full-size I/O devices in conjunction with your notebook (see Figure 7-2). With a port replicator you can enjoy the best of both worlds—portability plus the convenience of a desktop PC. The port replicator provides a quick and easy way to connect a notebook PC to other input/output devices and to a network connection. Once "docked," the notebook PC has A/C power and can use whatever is connected to *ports* in the rear of the port replicator. When my wife slips her notebook into the port replicator, her portable PC becomes a system unit that is linked to our home network and the Internet, an enhanced keyboard, a wireless mouse, a 19-inch flat panel monitor, and an all-in-one multifunction device.

The other downside to notebooks is that they frequently are stolen, to the tune of about a quarter million a year. So, be careful! Most are stolen from travelers passing through airports or staying in hotels/motels.

The notebook PC is closed and inserted from the front

Figure 7-2   Notebook PC docked in a port replicator

Which Platform?

In 1981, IBM introduced its *IBM PC* and it was that machine that legitimized the personal computer as a business tool. Shortly after that, other manufacturers began making PCs that were "100 percent compatible" with the IBM PC (actually more like 99.87 percent); that is, they basically worked like an IBM PC. Most of today's personal computers evolved from these original PC-compatibles. Long removed from the IBM PC, they are now nicknamed *Wintel PCs* because they use a Microsoft Windows operating system (*Windows 95, Windows 98, Windows Me, Windows 2000,* or *Windows XP*) and an Intel Corporation or Intel-compatible processor.

The Wintel PC, which represents the dominant PC platform, is the focus of this book, but there are other platforms. Most of the remaining personal computers are part of the Apple *Power Mac, PowerBook, iBook, eMac,* or *iMac* line of computers. These systems use the *Mac OS X* operating system and are powered by *PowerPC* processors developed jointly by Apple, IBM, and Motorola.

Generally, Apple computers are a little more expensive than comparable Wintel PCs. Apple has a long history of innovation and many loyal users, but the price differential and the sheer momentum of the Wintel PCs have kept Apple from realizing a larger share of the PC market. Apple manufactures a complete line of computers, but its strength is in the high-performance professional graphics/multimedia market.

There are many reasons I would recommend that you stay with the Wintel platform, but these are the main reasons:

- They are everywhere—at work, in your neighbor's home, in libraries, in public school labs, in coffee shops, in some airplanes, and so on.
- You won't need to learn another system once you understand the Wintel PC systems.
- There is a lot of relatively inexpensive software available for this platform.
- You get more for your personal computing dollar.

When making the platform decision, consider compatibility with the other PCs in your life: your existing PC (if you have one), the one at work/home, and/or the one in your college lab. If these are all Wintel PCs, I would recommend staying with that platform.

Who Will Use the PC and How Will It Be Used?

I know this is two questions, but they are closely related. Plan not only for yourself, but also for others in your home who might use the system. I would recommend you do this even if you think and hope that you will be the only user. It seems as if any system in any home ultimately becomes fair game when another family member needs its resources. Invite the input of others and consider their needs along with yours.

The typical off-the-shelf notebook or desktop personal computer, even a low-end one, has amazing capabilities and will do most anything within the boundaries of the digital world. Nevertheless, depending on how you plan to use the system, you may need to supplement the basic system with additional hardware and software. For example, if you plan on recording or editing video, audio, or digital imagery, you may need some additional hardware and software. The same is true if you want to have videophone conversations with your aunt in Alaska and friends in France. If you're purchasing a PC for a home with teenagers, you might want to consider a force-feedback joystick, game pad, and/or a high-quality sound card and surround-sound speakers. If you plan on telecommuting to work, your choices will be colored by many work-at-home requirements. All of these considerations are addressed later in the book.

Will the New PC Be Part of a Home Network?

The spread of PCs throughout the house has prompted the explosive growth of home networking. If home networking is in your future, the mix of hardware needs for your new system may change. For example, you might share a printer with an existing system. You'll need to configure your system with a network interface card (NIC) to link it to the network. To learn more about wired and wireless home networking, read Chapter 18, "Building a Home Network."

Things to Think about when Buying a PC

It's easy to overlook important considerations that could influence your PC system buying decisions. I offer these factors for consideration in hopes that you will avoid some of the problems that I and so many others have experienced when we purchased less (or more) PC than what we really needed or wanted:

- What software is preinstalled on the PC?
- What type of hardware/software support services are available?
- Is there a need to synchronize with handheld devices?
- How soon will the hardware/software become obsolete?

What Software Is Preinstalled on the PC?

One of the most challenging aspects of choosing between alternative PCs is appraising the worth of the software that comes with the system. A miscalculation in your assessment can easily skew the overall evaluation. And, that's the way PC vendors meant it to be. They want the quality or variety of their software bundle(s) to either confuse the buyer or be the difference maker, depending on the quality of their offerings.

If the PC purchase decision was based solely on hardware, we could compare oranges with oranges—but it's not. Frequently, the bundled software is the biggest variable in the PC-purchase decision process. The mix of software that PC vendors choose to offer with their systems can be substantially different between competitors and even within their own line of PCs.

It's not unusual for a PC vendor to advertise that they will provide $500 worth of software—with a $1000 PC. The keyword here is "worth." The advertisement may be technically true based on the manufacturer's suggested retail price (MSRP), but the real value of software is the "street price," which can be considerably less.

The Operating System: Windows

Every new PC is sold with an operating system, typically the latest version of *Microsoft Windows*, either the *home edition* or the *professional edition*. The home edition is sufficient for 95 percent of the home computers. The professional edition has a few security and networking features that might be reason enough for the telecommuter to pay extra, usually about $80, for this advanced version of Windows.

The Software Suite

Software suites are bundled with all new PCs except those with really low price tags. The latter has an operating system and little or no software. Most new personal computers are bundled with one of the following software suites:

- **Microsoft Office Standard 2003 Edition** The "Standard" version is designed for users who require only the core software productivity tools. Information is easily shared between the various applications within this suite, which includes Microsoft Word (word processing), Excel (spreadsheet), Outlook (e-mail and personal information management, or PIM), and PowerPoint (presentation). These software packages are de facto industry standards and anybody who makes anything electronic (hardware or software) will do so with an eye on compatibility with these office productivity tools. Recent releases of Microsoft Office include speech recognition software, too.

- **Microsoft Office Small Business Edition 2003**   The "Small Business" version includes all core Office 2003 productivity tools—Microsoft Word, Excel, Outlook, and PowerPoint—plus an extended business contacts version of Outlook and Microsoft Publisher, a desktop publishing program. Neither of these add-ons to the Standard version offers any real benefits for the home user.
- **Microsoft Office Professional Edition 2003**   The "Professional" version includes everything in the Small Business version plus Microsoft Access, the Office 2003 database solution that helps users store, access, and analyze their data. Over the years, I've maintained dozens of personal databases, but I've always used spreadsheet, word processing, and built-in PIM software— never database software, like Access. Unless you need Access for viewing and analyzing company databases, you probably won't need it.
- **Microsoft Office Basic Edition 2003**   This version is available only as a preinstalled option for participating PC manufacturers. This version includes only Word, Excel, and Outlook. This is a good mix of programs, but I would be concerned that you might regret not having PowerPoint at some time in the future.
- **Microsoft Works Suite**   This is a complete, easy-to-learn office suite combined into a single program. Works includes word processor, spreadsheet, database, calendar, e-mail, and Internet applications. If you expect your personal computing needs to remain relatively basic and within the confines of your home, Works will work. If this is not the case and you have the option to upgrade to a version of Microsoft Office, I would recommend the upgrade. The upgrade may add an additional $100 to $300 depending on which Office suite you choose.
- **WordPerfect Office**   This Corel alternative to a Microsoft suite comes in a standard and a professional version, like Office 2003. The two versions offer similar productivity tools to the Office 2003 Standard and Professional counterparts. WordPerfect offers speech recognition software, as well. The WordPerfect Office suite is an excellent product, considered by some observers to be better than its Microsoft counterpart. I've used them both extensively. Each has its strengths and weaknesses, but, overall, I rate them about the same in quality and usability. Occasionally, you will see a vendor offer the WordPerfect Productivity Pack, which is a scaled-back version of WordPerfect Office (WordPerfect and Quattro Pro being the main applications). The major software tools in the WordPerfect Office suite— WordPerfect (word processing), Quattro Pro (spreadsheet), and Paradox (database)—were at one time standards for personal computing until the overwhelming presence of Microsoft pushed them aside, one by one.

The function of office productivity and other software is described in Chapter 14, "Building a Software Portfolio."

Microsoft, with its considerable clout, has been grabbing market share for the past 15 years. Now, Microsoft Office is the world-wide de facto industry standard for office software suites, except in the legal profession where attorneys have remained loyal to WordPerfect. Unless you're a lawyer or are relatively sure that you will not be interacting with other PCs or sharing electronic documents, I would suggest that you choose a PC system that will allow you to bundle Microsoft Office 2003 with the system. Here's why. In all likelihood you will be interacting with other similar systems at school, at work, at your civic club, or at a thousand other possible locations. The chances are high that these systems will have Microsoft Office—just like yours at home. Also, it's likely that you will routinely send and receive Word, Excel, and PowerPoint files via the Internet.

These software suites may or may not be accompanied by other software or service incentives. For example, additional software preinstalled with Microsoft Office 2003 might include antivirus software, a personal finance package, or perhaps an online encyclopedia. Depending on how you configure your system, the typical PC system is accompanied by several other pieces of software in support of individual components, such as the DVD drive, DVD+RW drive, printer, or sound card. The latter may or may not be preinstalled.

Optional Software and Software Bundles

When you purchase a PC online or via telephone order through direct-marketer manufacturers, you may be given an opportunity to order additional software. These offerings are in two main categories: *individual software packages* and *optional bundles*. The bundled software might be in topical groups of two, three, or four software packages or it can be from three to six packages that you select from a list of up to 30 software packages.

Generally, any of the individual software packages can be purchased online or at retail outlets at the PC vendor's offering price or for a few dollars less. Don't feel as if you need to make a decision now on these individual software packages, except for antivirus software. If a vendor offers a quality antivirus package, I would recommend that you purchase it with the PC system. You want that protection before you go online or begin swapping disks with friends.

Demos and Free Services

Generally, free services and demonstration software add no value to a PC system because, with very few exceptions, these services and demos are available free to any potential customers. The PC system you're considering probably will include an Internet-access disk like America Online (AOL), possibly preinstalled, with an offer of free access for some length of time. These service offers are merely marketing hooks, so treat them as such in your decision making. The same is true of demonstration software, which is in some way restricted (for example, one versus ten game scenarios or limited to 30 days' use).

What Type of Hardware/Software Support Services Are Available?

PC hardware is very reliable. I've seen PCs operate continuously without incident for years in college PC labs, in steel mills, and in teenage boys' bedrooms, the ultimate test of endurance. Of the 25 or so PCs that I've purchased for myself, all have been amazingly reliable, except for one lemon notebook, which never did work the way it was supposed to work. After about $1000 of fruitless warranty repairs, the manufacturer eventually replaced it with a new upgraded notebook.

Even with a history of reliability, the possibility exists that one or several of the components eventually will fail and have to be replaced or repaired. Most retailers or direct-marketer vendors offer a variety of hardware service contracts from same-day, on-site repairs that cover all parts and service to a carry-in (or mail-in) service that does not include parts and can take several weeks.

Because hardware support services vary within and between vendors, I would suggest that you look over the options carefully and choose the one right for your circumstances. It's important that you understand *exactly* what you must do to get your system repaired. Be clear on this point before forking over any money.

As a rule of thumb, choose at least some level of repair service for the effective life of your system. Historically, a system begins its trek to technological obsolescence after about three years of service. I would recommend paying a little extra at the time of purchase and extending a standard one-year warranty to at least three years (usually about $100 to $150). The three-year comprehensive warranties vary somewhat between manufacturers, but most offer parts/labor, mail-in and/or on-site support, and call-in technical assistance. After the warranty period, you're on your own, just as you are with your car. Home office and small business users should consider paying extra for the convenience of same-day, on-site service.

Most hardware and software vendors offer telephone-based *technical support.* The extent of the "tech support" service varies. Some companies provide their licensed users with a toll-free 24-hour hot line—free of charge for as long as they own the product. At the other end of the spectrum, companies charge their users as much as $3 a minute for telephone technical support.

Typically, PC manufacturers provide tech call-in support service for the length of the warranty, then charge after that. Vendors also offer tech support via a free web site that might include online tech support, answers to frequently asked questions, and solutions to common problems.

Is There a Need to Synchronize with Handheld Devices?

The electronics world is doing everything possible to keep us connected, especially in this new era of wireless digital communications. Millions of people now own a variety of portable electronic devices, including pocket PCs, PDAs, and cell phones. Most of these devices are designed such that *personal information management* data, such as a *contact database, calendar,* and *to-do list,* can be synchronized between the portable device and a personal computer. If you have one of these devices and wish to synchronize it with your personal computer, make sure that the PC you wish to purchase and its software are compatible.

How Soon Will the Hardware/Software Become Obsolete?

Today's PC costs half as much and offers a 20,000 percent improvement in performance over a 1990 PC. Obsolescence comes quickly in the PC world, so it's important to remember that some new PCs are a year or so closer to obsolescence than others. If you plan to be a frequent PC user at school, home, or work, focus your search on PCs with state-of-the-art technology. You may get a substantial discount on a PC with dated technology, but will it run next year's software or offer enough disk capacity for your extended personal computing needs?

Software vendors are continually improving their software packages. Consequently, software follows the same pattern of obsolescence. Software changes with the technology, so software companies will routinely release new versions of their software, sometimes as often as once a year. Would online and storefront retailers sell software that is not the current version? Yes, they would. So it pays to do a little research to ensure that you are buying the most recent release of a particular software package. Purchasing software and growing your software inventory are covered in detail in Chapter 14, "Building a Software Portfolio."

CHAPTER

8

What and Where to Buy

All too often, first-time PC buyers, and even veteran PC enthusiasts, don't buy exactly what they want or need because they go about it in a less than rigorous way. Perhaps they bought systems with too little memory, the wrong sound card for the speakers, insufficient backup capabilities, not enough USB ports, a mouse that causes repetitive-stress problems, a system unit with no room to grow, and on and on. Oversights are equally common: failure to consider needs of other users, failure to consider compatibility with the PCs at work, failure to assess the kids' gaming needs, and so on.

Buying a PC can be a traumatic experience or it can be an enjoyable and fulfilling one. It depends on your approach. The two-chapter combo, Chapter 7 and this one, is intended to give you the structure and information you need to purchase a personal computer system with confidence. Chapter 7 sets the stage for buying. Now, it's time to go shopping.

Hey Larry! What Computer Do I Buy?

Many friends, friends of friends, relatives, children of long lost acquaintances, my doctors, my lawyer, my plumber, my accountant, people I've never met, and literally hundreds of others have asked this question in one form or another: "Hey Larry! What computer do I buy?" I'm always happy to respond because I will eventually seek their help when I shop for a fly-fishing rod, a grand piano, a boat, or any of those things I know little about.

From the moment we press the on button for the first time, we are committed to a lifetime of buying newer and better PCs, PC peripherals, and PC software. It doesn't take long before we are caught up in an endless loop of PC upgrades, supplies, accessories, and services. The personal computing adventure is great fun, but it isn't cheap. But neither is Disney World.

What Do You Get when You Purchase a New PC?

For a number of years, the prices you saw for new PCs generally included the system unit (a working PC) and a standard set of input/output devices. Typically, the mix of peripheral devices included a keyboard, a mouse, a monitor, speakers, and, perhaps, a microphone. All other I/O devices were purchased separately.

Today, there are no standards that define what comprises a new PC. What you see in the picture in the catalog or on the web site may not help either. The only way to know what you are actually getting for the advertised price is to read thoroughly the list of included items and their specifications. Often that list may not include a monitor or speakers, even though these may be shown in a picture above the system price. Occasionally, the only item for sale is the system unit—no I/O whatsoever. PC vendors recognize that many people are purchasing their second, third, and fourth PCs, and they may already have perfectly good I/O devices they plan to use with the new system. This is especially true of the monitor and the speakers, whose useful lives often span several PCs.

When you purchase an off-the-shelf PC at a department store, you put the boxes in the cart and check out. What you see on the shelf is what comes out of the boxes. However, if you purchase a PC online from the manufacturer or selected specialty stores, you might have the flexibility to customize an advertised PC by upgrading system unit components (processor, RAM, hard disk) and some or all of the I/O devices—at extra cost, of course.

General Categories of Personal Computers

Anyone shopping for a new PC is at one time or another confused, especially first timers. It's part of the process. It doesn't make any difference whether you visit a retailer or an e-tailer (online retailer). There are so many options and the PCs look pretty much the same. At first look, the most apparent difference between a $600 PC and a $2000 PC is $1400. They may look alike on the outside, but there is a significant difference on the inside. To help sort out these differences, I would propose that you conceptualize PCs into three general categories based on cost and performance:

- Entry-level PCs
- Midlevel "sweet-spot" PCs
- Performance PCs

Keep in mind that technological innovation continues its relentless march toward defining a new level of across-the-board performance each year. This means that what was a performance PC a couple of years ago could be today's entry-level PC.

The entry-level and performance PC categories need little explanation; however, the midlevel sweet-spot PC category may require a little clarification. In sports, the "sweet spot" is the most effective hitting area on a baseball bat, a tennis racket, or a golf club. The PC market's sweet spot is that portion of the market that offers the greatest value. When you purchase a sweet-spot PC, you get near leading-edge performance without the leading-edge price tag.

The PC market's sweet spot is a desktop PC that is about 6 to 18 months off the technology; that is, the major components in the system, such as the processor and hard disk, were introduced up to a year and a half earlier. I'll talk about PCs at the two extremes first, and then I'll talk in some depth about sweet-spot PCs.

Entry-Level PCs

Budget limitations and/or family priorities may dictate that you purchase an entry-level system or a used PC. "Affordable" PCs offer good value and solid performance, but you may not have much flexibility to customize the PC at the time of the sale. For example, you may have only one or two choices for the monitor. Often, entry-level PCs are sold "as is" with no upgrade options.

Fewer, slower, less, and older describe entry-level PC system components. For example, an entry-level PC system might have fewer USB ports, a slower DVD+RW drive, less RAM, and a processor that has been on the market for a couple of years. But you have to put these descriptors into perspective. Even though the processor is 50 percent slower than a performance PC's processor, 50 percent of blazing speed is still very fast.

The major downside of an entry-level system is that it may be one or two years closer to technological obsolescence than intermediate or high-end PCs. People who buy entry-level PCs forfeit technology bragging rights, but they can brag about saving enough money to purchase a big-screen TV.

The Performance PC

If you are a power user with special processing needs, the performance PC is probably the answer. The leading-edge performance PC is the foundation tool of video editing, computer-aided design (CAD), web design, software development, IT writing/publishing, graphics/illustration, and other power-hungry applications.

The key descriptors for performance PCs are more, faster, greater, and newer. The performance PC has the full gamut of ports, and plenty of them. It has two or more optical drives, including a DVD±RW drive. All have at least 1GB of RAM and some have up to 4GB. It has at least one state-of-the-art processor. The performance PC is feature rich, with high-end graphics and sound cards that could add as much as $700 to the price of the system. The system might be configured with a video editing package that would include a video capture card and related software. The system unit would include an enhanced power unit and extra fans for cooling the many heat-producing components.

Sweet-Spot PCs

My pat answer to the question, "Hey Larry! What computer do I buy?" is "Buy at the sweet spot." Most people looking to buy their first PC or a supplemental PC want a good, solid PC that will run all current and future applications over the next two or three years—that's a sweet-spot PC.

To me, PCs in the middle of the current market, the sweet spot, offer the greatest value. The savings you might realize when you purchase a low-end, entry-level system will evaporate quickly with premature obsolescence. If you buy at the high end, you pay a premium for high-demand state-of-the-art PC components. Performance PCs might be 30 percent faster and capable of storing twice the information, but their price might be double that of a sweet-spot PC.

To "hit" or find the sweet spot, go to the web site for any major PC vendor that markets directly to the public (for example, Dell, Hewlett Packard, Compaq, IBM, Gateway, and others), then go to the page that features their home/small office desktop PC options. The PC or PCs in the middle of the price range are the current "sweet spot." Once you look over the specifications for these midlevel PCs at three or four vendor web sites, you should have a good feel for the PC market's sweet spot. Remember, though, the sweet spot is continuously moving with the technology. Today's high-end PC is on track to be tomorrow's sweet-spot PC.

Also, the sweet spot is apparent at any major PC retailer, such as Best Buy or Office Depot. The sweet spot is represented by those similarly priced PC systems in the middle price range.

Customizing a PC

Most PCs sold in retail stores are offered as a package deal. However, since service and price are what differentiate one retailer from another, some retailers are willing to one-up the competition by giving you the flexibility to tweak the system a little. If you wish to buy and have another 128MB of RAM, ask if they will install it for you. On the other hand, PC manufacturers that sell directly to the public give you plenty of flexibility to customize your order.

If you find an acceptable PC and it is customizable, I would recommend that you revise the options to meet your needs and your pocketbook. This means adding extra features or capabilities you might need to meet specific personal computing needs. For example, if you have a couple of gamers in the house, you might wish to upgrade a dual-speaker system to surround sound with four or five speakers and a subwoofer (4.1 or 5.1 speaker systems).

In an all-out effort to keep the price low in a very competitive market, manufacturers invariably configure their advertised systems to save $20 here and $50 there. What that means to you, the consumer, is that several of the system components are not up to the level of the overall system. For example, the system might be configured with 128MB of RAM, the minimum to run Windows and not nearly enough for modern-day personal computing. Or, the system might come with inexpensive desktop speakers that provide more noise than audio. Your challenge is to identify and upgrade unworthy components.

You would be the exception if the come-on price of a customizable system gave you exactly what you needed in a PC. The more likely scenario is that you will want to add some important upgrades that have the potential to add considerable value to your PC and your personal computing experience. What follows is a list of recommended upgrades to the system unit of a customizable PC system (I/O upgrades are covered later). Evaluate these upgrade recommendations based on your budget, priorities, and personal computing needs. My recommendations are listed by value, here and in Table 8-1, with the *biggest payout for your PC dollar listed first*. I've included price range estimates to give you a feel for costs. Prices change, so what you experience at the time of sale might be more or less than my estimates.

Priority	Recommended Upgrades to Basic System Unit	Recommendation
1	RAM	To 512MB, 768MB, or 1GB if running multiple applications or gaming
2	Extended warranty	To at least 3 years
3	Hard disk capacity	To double the capacity of the system's basic hard disk
4	DVD-ROM drive	To a rewritable drive (CD-RW and/or DVD±RW), if needed
5	Sound card	To 5.1 Dolby Digital capability
6	Graphics (video) card	To one with 128MB or 256MB of video RAM

Table 8-1   Recommended Upgrades to a Basic PC

Upgrade RAM for Improved Performance

The least expensive and most effective way to improve performance of a PC is to increase its RAM. A $100 to $150 investment in additional RAM can improve system performance by as much as 50 percent. Modern PCs operate reasonably well at 256MB. Having 512MB is better, but not as good as having 1GB.

When available RAM fills up, active programs and data must be swapped between relatively slow, mechanical hard disk and high-speed, solid-state RAM. When the hard disk is used for supplementing memory, processes that would normally take microseconds or nanoseconds begin to take milliseconds, a thousand to a million times slower. If your plans include running three or more applications at once or playing games, then I would recommend at least 512MB RAM. If you expect to be doing sophisticated multimedia work, such as music and video editing, I would recommend you have at least 1GB of RAM.

Buy an Extended Warranty for Peace of Mind

This is the best deal of all the manufacturers' options at the time of purchase, especially for notebooks. You usually get a one-year warranty with the purchase price, but for less than $100 a year you can extend the warranty for two or three years. This extra insurance gives you peace of mind that you have somewhere to go when something goes wrong or you need some answers—and, it's quite possible that it will and you will. A three-year warranty should suffice.

Upgrade the Hard Disk for More Storage Capacity

Just as you can never have enough closet space, you can never have enough hard disk capacity. This is especially true if you have gamers in the house and/or you plan on storing lots of digital images and/or videos on the PC. As a rule of thumb, I would recommend choosing an option that roughly doubles the basic system's hard disk capacity. For example, if the advertised system is configured with 60MB hard disk, you might wish to consider upgrading to a 120MB hard disk. If you do this at the time of purchase, a hard disk upgrade can be purchased for an additional $50 to $100.

Upgrade the DVD-ROM Drive to a Rewritable Drive

Anymore, it's unusual that any sweet spot or performance system would not be configured with a rewritable disc drive for burning CDs and DVDs, and for use as backup. Some entry-level PCs may not have the rewritable disc option. If your chosen system does not have a CD-RW and/or DVD±RW drive, you should consider upgrading the read-only drive to one of these or adding that capability to an empty drive bay. I recommend the latter so that you have the processing flexibility that is made possible with two optical drives. The cost of a rewritable upgrade ranges from $50 for a CD-RW drive to $200 for a high-end DVD±RW drive.

Upgrade the Sound Card for Superior Audio

Your new PC has the potential to be an entertainment center. If you enjoy superior audio quality, you may wish to consider a sound card upgrade. Many new PCs have integrated audio built into the motherboard. In general, integrated audio offers only minimal audio functionality. To enjoy high-fidelity Dolby Digital 5.1 surround sound, you may need to upgrade to a sound card with expanded capabilities. This adds from $20 to $150 to the cost of the system, depending upon the features you desire.

Upgrade the Graphics (Video) Card for Enhanced Viewing

Any modern graphics card can handle the display tasks for a typical user; however, if you expect to be involved with sophisticated multimedia applications and/or serious gaming, you should consider upgrading to a better graphics card with at least 128MB of video RAM. Enhanced graphics capability enables the presentation of visually stunning graphics. A reasonable graphics card ups the cost from $50 to $100 and a top-of-the-line graphics card (for multimedia professionals and zealous gamers) can add up to $400 to the cost of a PC.

What Input/Output Peripheral Devices Do You Need?

A healthy mix of I/O peripheral devices can really spice up your computing experience. Input/output devices come in a variety of speeds, capacities, and qualities. Some have features their competitors don't have and vice versa. This section continues to emphasize what to buy, not so much the technology and functionality. Common I/O peripherals and their technologies are covered in detail in Chapter 3, "Getting Information In: Input," and Chapter 4, "Getting Information Out: Output."

Which I/O peripherals you should select depends on your *specific needs* (for example, a scanner with a bed large enough for legal-size paper), *quality requirements* (for example, near photo-quality printing), *usage volumes* (for example, 500 printed pages per week), and the *amount of money you are willing to spend*. Each increment in expenditure gets you a device that is faster, bigger, more durable, and/or provides higher quality I/O. In truth, however, not all of us need bigger, better, and faster.

Budget permitting, I would recommend that you upgrade certain I/O devices that might be packaged with the PC system and purchase several other popular I/O devices to complete the system. I've listed several suggestions in the following sections, with priority suggestions listed first. These are summarized in Table 8-2.

Priority	Recommended I/O Device Upgrades or Purchases	Recommendation
1	Upgrades to prepackaged I/O: • Keyboard • Mouse • Monitor • Speakers	Upgrade to: • Cordless, USB • Cordless, optical, ergonomic, and USB • Minimum 17-inch, flat panel preferred • 2.1 or to 4.1/5.1 for surround sound
2	Printer or All-in-one multifunction device	Inkjet (speed, quality, features as required) Get print, scan, copy, and/or fax in one device and save money
3	Headset with mike	Approved for speech recognition; noise-canceling capability
4	Scanner or All-in-one multifunction device	Speed, quality, and features as required Get scan, print, copy, and/or fax in one device and save money
5	Desktop video camera or webcam	Quality and features as required
6	Game controllers	Two game pads for gamers

Table 8-2   Recommended Input/Output Upgrades and Purchases

1. Upgrading Prepackaged I/O Devices: Keyboard, Mouse, Monitor, and Speakers

Typically, the cost of a desktop PC system includes the system unit with a keyboard, mouse, monitor, speakers, and, possibly, a microphone. Generally, these I/O devices are of low to medium quality. If you have some budget flexibility and the vendor gives you I/O upgrade options, I would recommend an across-the-board upgrade for some or all of these I/O devices.

Keyboard Recommendations

For an extra $20 to $40, you can get a longer-lasting enhanced keyboard and an ergonomically designed mouse that should last the useful life of the system. Given a choice, choose a USB keyboard over a PS/2 keyboard.

If you don't want to be tethered to the workstation area, you might want to consider a cordless keyboard and mouse. Some PC vendors do not offer a cordless upgrade, so if you want this upgrade, downgrade to "no keyboard" and "no mouse." You can then purchase a quality cordless keyboard/mouse at any retail source for around $70 to $90.

Mouse Recommendations

The manufacturer's grade mouse may be quick to wear out. I recommend that you get a mouse with an optical sensor, thereby eliminating the mechanical mouse ball (the reason for most failures). A mouse with a few extra buttons is a plus, especially for gamers. The better mice, which may add $10 to $25 to the system price, offer greater accuracy and are noticeably more responsive. I would suggest that you eliminate the tail and go cordless.

Monitor Recommendations

With increasing frequency, the monitor is not included with the system price; if it is, it's usually a 17-inch manufacturer-grade CRT monitor. These are OK for home use and probably will work well for many years. However, with so much of what we do being presented as multimedia, I would recommend a bigger, better monitor. Considering how much time you and your family will spend in front of the computer, the extra viewing area will surely enhance your personal computing adventure. You'll pay about $100 per extra inch for a CRT-style monitor.

If you can afford it, I believe you will find the space-saving, flat panel LCD monitor worth the extra money. Expect to pay a premium for flat panels, probably double what you would pay for a similarly sized CRT. A quality 17-, 18-, or 19-inch display can add from $300 to $800 to system cost.

If your personal computing applications demand extra viewing area, why not try a dual-monitor setup (see Figure 8-1)? The cost of upgrading the size of the primary display from 17 inches to 20 inches can be more than the cost of an additional 17-inch display. When you work out the numbers, the cost per square inch of viewing area is significantly less with a dual-monitor setup. If you choose the dual option, you may need to upgrade your graphics card to one that accepts dual monitors.

Figure 8-1   Dual-monitor setup with a video editing application spread across two screens

If you purchase a quality monitor (or perhaps a pair of them), it's not unreasonable to expect it (them) to last for eight or more years. The monitor cost for your next PC may be zero.

Speaker Recommendations

If speakers are included with the price of the PC (and sometimes they are not), they probably would be the kind that can provide mediocre audio for music and video. Most manufacturers offer several alternative upgrades. At a minimum, I would recommend that you go one step up from the basic offering and get a 2.1 system (dual speakers with a subwoofer) for another $30 to $50.

If you want to see the walls shake and actually feel the music or the sound track, you want a 4.1 or 5.1 alternative, which bumps the price of the computer another $75 to $150. Stereo buffs and serious gamers may want to consider 6.1 or 7.1 speaker systems from external sources for $150 to $400. Most modern sound cards can handle 4.1 and 5.1 speaker systems; however, you may need a sound card upgrade for 6.1 or 7.1 speaker systems.

2. Printer or All-in-One Multifunction Device

Every PC system needs access to a printer. The keyword here is "access." If you already have a good printer on another PC system in your home, you probably don't need another. Printers are easily shared on a home network or via "walknet," the transfer of print files on a disc, diskette, or USB flash drive.

A significant percentage of PC buyers are opting for an all-in-one multifunction device instead of a stand-alone printer—or a stand-alone fax machine, scanner, or copier—because it does it all. All-in-one devices are popular in any setting where the volume for any of their functions is relatively low.

Printer Recommendations

The color inkjet printer is the overwhelming choice of people buying printers for the home/home office. The cost of these printers ranges from about $40 to $300. You can buy a high-volume, black-only laser printer for the price of a high-end inkjet, but who wants black-only?

A printer may last you through a couple of PCs and/or be shared with other PCs in the house. Any brand-name printer, such as HP, Canon, Epson, Dell, or Lexmark, that costs in excess of $150, will give you quality output at an acceptable speed and capacity for home use, plus the capability to print on different sizes and grades of paper and on envelopes. However, if you're on a budget, a printer in the $75 to $100 range will fit most home-use needs—just a little more slowly. Each increment in cost over $150 gives you more output speed, better resolution, and extra features, such as being network ready, two-sided printing, or offline printing (from a digital camera's memory stick). Before you buy, read the specs and features list, and then compare them with similarly priced alternatives. Usually, you must purchase the printer cable separately.

For what they do, printers are reasonably priced. Printer pricing is based on the assumption that you will spend from $500 to $2000 on printer (ink) cartridges and, possibly, print heads over the life of the printer. Of course, the company that makes the printer also makes the cartridges and print heads.

All-in-One Multifunction Device Recommendations

When they first came on the market, all-in-one multifunction devices didn't print, scan, fax, or copy as well as the stand-alone units. Nevertheless, people were more than willing to give up speed and resolution to save a significant amount of money. The specifications for modern all-in-one devices stand up well to their stand-alone counterparts. We have an all-in-one that serves as our household network printer and as the service center for scan, fax, and copy jobs. It wasn't too many years ago that color copiers cost thousands of dollars. Now, they are part of the all-in-one peripheral package. I guess you can say I am an all-in-one convert.

Some all-in-ones have fax capability and some don't. If the all-in-one is for a home office, you probably want the fax function. If it's just for general home use, the fax function is nice to have for those rare occasions when you need to send or receive a fax. However, it will cost you another $50 or so.

All-in-one multifunction devices are available for under $100 (without fax), but the best ones can cost in excess of $400. A device that has so many different capabilities is difficult to evaluate relative to the alternatives. The most straightforward buying strategy for an all-in-one is to purchase one with a flatbed scanner (versus a sheet-fed scanner) with the best print quality that your pocketbook will allow. The capabilities of the other functions are in line with those of the printer.

3. Headset with Mike

All notebook PCs and some desktop PCs come with a microphone, but if you want to take advantage of the speech recognition capability made available with the newer Microsoft Office suites, you need to purchase a quality headset with a mike (from $15 to $40). If you purchase speech recognition software separately, the headset comes with the product.

PC Headset with Mike Recommendations

Whether you use speech recognition or not, I would recommend that you have a quality headset-mike combo on hand for online chat, videophone, game interaction, and other audio applications. Any headset-mike with noise-canceling capabilities that is approved for speech recognition will do. The money you spend above $15 will buy you a more comfortable fit and a more visually appealing product. If your primary application is speech recognition, I recommend that you get one with only one headphone.

4. Scanner

If you opt for an all-in-one multifunction device, you won't need a stand-alone scanner. Digital imaging has emerged as one of the mainstays of personal computing and the scanner has become a very popular PC peripheral. With a scanner, you can convert any color hard copy document and small 3-D images to a digital image that can be integrated into anything from a newsletter to a greeting card. The scanner can also read text and speak the words with the help of text-to-speech software. Used in tandem with a printer, the scanner doubles as a copy machine for small-volume copying.

Scanner Recommendation

You can purchase a scanner for under $100 that produces electronic images in brilliant color. For most home applications, any name-brand flatbed scanner with an 8.5×11.7-inch scanning area and 1200×2400 dpi (dots per inch) resolution will satisfy home scanning needs. If you are willing to pay more, you get better resolution (for example, 3200×4800), faster scans, larger bed (14 inches long for legal-size scans), and a variety of features, such as sheet feeders or adapters for scanning negative and 35 mm slides. If you're just looking for a good home scanner, you can simplify the decision by purchasing a good all-in-one multifunction device.

5. Desktop Video Camera or Webcam

The desktop video camera, sometimes called a web camera or *webcam,* certainly isn't a PC system necessity, but for as little as $20, it can add some zing to your personal computing. These versatile little cameras are smaller than your fist, but can capture still images and record video. They let you have interactive videophone conversations and do videoconferencing, too. You can use them for many other tasks, including sending video e-mail via the Internet, setting up a webcam so you can broadcast live video over the Internet, maintaining security, or monitoring your children's activities in the back yard.

Desktop Video Camera or Webcam Recommendations

A $20 desktop video camera will do the job. A webcam in the $100 range will give you near-photographic, megapixel still images, video images with 640×480 resolution clarity, and, possibly, digital zoom capability. For a little more, you can purchase a webcam that will follow a person's movement about the room. Remote webcams can be placed in other rooms or outside.

6. Game Controllers

Gaming is a world unto itself and is discussed in detail in Chapter 17, "PC-Based Gaming." If you have gamers in the house, game controllers are must-have items. Game controllers come in all shapes and sizes, including game pads, steering wheels, joysticks, and more.

Game Controllers Recommendations

The more sophisticated game controllers, such as force-feedback joysticks, can cost $100 or more, but not every game uses this type of device. Most games are set up to use an inexpensive game pad (from $15 to $40), so I would suggest you buy at least one USB game pad (minimum of ten action buttons).

What Special Hardware Do You Need for Internet Access and Home Networking?

We've talked about the hardware that you might expect to see, both inside and outside your stand-alone personal computer. PCs, however, seldom stand alone anymore. Most are linked to the Internet and, by extension, thousands of computers throughout the world. A growing number are part of a home network, as well.

There are a number of ways to gain access to the Internet and a variety of communications hardware devices, including a *modem,* associated with that link. All Internet access options and hardware are discussed Chapter 11, "Internet Basics: Going Online." The communications devices needed for home networking, including the *network adapter* or *NIC (network interface card)*, are discussed in Chapter 18, "Building a Home Network." A network adapter, which is installed on each PC, is in the $10 to $25 range for a wired network and in the $40 to $90 range for a wireless network. You also need a central base unit that will cost around $100 for a wired network and about double that for a wireless network.

Where to Buy Hardware and Software

Twenty years ago PCs were considered high-tech specialty items and were sold almost exclusively through retail computer stores. Today, PCs and PC software have emerged as popular consumer items. PCs and associated hardware and software can be purchased at thousands of convenient bricks-and-mortar locations and from hundreds of retail sites on the Internet—electronic retailers or e-tailers. The various types of PC retailers are discussed in this section and summarized in Table 8-3.

Where to Buy Hardware and Software	Considerations
Bricks-and-mortar PC retailers with comprehensive service centers	Expert service and help; can custom-build a PC
Bricks-and-mortar PC retailers with upgrade service centers	Can upgrade system to meet growing needs
Bricks-and-mortar PC retailers without service centers	PC sold as a consumer item with little in-store technical support
Direct marketers	Customizable PCs with manufacturers' support
Online and telephone-order retailers	Wide variety of prepackaged systems at good prices
Retailers of pre-owned computers	Inexpensive older systems, usually 3 to 4 years old
Online auctions	Hundreds of low-cost, high-risk "working" PCs 2 to 5 years off the technology (available 24/7)

Table 8-3   Where to Buy Hardware and Software

I would like to think a retailer has your best interest in mind when they make recommendations, but this may not be the case. To be sure, they can be helpful, but keep in mind that they want to sell you something—anything.

Bricks-and-Mortar PC Retailers with Comprehensive Service Centers

There are thousands of independent computer stores with no chain affiliation, several national retail chains, and many regional chains that specialize in the sale of PC hardware and/or software. Most of these stores market and service a variety of PC systems and many are happy to custom-build one for you. Their authorized service centers are set up to address any PC concern. These dealers are easy to find; just look under "Computer and Equipment Dealers" in the yellow pages.

Computer retailers have their advantages, the big one being that they provide readily available personal "expert" service. Often computer retailers will help you install your system and, possibly, offer a range of hardware and/or software training classes (both free and for a fee). Most computer retailers are authorized service centers for the computers they sell. I purchased all of my PCs from a local computer retailer during a five-year period in the 1990s. The custom systems worked well and I enjoyed the personal touch of my friends at the "shop."

Bricks-and-Mortar PC Retailers with Upgrade Service Centers

Many audio/video/computer chains, such as Best Buy, college bookstores, and other specialty retailers, sell PCs and provide upgrade services. Mostly they sell prepackaged systems, but their service departments have the capability to make minor changes to off-the-shelf PCs. For example, they can upgrade your RAM, add a second hard disk, insert a network adapter, and so on. They may offer a "clean and tune" service, as well. As an expression of goodwill, some stores may help you troubleshoot minor problems, but their service departments are not intended to be "full" service. It's unlikely that this type of retailer will upgrade I/O components that come with a packaged system, such as the mouse or keyboard.

Bricks-and-Mortar PC Retailers without Service Centers

Computer/electronics departments of most department stores, "big box" discount stores, and office supply stores sell PCs. For the most part, these stores treat computers as they would any consumer item. When you walk out the door, you are covered by the manufacturer's warranty, unless for some reason the system is obviously defective when you first attempt to use it. When this happens, a responsible merchandiser will exchange the system for one that works. Any support or advice from these types of establishments pretty much ends when the sales clerk hands you a receipt. If you are given the option to purchase an extended warranty, I recommend you do so (at least three years). These types of retailers tend to cater to the masses, so they specialize in low-end and sweet-spot PCs.

Direct Marketers

Most major PC manufacturers, PC peripheral manufacturers, and PC software companies sell directly to the customer. The direct marketer's "store window" is a web site on the Internet, an advertisement in a magazine, or a direct-mail piece. Most orders are placed online via the Internet, but orders can also be submitted by telephone and fax. Usually orders are shipped within a day or two and deliveries are two to four days later.

Software companies not only sell software over the Internet, they also deliver it over the Internet. Many software companies give you the option of purchasing a boxed product, which must be physically delivered, or a download of the software. The entire transaction is online—that is, the payment and the subsequent downloading of the software. Often the download software is sold at a reduced price because everything is electronic, thus eliminating the cost of packaging and delivery.

The strength of the direct marketer's sales program is online sales via the Internet. Every major vendor has a comprehensive web site that presents an easy-to-understand hierarchy of PC systems. Even if you buy locally, these web sites are a good place to gather pricing information. Although the labeling might vary between vendors, you would normally navigate to the "home/home office" or "home/small-business" page and then select either the desktop PC or notebook PC to view the various options.

Once you decide which system you want, *customize* or *configure* it so you can pick exactly the options you want with your PC system. When you have selected your options, click "update price." If you are like most online PC shoppers, you make choices, then look at the price, and then you repeat the process until you're satisfied with the balance between features, performance, and price.

Some major computer manufacturers also sell "refurbished" systems. Typically, such systems are current models returned during the satisfaction-guaranteed period, usually 30 days. The returned systems are remanufactured and offered for sale via the company's web site at about 85 percent of the new-system price, usually with a full warranty.

If you have access to the Internet, I would recommend that you consider purchasing your PC system online. I've purchased a number of PCs online and my experiences have been uniformly positive. All of the systems were received within five days of when I clicked the "check out" button.

Buying directly from the manufacturer via the Internet has many advantages. The manufacturers' web sites are comprehensive in that they present all available options, plus, they provide enough easily accessible information to answer most questions you might have. This information often includes table comparisons between systems and between the various component options so that you can make truly informed decisions. If you have further questions, you can call the company directly or send your question via e-mail.

Online and Telephone-Order Retailers

The online/telephone order retailers provide an alternative to buying a PC and related products at a bricks-and-mortar retail outlet. Virtually all telephone-order retailers support online sales, and vice versa. Most major bricks-and-mortar department stores, discount warehouses, electronics stores, and so on have a presence on the Internet, too. You can buy a PC at any Wal-Mart or Best Buy store or you can go to WalMart.com or BestBuy.com and get it there, too.

A number of online retailers specialize in the sale of PCs and electronics. E-tailers such as CDW, TigerDirect.com, Newegg.com, PC Mall, and many others have large online catalogs with literally thousands of items. You can easily search their catalogs to find what you need. I've ordered online scores of times over the years from many different e-tailers and I always get what I ordered, usually within two to four days.

Online retailers are like bricks-and-mortar retailers in that when you click "buy," any further problems are between you and the manufacturer and are conducted within the restrictions of the warranty.

One of the beauties of Internet shopping is that comparison shopping is automated. Several Internet sites let you search dozens of online retailers to find the best price for a given item (see Figure 8-2). It's a dream scenario for the smart PC shopper.

HP OfficeJet 6110

Lowest price: $265.00
Manufacturer: Hewlett-Packard Co.
Part number: Q1638AABA
View my list | Add to my list

See more images   Read CNET Editors' review

Total cost calculated for zip code 72701 (Change)

Sort by: Merchant	CNET Certified	In Stock	Price	Tax + Shipping	= Total cost
Page Computer Store Profile | Buy Now	★★★★ Store rating	Yes	**$265.00** as of 01/15/2004	Tax: $0.00 Ship: $21.24	**$286.24**
2Buystore.com Store Profile | Buy Now	★★★★☆ Store rating	Yes	**$274.75** as of 01/15/2004	Tax: $0.00 Ship: $3.99	**$278.74** Your best price
Mwave.com Store Profile | Buy Now	★★★★★ Store rating	Yes	**$279.68** as of 01/15/2004	Tax: $0.00 Ship: $13.00	**$292.68**
Ebuyer Store Profile | Buy Now	★★★★★ Store rating	408	**$280.59** as of 01/15/2004	Tax: $0.00 Ship: $10.59	**$291.18**
TheNerds.net Store Profile | Buy Now	★★★★★ Store rating	703	**$281.53** as of 01/15/2004	Tax: $0.00 Ship: $15.91	**$297.44**
Buy.com Store Profile | Buy Now	★★★★★ Store rating	YES	**$284.34** as of 01/15/2004	Tax: $0.00 Ship: See Site	**See site**
pcRUSH Store Profile | Buy Now	★★★★★ Store rating	Yes	**$284.35** as of 01/15/2004	Tax: $0.00 Ship: $19.70	**$304.05**

Figure 8-2   Comparison shopping on the Internet

Retailers of Pre-owned Computers

Some retailers specialize in used computers. They purchase them from a variety of sources: school districts, companies upgrading their computers, individuals, auctions (online and off), and so on. Used-computer retailers are easy to find; just look under "Computer and Equipment Dealers—Used" in the yellow pages.

Used-PC dealers buy computers and their software in bulk, often at very low prices. They identify those PCs and components that work, and the rest are salvaged or recycled. In all cases, user files are removed. Invariably, these computers, which may have been in continuous use for three or four years, need work or, at a minimum, a good cleaning. Usually, parts from several computers are combined to make one good computer. Often, workable computers are enhanced to make them more salable. For example, a modem and an extra hard drive might be added.

Buying a used computer is akin to buying a used car. How much risk are you willing to accept? You probably don't know who owned it or how it was used. Nevertheless, if you're on a tight budget and you want a PC to do basic personal computing applications, a used computer may be the answer. If you decide to go this route, settle for no less than a full 30-day warranty on everything.

Online Auctions

A great source for anything is an online auction. PCs and electronics are among the most popular items up for auction on the Internet. Online auctions go on 24 hours a day, with people all over the world registering bids on thousands of items. Each item has its own bidding period, and, like any auction, the item goes to the highest bidder.

At any given time, eBay, the most popular online auction site, lists hundreds of "working" PCs that are two to five years off the technology. Most winning bids are anywhere from $50 to $400. I would avoid bidding on a system that is deinstalled— that is, it offers no software. Make sure the system has an operating system. Having office suite software, such as Microsoft Office, is a real plus.

Build Your Own PC

You're probably saying, "I can't build a computer!" Maybe not, but what about your computer-savvy children or friends? The one I use was built by my teenage son, Troy, who has built others in our house and many for his friends. Troy is among tens of thousands of individuals who order their PC components, just as manufacturers do, and assemble their own desktop PCs. They do it to save money, to get exactly the PC they want, and to have fun. Once he has all the parts together (see Figure 8-3), it takes Troy from two to three hours to assemble a PC and load the software. The only tool he uses is a screwdriver.

Figure 8-3   The components for a home-built PC

Anyone who is willing to do a little personal study can purchase the individual components and build his or her own personal computer—it's not nearly as difficult as it sounds. When you build your own PC, however, there is no help desk. The individual components have warranties, but there is no warranty on the overall system.

Which PC Manufacturer Is Best for You?

The personal computing industry is always changing with the technology and PC market demands. Consequently, PC manufacturers are continually updating their product lines and adjusting their prices. Any decision about which PC manufacturer is best must be made at a particular moment in time and for the circumstances of a particular buyer. All big-name manufacturers, such as Dell, Gateway, Hewlett-

Packard (merged with Compaq in 2002), Apple, and IBM, produce quality PCs that can be expected to last well beyond their useful life. Surprisingly, however, these big-name manufacturers account for a little over 40 percent of PC sales.

The bulk of PC sales are by small "white box" PC vendors. Many small PC companies have emerged that custom-build and sell "no-name" PCs to school districts, city governments, small companies, and individuals. Some of these small players are excellent and have a solid record of providing good service, price, and flexibility. And, they usually sell for less than name-brand manufacturers. To do so, however, white box vendors may use components of lesser quality.

Ultimately, the answer to the question "Which PC manufacturer is best for you?" is the manufacturer that offers systems that provide the best match for your personal computing needs and your bank account. Not surprisingly, the manufacturer changes from system to system. Over the past 25 years, I have purchased PCs from eight different "best PC manufacturers."

9

Supplies, Services, and Accessories

As soon as you get your system, you will want to stock up on supplies, subscribe to vital services, and purchase helpful accessories. Most personal computing consumables are associated with the printer and interchangeable disk/disc drives (DVD+RW, CD-R, Zip disks, and other storage media). In this chapter, I'll discuss these and other supplies, subscription services (Internet access and virus protection), and identify accessories that can give you peace of mind protection and enhance your personal computing experience.

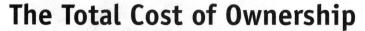
The Total Cost of Ownership

The amount shown on the price tag for a new PC system is only part of what you must pay to enjoy the breadth and depth of personal computing. For example, consider the must-have printer. Rarely does the PC price tag include a printer. The printer cable, sold separately, is another expense. Of course you will want paper on which to print, probably in several different qualities, sizes, and colors. When your printer runs out of ink, possibly two to four times a year, you will need to purchase and install new printer cartridges.

It's easy for a teenage boy to spend $500 a year on gaming software (about a game a month)—I know. You'll need a place to put the PC and a comfortable chair. Access to the Internet will cost you from $20 to $70 a month. These are just a few of the many costs that comprise the *total cost of ownership* for a PC, which can be as much as $5000 per year for a PC power user on a home network. Of course, the TOC can be as low as $1000 for those who exercise a little frugality and show some restraint.

The cost of the actual PC system is the major expense ($500 to $4000), but there are many incidental expenses that can mount up and influence your selection of a PC. Table 9-1 gives you some ballpark figures on what you might expect to spend on

One-Time Costs:	Low	Avg.	High
Desktop personal computer system (with keyboard and mouse)	$500	$1000	$2000
Monitor Second monitor	$100	$350	$800 $800
Speaker system	$30	$60	$400
Printer	$75	$150	$300
Scanner	$100	$150	$300
All-in one multifunction device—print, scan, fax, and copy (Add $175, $275, or $500 in lieu of printer/scanner)	$0	$0	$0
Headset with microphone	$15	$25	$30
Webcam	$20	$60	$100
Game controllers	$0	$50	$300
2 PC home network (2 NICs and a hub)	$0	$150	$400
Totals (single monitor) **Totals (dual monitors)**	**$840**	**$1995**	**$4630** **$5430**

Table 9-1 Estimated Cost of a New Desktop PC Computer System

a desktop PC system (the hardware plus the bundled software). Table 9-2 does the same for a notebook PC. The estimated incidental costs are shown in the Table 9-3. The cost ranges that are listed are for a first-time user. The low end of the ranges is representative for casual home users and the high end of the ranges is applicable to sophisticated users with home offices. The average category is representative of the typical PC buyer.

The overall range presented in these tables shows the extremes for the PC, the various peripheral devices, and the incidental expenses. It's unlikely that anyone would be at or near all of these extreme estimates. Even someone on a very limited budget will spend in excess in several categories, and the home office power user will have little use for some of the items.

One-Time Costs:	**Low**	**Avg.**	**High**
Notebook PC	$700	$1300	$4000
Port replicator or docking station	$0	$200	$400
Auxiliary monitor	$0	$350	$800
Second auxiliary monitor			$800
Auxiliary keyboard/mouse	$50	$70	$90
Speaker system	$0	$60	$400
Printer	$75	$150	$300
Scanner	$100	$150	$300
All-in one multifunction device—print, scan, fax, and copy (Add $175, $275, or $500 in lieu of printer/scanner)	$0	$0	$0
Headset with microphone	$15	$25	$30
Webcam	$20	$60	$100
Game controllers	$0	$50	$300
2 PC home network (2 NICs and a hub)	$0	$150	$400
Totals (no auxiliary I/O or replicator)	**$960**	**$1945**	**$5830**
Totals (auxiliary I/O, single monitor)		**$2565**	**$7120**
Totals (auxiliary I/O, dual monitors)			**$7920**

Table 9-2   Estimated Cost of a New Notebook PC System

	One-Time Costs:			Annual Costs:		
	Low	Avg.	High	Low	Avg.	High
Software	$100	$600	$1500	$100	$400	$800
Cables	$15	$15	$50			
Supplies: Printer cartridges and heads Printer paper Storage media				$100 $25 $30	$200 $40 $100	$300 $60 $200

Subscriptions:
ISP (Internet
  service provider)
Virus protection
  service
PC magazines
				$240
				
				$25
				$0
					$500
					
					$50
					$25
						$1000
						
						$100
						$60

Internet access (setup fee plus hardware)	$0	$200	$600			
Additional data/fax telephone line (optional)	$0	$50	$50	$0	$360	$360
Furniture	$30	$150	$500	$30	$60	$100
Desktop PC accessories	$50	$150	$300	$25	$50	$100
Notebook PC accessories	$100	$200	$400	$50	$100	$300
Power protection: UPS Surge protectors (2)	$0 $60	$150 $80	$250 $100	$0	$50	$125
Electricity				$60	$150	$250
Insurance				$0	$40	$100
System maintenance				$25	$50	$100
Total estimated incidental expenses	**$355**	**$1595**	**$3750**	**$710**	**$2175**	**$3955**

Table 9-3   Estimated One-Time and Annual Incidental PC Expenses

This total cost of ownership information is an eye opener for some people, even people who have been doing personal computing for a long time and never stopped to tally the costs. Personal computing done with imagination and purpose will return your investment many times over, but it's important that you know the costs. There's a reason that the PC is the third largest expense in most PC-ready households and the biggest expense in many households. Tables 9-1, 9-2, and 9-3 give you ranges for expected costs so you can prepare more realistic personal computing budgets.

PC Supplies

Most consumable PC supplies are associated with the printer or interchangeable storage media, as described in the following sections.

Printer Supplies

Over the life of a PC, the printer may be its most expensive component, because you must feed it with paper and keep the ink flowing with replaceable printer cartridges. Manufacturers sell their printers for close to their cost because they know that you will be using their printer and their patented printer cartridges for five or more years. It's not unusual for a family to run through $100 to $350 worth of printer cartridges a year. That amount doesn't include the paper, which can be from $25 to several hundred dollars a year, depending on applications and usage. To get you used to the printer being a money sinkhole, printer manufacturers seldom include the required USB cable with the sale price. That, you must purchase separately.

Most printers require two ink cartridges, one for black and one for color. Some printers have only one print cartridge. It's a good idea to have at least one set of cartridges on hand in case you run out while printing a project that is due at 8:00 A.M. Also, you will want a healthy supply and variety of paper on hand. Here are some suggestions:

- **Standard letter-size printer/copy paper**   I buy standard printer paper by the box (ten reams of 500 sheets). For a few dollars extra, you can purchase quality paper and avoid most of the jams that are inevitable with bargain paper.
- **Legal-size printer/copy paper**   Inevitably you'll run into a situation in which you want to print everything on one page but it won't fit on one page of standard letter-size paper. So you may as well have a ream of white 8.5×14-inch paper on hand.

- **Colored paper**   Over the years, I've found the best strategy is to buy reams that contain several colors, 100 each of five colors.
- **Photo paper**   There are many types of photo paper, ranging in cost from $.20 to almost a dollar a sheet. I buy packages of 100 of three different qualities. I print images on the less expensive paper that are bound for a short stay on the refrigerator. The midrange prints are fine for the photo album. The costly paper is saved for the photo images that go to grandmother or get framed.
- **Social expression paper**   You can get paper made specifically for greeting cards (quarter-fold, half-fold, textured, and so on) and banners.
- **Envelopes**   Printers do an excellent job of printing addresses on envelopes, so take advantage of this feature during the holiday seasons. If you prefer stick-on labels, you can purchase and print address labels for less than a penny each.
- **Iron-on transfers**   You print the iron-on transfer as a mirror image, and then iron it on a piece of clothing. For example, I've found that it's a fun way to create a T-shirt sporting a picture of my kid's soccer team or for making a social, political, or humorous statement.
- **Magnetic paper**   This paper attaches to most metal surfaces and is great for decorating the refrigerator with images of family adventures and for arts and crafts projects.

Storage Media Supplies

You can still get PCs with the traditional 3.5-inch floppy disk drive, but you probably won't need it, especially if you have a rewritable optical disc drive. If you need interchangeable storage, you would be better of with an inexpensive high-capacity USB flash drive. The floppy disk is just too slow and its capacity is too little (1.44MB) to be of much value in twenty-first century personal computing.

In 1980 the 100MB Zip disk emerged as the successor to the floppy disk for interchangeable storage capacity. It eventually grew to hold 250MB, then 750MB. However, because most new PCs are configured with rewritable optical disc drives (CD-RW or DVD±RW), the Zip disk is unnecessary.

Most new PCs are sold with a CD-RW drive, a DVD-RW drive, or a DVD+RW drive. The CD-RW drive is capable of "burning" an audio or video CD or a data CD-ROM from read-only CD-R media. The unit can also read and write to CD-RW media. If your PC system comes with a CD-RW drive, I would recommend that you purchase 50 blank CD-R discs and at least 5 CD-RW discs. Fifty CD-Rs sounds like a lot, but it's amazing how fast a family can run through them, especially if you have children burning audio CDs and parents sending and archiving digital photos and videos. You'll need the CD-RW discs for archival storage and system backup.

The DVD+RW and DVD-RW drives can do everything that a CD-RW drive can do, but they can also "burn" audio and video DVDs from read-only DVD-R media. Plus, these versatile drives allow you to write, erase, and rewrite media up to 1000 times on rewritable DVD media. Making inventory recommendations for this type of device is more of a challenge. I'm sure that you'll need some CD-Rs, as these are compatible with most PC systems, should you wish to use them on other PCs. You'll probably want a stack of DVD-Rs, too. You may want to go directly to DVD-RW for archival storage and system backup because of their greater storage capacity (4.7GB). However, if your read/write archive and backup requirements are small, you may as well go with the less expensive and more common CD-RW media.

Note whether your rewritable DVD drive is DVD+RW (plus), DVD-RW (minus), or DVD±RW (both plus and minus). Depending on what you have, buy either "+" or "−." If your drive is ±, it can handle either format, but I would recommend that you choose the + standard, which is emerging as the de facto DVD standard.

Subscription Services: Internet Access and Internet Protection

Two subscription services are vital to happy and healthy personal computing. I can't imagine living the personal computing adventure without *Internet access.* Equally essential is a *virus protection subscription service,* which enables you to protect the valuable resources on your hard disk. At any given time, hundreds of computer viruses are circulating around the Internet seeking vulnerable PCs.

Internet Service

Your PC can be a window to the world once you are linked to the Internet. To look through that window, though, you need to subscribe to an *Internet service provider (ISP).* An ISP is a company with an Internet account that, for a fee, provides individuals and organizations access to, or presence on, the Internet. There are hundreds of national/international, regional, and local ISPs, such as Earthlink, MSN, and America Online at the national/international level.

Subscribing to an ISP can cost from $240 to around $1000 per year, depending on the access speed you choose. Costs for Internet access can vary by as much 50 percent for the same service, depending on where you live.

Internet access is made available via a communications channel, the link through which information travels to get from one location on a computer network to the next. The most popular channels are your telephone line and TV cable. Internet access is made available over these channels in a variety of *bandwidths,* the number of bits a channel can transmit per second. People link to the Internet via *dialup access* on telephone lines at a maximum speed of 56 Kbps (thousands of bits per second) or via high-speed *broadband access,* which can be 50 times faster than the traditional dialup access. Low-bandwidth dialup access is sometimes called *narrowband access.*

Narrowband: Dialup Internet Service

A dialup link is a temporary connection that is established by using a modem to dial up the number of the ISP's remote computer. This is done in the same way you would call a friend over a regular telephone line. Dialup access is available to anyone with *POTS—plain old telephone service.* This narrowband service, which is in just about every home and business in the United States, permits voice conversations and digital transmissions (with the aid of a modem).

Broadband: High-Speed Internet Service

Dialup service was the only option for most of the public Internet era. Cable Internet service was first made available in 1998 and quickly had 1.5 million cable-modem subscribers. Now millions are enjoying broadband access, but thousands of cities and parts of cities are still without this service. You may not have broadband service even if you have a telephone and cable TV.

As anyone who is familiar with click-and-wait narrowband access can attest, broadband offers an entirely different experience. A web page that might take one minute to fill at narrowband speeds takes only a couple of seconds on a broadband line.

Broadband is *always on,* so there is no need to dial up and log on. Generally, the broadband access fee is two to three times that of narrowband. The most common broadband options are, in order of popularity, cable, DSL, and satellite.

Cable-Modem

Cable companies everywhere are updating their analog cable infrastructure to enable delivery of digital service that offers crystal-clear television signals and high-speed Internet access. Cable Internet access, referred to as *cable-modem,* offers service at anywhere from 1 Mbps up to 10 Mbps (the *downstream rate*). The *upstream rate* (sending) is 384 Kbps to 1.5 Mbps. A 1 Mbps channel capacity is very inviting to the millions of people who are chugging along at 56 Kbps over POTS lines. Cable Internet access requires a *cable modem.*

Cable, DSL, and satellite modems do not actually modulate and demodulate signals. Tradition resulted in the term modem being added as a tag-along descriptor. Broadband modems deal exclusively with digital signals, so analog/digital conversion is not needed.

DSL

DSL (Digital Subscriber Line) service is delivered over POTS lines at 1 to 9 Mbps. The upstream rate is similar to cable-modem. DSL requires a special *DSL modem*. DSL can share an existing telephone line such that voice conversations and digital transmission can occur at the same time. Cable-modem was first and has three times the number of subscribers, but DSL is gaining ground as it is made available to new markets.

Satellite

Not everyone has access to cable or DSL broadband service, even people living in some metropolitan areas. However, satellite service is available to anyone in America with a southern exposure to the sky and the necessary equipment, a digital *satellite dish* and a *satellite modem*. Digital satellite access offers downstream speeds of 400 Kbps to 1.5 Mbps and upstream rates of 56 Kbps to 1.5 Mbps.

Satellite's big advantage is that it is universally available; however, it has several disadvantages. I used satellite for three years, but because it was my only broadband option. I paid almost twice what my friends across town were paying for DSL or cable-modem. Satellite has a built-in latency of about a quarter of a second because of the time it takes the signal to travel to the satellite and back (about 47,000 miles). This latency usually is not a problem, but it can cause problems for real-time interaction, such as in online multiplayer gaming. Also, it was frustrating to lose my signal when the cloud cover was dense or during thunderstorms.

These Internet access options, along with the required hardware, are discussed further in Chapter 11, "Internet Basics: Going Online."

Virus Protection Service

A computer virus can cause anything from a minor inconvenience to major devastation. Computer viruses are passed from a computer system to other systems, including PCs, over the Internet and via interchangeable storage media. Our best protection against malicious people who create viruses is the *antivirus program,* but it is only as good as its list of *virus definitions*. Many new computer systems come with an antivirus program installed, such as Norton AntiVirus (Symantec Corporation) or VirusScan (McAfee Security). If yours doesn't have antivirus protection, I would recommend that you get it at your earliest convenience, preferably at the time you buy your PC.

Antivirus software vendors offer a virus protection subscription service that allows you to download protection for recent viruses, including the virus du jour. Antivirus software and protection service can cost from $25 to $50 (software included) a year and must be renewed annually. Chapter 13, "Internet Security: Protecting Your PC," contains more information on viruses and antivirus software.

PC Accessories

We accessorize everything else, so it stands to reason that we would do the same with our personal computers. Most accessories would be considered optional, but a few, such as power protection, are essential.

Power Protection

I would not plug in a PC without first providing it with minimal protection from AC power disturbances, such as "dirty" power (sags and surges in power output), brownouts (low power), or power outages. Power surges, in particular, are a serious problem for PCs. At least a hundred people have told me about losing major electrical components, including the motherboard and processor, as a result of electrical storms. Dirty power can be delivered directly from your power company or it can surface when your PC shares a circuit with a power-hungry appliance, such as a toaster oven or a washing machine. Dirty power and brownouts can cause errors in data transmission, disk read/write operations, and program execution.

There are several levels of protection against electric problems delivered over AC power lines, TV cables, or telephone lines that connect to PCs. The relatively inexpensive *surge suppressor* ($30 to $50), considered the most basic level of protection, will protect your system from most lightning hits and other electrical aberrations. The surge suppressor (see Figure 9-1), sometimes called a *power strip,* is placed in line with your PC system's power supply so that it can absorb the shock of voltage spikes and surges. Having lost several system components, I learned the hard way that having just any type of surge suppressor does not guarantee protection against serious surges in electrical current. You must have a good one. The better surge protectors are more likely to thwart a damaging electrical surge over both your power source and the phone line that links to your modem. The quality of surge suppressors is proportional to cost, with those on the low end being virtually useless. Surge suppressors are rated in *joules,* the energy they can absorb. Five hundred joules is basic protection and 1000-plus joules is superior protection. I plug a printer, speaker system, scanner, one monitor, and webcam into a surge protector.

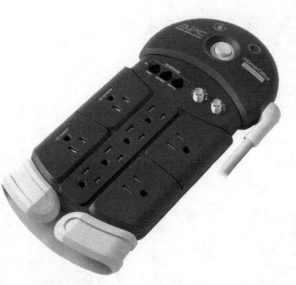

Figure 9-1   Surge protector (AC power and communication channels)

(Photo courtesy APC Corporation)

Flip the switch on most surge suppressors and everything plugged into the unit is either turned on or off. A variation on the surge suppressor is the *power station,* which enables you to control power to individual devices.

If your finances will allow, spend another $60 to $250 and buy an *uninterruptible power source* or *universal power supply (UPS)* (see Figure 9-2) for your system unit and its expensive components. I plug my primary monitor and my system unit into a UPS unit. The function of a UPS unit is to provide uninterruptible power by offering a secondary source of power. The UPS has a battery that is continuously recharged by AC power. Upon detecting any type of power disturbances, the UPS unit beeps a warning and instantaneously switches to battery power to provide clean, continuous power for several minutes. This time cushion allows you to "shut down" normally. If you experience regular power flickers that force you to reset digital clocks, then you should consider a UPS. Those power flickers reset your PC, and any changes to un-saved files are lost. The manufacturers of high-end UPS units will replace your computer if their device fails to protect it from power disturbances.

You need to match your system's power requirements and your desired run time (the amount of time your system will run on the battery) with the rated output of the UPS unit. For example, to get ten minutes of run time for a desktop PC system unit with a Pentium 4 processor, you might need a 500 VA (voltage-ampere) UPS unit.

Figure 9-2 An uninterruptible power source (UPS)

(Photo courtesy APC Corporation)

Accessories for Notebook PCs

A notebook PC is self-contained by design. It has everything you need to enjoy personal computing; however, you can enhance your experience with any or all of these notebook accessories:

- **Security lock** One end of the security lock cable ($25 to $50) is looped such that it can be lassoed to any secure object (see Figure 9-3) and the other end is slipped into the notebook PC's built-in security slot.
- **An additional battery** If much of your processing time is without AC power, you might consider purchasing one or more additional batteries.
- **DC/AC adapter for car** With a DC/AC adapter (around $30), you can convert your car into an office, a game room, an interactive route planner, a movie theater, and even a study hall.

Figure 9-3   Security cable lock

(Photo courtesy Kensington Technology Group)

- **Port replicator or docking station**   If you choose a notebook PC, you might consider spending a little extra (around $200) to purchase a *port replicator*. The port replicator, which is introduced in Chapter 7, lets you enjoy the best of both worlds—portability plus the expanded features of a desktop PC. An upscale variation on the port replicator is called a *docking station* (around $400). It may have additional functionality, such as a media bay for interchangeable notebook media modules (for example, a DVD+RW drive) or a PCI slot for an expansion card.

- **Auxiliary monitor, keyboard, speakers, and mouse**   A notebook PC looks, feels, and handles differently than a desktop PC. If you would prefer to have a larger monitor, a full-size 104-key keyboard, quality speakers, and a mouse, then you may wish to purchase a port replicator and as many of these peripheral devices as you desire.

- **Sound adapter for car**   If you have a tape player in your car, you can purchase an adapter ($15 to $20) that allows you to route your notebook PC's audio through the car's stereo system. We use the adapter when the family watches DVD movies in the car. When the kids play their computer games, I ask them to use headsets.

- **GPS receiver and street map software**   If you purchase a GPS (global positioning system) receiver (about $80) and associated street map software (about $50), you will never be lost again.

- **Carrying case**   The major PC companies offer several options, usually a nylon case for around $50 or a leather case for double or triple that amount. A nylon backpack case may be another option.

Miscellaneous PC Accessories

You can expect to see these PC accessories somewhere in the vicinity of most PCs:

- **Mouse pad**   In theory, the optical mouse is supposed to work on all types of surfaces, but in practice, they seem to work better and are more comfortably maneuvered on a mouse pad ($5 to $10). I recommend that you try one with a built-in wrist pad ($10 to $15).
- **Keyboard wrist pad**   The keyboard wrist pad/rest is a soft strip of gel or foam that is placed in front of the keyboard to help prevent repetitive stress injuries ($10 to $20).
- **Disc holder/tray**   CD/DVD disc holders come in all imaginable shapes, sizes, capacities, and designs.
- **CD/DVD carrying case**   Portable CD/DVD carrying cases range in capacity from ten to several hundred CDs/DVDs.
- **CD/DVD sleeves and jewel cases**   CD/DVD blanks often are sold in bulk without any protective covering, so you might want to buy some soft sleeves or the hard plastic jewel cases.

You probably will find and buy other PC accessories, but these are the main ones you will want to consider at or near the time of purchase.

CHAPTER

Installation, Maintenance, and Troubleshooting

When you purchase a new dishwasher, an installation crew comes to your house, installs it, tests it, and thanks you for your business. When you purchase a PC, *you* unload and unpack the boxes, *you* connect the devices, *you* flip the on switch, and *you* hope everything works. Also, *you* are responsible for system maintenance and troubleshooting duties. This chapter contains many tips and hints that help make user duties go a little more smoothly.

System Setup and Installation

The room with the PC often becomes a hub of household activity. If your family is like others, family members can expect to spend plenty of time in front of and around the PC, so you want to pick the right place—the first time.

Set Up Your Workspace

Your first task in the installation of a new PC is to select a good location. The location should have these qualities:

- Be away from people traffic
- Have access to a telephone line and/or cable TV
- Have plenty of no-glare lighting
- Be within an environment that controls temperature, dust, and humidity
- Allow for growth

Once you have settled on a location, you need a desk that is designed to accommodate PC hardware and wiring. Arguably, the most important health consideration is that the keyboard and mouse be located so that the upper arm and forearms are at a 90-degree angle. The best way to make this happen is to ensure that the desk has an elbow-height shelf for the keyboard and mouse and/or the chair has a height adjustment.

Unpacking

When you purchase a PC, you receive several boxes containing the various pieces of the system. Here are some recommendations that can save you time and money:

- *Read the instructions.* Generally, a new PC is ready to run right out of the box. Nevertheless, I recommend that you read the device's installation instructions *before* beginning any PC system installation procedure. Most installations are intuitive, but occasionally the instructions include an important tip that may impact your system configuration and/or the operation of the hardware or software.
- *Save all sales documentation.* Keep all shipping invoices, sales receipts, delivery information, credit-card statements, and other documents that relate to the sale. You might need them for rebates, warranty work, or returns.
- *Note any visible damage to shipping cartons.* If a shipping carton appears to have been opened or damaged, ask the delivery person to properly document the problem.

- *Register all hardware and software.* Product registration may be important for warranty protection and for long-term access to technical support. Most modern PC hardware and software packages let you submit your registration online during or after installation, or you can do it the old-fashioned way and mail it.
- *Clearly label all external connectors.* The manufacturer usually labels the connectors; however, I would suggest that you use a permanent marker pen and label sound card connectors, speaker cables, and others so that you are clear on what goes where.
- *Keep the shipping material.* Keep all boxes and packing materials for a few months in case the hardware fails and you need warranty work.

Hardware Setup

Setting up the hardware is a relatively straightforward process. Just follow the vendors' monkey-see, monkey-do instructions. These colorful map-size instructions graphically illustrate each step in the installation process. The PC vendor's system-oriented instructions will lead you through the process of connecting the color-coded cables between the system unit and the keyboard, mouse, monitor, and speakers. If your system has a modem, you might wish to insert a telephone line from a wall jack into the "line in" modem jack to enable online registration. The last step is to plug the various components into AC power. After you confirm that all connections are tight and secure, turn it on and begin doing personal computing.

Other peripheral devices, such as the printer, scanner, and webcam, come with the same explicit, pictorial instructions. Remember, each I/O device comes with its own *device driver software* and, possibly, applications software. The device driver provides instructions needed by Windows to communicate with the peripheral device. Depending on your device's instructions, the software is installed either prior to connecting the device or after connecting the device. If you are asked in the instructions to connect your device before installing any software, then Windows will detect the new hardware device and display the Add Hardware Wizard. Follow the wizard's directions to complete the hardware installation process. Once you have installed all peripheral devices according to instructions, you can plug/unplug USB plug-and-play devices at any time. However, you must shut down the system to connect/disconnect other devices.

CAUTION: *Don't get all hung up in hardware manuals at this time. Now is the time to get the hardware up and running. The operational explanations in the manuals make a lot more sense when the software is installed and the peripheral devices are functional.*

Installing Software

The typical PC is sold with Windows and a few applications, such as Microsoft Office, already installed on the hard disk and ready to run. Even if your new system includes some software, you will likely install other software as well (for example, antivirus software). Software installation involves copying the program and data files from the vendor-supplied CD-ROMs to the hard disk. All operational instructions are integrated into the online Help feature.

Commercial software is distributed on one or more CD-ROMs or DVD-ROMs. This normally straightforward installation process can take from a few minutes to an hour, depending on the complexity of the software, the distribution media, and the speed of the PC. Here are the general steps to follow:

1. *Close all Windows applications*. Some programs will not install with open applications.

2. *Insert the CD/DVD*. Insert the "Disk 1," "Program," or "Install" disc into a disc drive.

3. *Run the setup program*. Most commercial software packages have an autorun feature that starts the installation program automatically when the disc is inserted. If nothing happens, click Start and then Run. Enter **D:setup** or **D:install** (where *D* is the letter of the CD-ROM drive) at the Run command line. Typically, applications software is installed in the Program Files folder on hard disk drive C: unless you indicate otherwise.

4. *Respond to install inquiries*. An installation wizard leads you through the installation process (see Figure 10-1). Depending on the software, you may be asked to respond to several questions. You also may be asked to choose a Full, Typical, or Custom installation. The Full installation requires more disk space—often, a lot more. Unless, you intend to use the product's more sophisticated features, choose Typical and save some disk space. The Custom option is for users who are already familiar with the product and may wish to install or uninstall specific application features.

Once installed, run the program by selecting Start | All Programs | *Program Group* | *Program Name*, where *Program Group* is usually the software vendor's name.

Uninstalling Software

The program's uninstall program must be run to remove all related files and changes to other files. Don't just delete the program folder, because that may cause the sys-

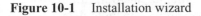

Figure 10-1   Installation wizard

tem to rebel against you for not doing a proper uninstall. Some programs list an uninstall program icon along with the program icon. If this is the case, simply run the uninstall program. If not, use the Windows Add or Remove Programs feature in the Control Panel to remove the software (select Start | Control Panel | Add or Remove Programs). The Add or Remove Programs dialog box shows a list of all installed programs (see Figure 10-2). Scroll down and highlight the program you wish to uninstall, and then click the Change/Remove button to uninstall the program.

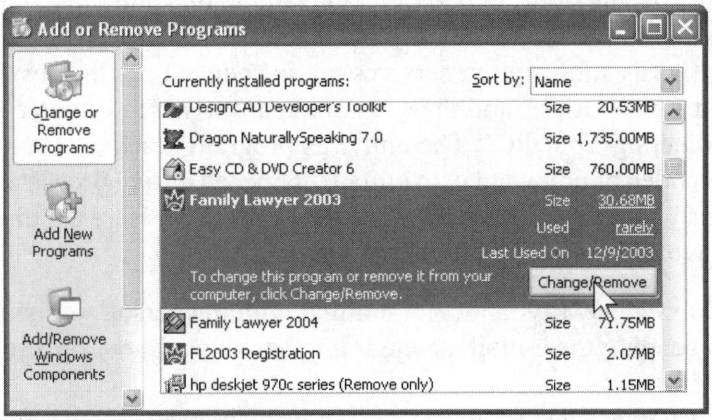

Figure 10-2   Add or Remove Programs dialog box

Testing Your New PC

All PCs and peripherals are "burned in" for several hours before shipment, to lower the infant mortality rate and ensure that your new computer and its components will work properly. They usually do, but you need to continue the test at home. The best way to do that is to drive your system hard for a few weeks in a way that tests the limits of all system components, including I/O devices. If you encounter no problems, your system will most likely be fine for years of normal use and abuse.

Maintaining a PC System

One of the easiest ways to enhance your personal computing experience is to make a commitment to properly maintain your PC system. A good PC maintenance program will include protecting the system and its contents, keeping the hardware running at peak performance, and ensuring that the software is up to date.

Protecting Your PC and Your Files

When we talk about protecting a PC, we're talking about protecting it from computer viruses, unauthorized access or use, and loss of information. Much of personal computing is disaster preparedness.

Protection from Computer Viruses

Viruses are the plague of the cyberworld. One of the first and most important tasks associated with maintaining a healthy PC is to purchase and activate an antivirus program. Antivirus subscription services are introduced in Chapter 9, "Supplies, Services, and Accessories," and the software is discussed in Chapter 13, "Internet Security: Protecting Your PC." The antivirus program scans all files in transition (being downloaded or uploaded with e-mail, or opened during processing) and periodically scans your disks to maintain virus-free operation. Here are three important maxims for avoiding viruses sent via e-mail:

- *Know the sender.* If you are not familiar with the person or distribution facility sending the e-mail, delete it immediately without opening it or any attached file.
- *Look for inconsistencies.* If the subject is in any way inconsistent with what you might expect from the sender, delete it immediately.
- *Question any suspicious attached file.* Never open a file with an executable or suspicious extension (for example, .exe, .com, .inf, .pif, .sys, .vbe, .scr,

and so on) that is attached to an e-mail unless you are expecting it and are absolutely sure of its origin and purpose.

If you notice any of the following signs that your PC may be infected with a virus, run your antivirus software immediately to remove the virus and deter any further damage:

- Strange messages pop up on your display, such as "Gotchya"
- Diminishing system performance
- Databases or files are missing data
- Inability to access the hard drive

Protection from Unauthorized Access

If more than one person will be using the PC, it's probably a good idea for each user to have a password-protected user account. As discussed in Chapter 6, "Working with Files," setting up multiple user accounts lets each user have his or her own personal My Documents folders. To add user accounts to a PC, select Start | Control Panel | User Accounts. When you log on, the PC verifies that you are an authorized user and changes the settings as needed for your personalized user account.

Protection from Loss of Information: Back Up Critical Files

PCs are amazingly reliable. For example, on average, a hard disk has an unrecoverable read error only once in every 100 quadrillion read operations. Nevertheless, this one in 100,000,000,000,000 chance, the threat of viruses, and our own propensity to do dumb things are enough that we should adopt a rigorous file backup program.

The most critical component of any computer system is the hard disk, because it contains your user files. You invest many hours, weeks, even years, in creating these files—so protect them! Everything in a computer system but your user files can be replaced. Practice good backup procedures and they, too, can be restored in the wake of a disaster.

Anyone who has ever used a PC for any length of time has lost one or more critical files. It happens. It doesn't have to be something as exotic and chaotic as a disk crash (a scratched disk); sometimes it's the result of a couple of errant keystrokes.

I highly recommend that you routinely back up important user files, such as your financial records, work files, children's projects, contact database, family photo images, and so on. Back up these files regularly to interchangeable disk, such as Zip disk, CD-R, CD-RW, or DVD±RW. If your PC system is on a network, you can back up folders and files to the server or another PC system.

The frequency with which you back up user files depends on the level of risk you're willing to accept. If you work at home, you might wish to back up volatile files (those which you modify frequently) on a daily basis and do a full backup every week. The CD-RW or DVD±RW disc backup rotation shown in Figure 10-3 is common with individuals whose files have high volatility. A full backup is done every Monday and taken to an offsite location, perhaps to your office or a neighbor's house. Only incremental backups (files that are modified on a given day) are made for each of the other weekdays. If all files are lost on Friday, the full backup from Monday is restored to the hard disk, and then incremental backups are restored for Tuesday through Thursday. Always keep two sets of backup discs, a *first generation backup* (the most recent) and a *second generation backup,* then alternate between the two each week.

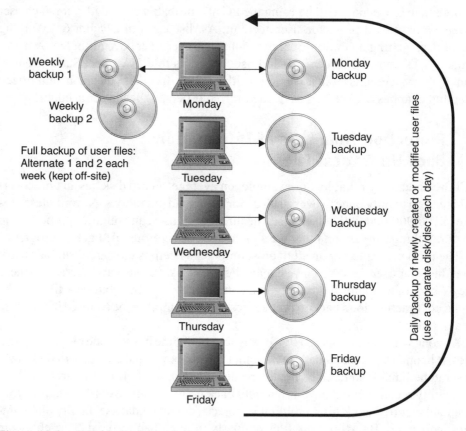

Figure 10-3 Weekly backup rotation

To make backup easier, I put almost all of my user files in one of three folders:

- **Active folder** This folder contains all active folders and files, except those containing disk space–eating images and video files. An active folder is one in which files/subfolders are added/deleted. An active file is one that I might at some time modify.
- **Static folder** When I wrap up a project or end my association with an organization, I create a permanent backup of related folders and move the associated folders to this folder. I never modify these folders/files.
- **Images folder** I treat image and video files differently because of their large size and the fact that I do not modify them. Our family photo album, which I maintain by activity within each month and year, contains thousands of images.

Hardware Maintenance

PCs are like bicycles, swimming pools, and charcoal grills in that they work better and last longer when they are well maintained. Maintenance always begins with cleanliness.

Keeping Your PC System Clean

A system that is clean throughout will run longer and with fewer problems than a system that gathers dirt and grime. At a minimum, make an effort to keep all components as free from dust as you would a living room coffee table. There are, however, some special cleaning needs:

- **Interchangeable disk drives** To keep interchangeable Zip disk and CD/DVD drives at peak performance, periodically use a disk-cleaning kit ($5 to $10) to remove dust, debris, and other containments from read/write heads and other mechanical elements of the drives.
- **Monitor** Use monitor cleaning wipes or a special cloth and cleaning solution ($5 to $10) designed for use on monitor screens to maintain a dust-free, static-free screen for better viewing.
- **Keyboard and mouse** With the system off, use the soft brush attachment on a vacuum cleaner and periodically remove lint and dust from around the keys to extend the life of your keyboard. The typical keyboard has up to 400 times more bacteria than a typical toilet, so you might want to wipe it and the mouse down with disinfectant every week or so.
- **System unit** Between three and ten fans continuously circulate air and everything that comes with it through the system unit. Every six months or so, I take the panel off the system unit case and use the blow end of a vacuum

cleaner or compressed air to blow out accumulated dust and debris, with the objective being to clean anything that might impede the free flow of air.

- **Printer**   Generally, printers do not require any scheduled maintenance; however, some vendors encourage customers to purchase cleaning kits (around $10), mainly for the pick-up rollers, which can lose their tack over time.

Upgrading System Unit Hardware

If you plan to update system unit hardware, Windows provides a handy summary of what's under the hood of your PC. Select Start | Help and Support | Tools (under Tasks), and choose My Computer Information. Select *Find information about the hardware installed on this computer* or any of the other options to view all kinds of interesting hardware information, such as the sound card's manufacturer, model, and last driver update.

Part of hardware maintenance is growing the hardware with your personal computing needs. Generally, desktop PCs, and to a lesser extent notebook PCs, have room to grow. Look for empty DIMM slots, PCI slots, and bays. The upgrade might involve switching processors (for example, an Intel Pentium 4 3.0 GHz to an Intel Pentium 4 4.0 GHz), adding a hard drive, installing a PCI expansion board (for example, a home networking adapter), or adding additional RAM (see Figure 10-4).

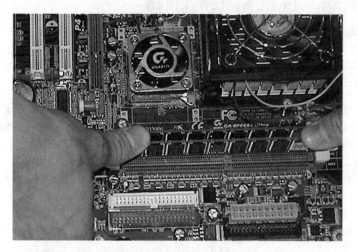

Figure 10-4   Inserting a 512MB RAM module in a DIMM slot

Upgrading a processor, adding a hard disk, or adding an expansion PCI card involves delving into the inside of the computer. If you have trouble programming your VCR, you probably should refrain from opening the system unit. These upgrades, however, are not difficult or expensive and can be accomplished in a few minutes at any authorized PC service center.

Although people routinely remake their PCs into more capable machines, I'm not convinced that spending major dollars on an old machine will stand muster to cost-benefit analysis. When you're finished, it might run faster and/or have more disk storage capacity, but it's still an old computer with old software, a dated chipset, and well-used components. Would it have been better to invest that money in a new PC system? I've upgraded my CD-ROM drive, added RAM, added many expansion cards, and added a hard disk, but I have never been able to economically justify doing major surgery on my PC, such as switching out a motherboard or processor.

Upgrade BIOS

When you turn on a PC, built-in software called BIOS (basic input/output system) stored in flash memory takes control of the keyboard, monitor, disk drives, and other functions required to load the operating system. The BIOS handles known technologies, but if you add a second hard disk or upgrade the processor after a few years, you may need to upgrade the BIOS software so it can accommodate recent innovations in hardware design. However, if new hardware devices install successfully or you don't change anything on your system, you don't need to upgrade the BIOS.

If you need a BIOS upgrade, download the most recent version of the flash BIOS program from the PC manufacturer's web site and install it on your PC. The download web page contains installation instructions. It is critical that you download the correct program for your PC system, and then follow the upgrade instructions—exactly. You will need the model and number of your motherboard. Click the Support button in Help and Support and choose *View general system information about this computer* to obtain this information.

Disk Maintenance

Maintaining a healthy disk is one of the keys to keeping your system at peak levels of performance and to overall enjoyment of personal computing. Disk maintenance involves periodically running these three Windows utility programs:

- **Disk Cleanup** This program searches your hard drive and then displays temporary Internet files, Recycle Bin files, and unnecessary program files that you can safely delete to free up space on your hard drive.
- **Check Disk** This utility scans a disk for problems, including bad sectors. The program can automatically fix file system errors and can attempt to recover bad sectors, thus recovering disk space.
- **Disk Defragmenter** Defragmentation involves rearranging file fragments on the disk such that files are contiguous on the disk. Contiguous files can be accessed more quickly and stored in less space. Figure 10-5 shows the disk image before (top) and after (bottom) "defrag."

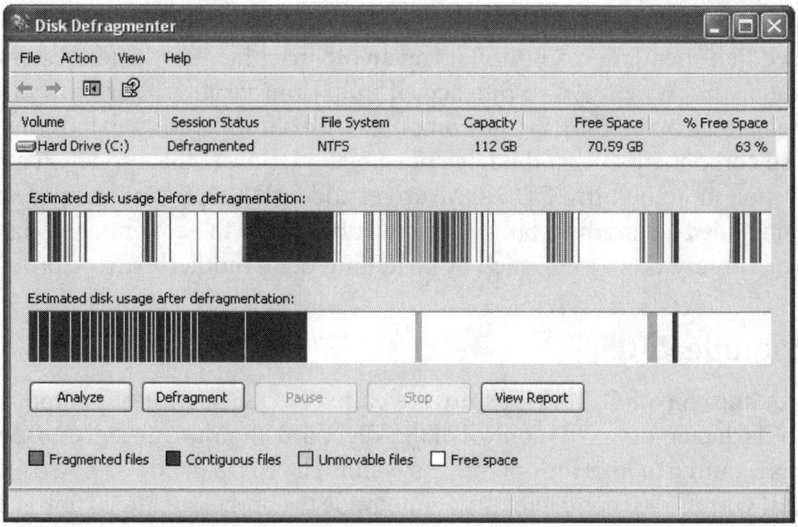

Figure 10-5 Disk Defragmenter utility

To run these utilities, right-click on the disk drive icon in My Computer and select Properties. Click Disk Cleanup in the General tab or choose the Tools tab and click Check Now or Defragment Now.

Power Management

Modern hardware and Windows have given us the flexibility to manage power usage on our PCs. Judicious power management can save power and help to minimize wear and tear on the computer. An always-on desktop PC and its peripheral devices can consume several hundred dollars' worth of power a year. Of course, power management is critical when using a notebook PC on battery power.

The power management function lets us direct that the monitor, the hard disk, and the entire computer be shut down according to preset or user-defined power schemes. A *power scheme* is a group of preset power-management options. A scheme might define elapsed times for when the PC goes on standby and/or the monitor or the hard disk is shut down. To choose or create a power management scheme, open the Power Options Properties dialog box in the Control Panel.

You can put your computer on *standby* or in *hibernation*. While on standby, a PC switches to low power and the hard disk and monitor(s) are shut down. When you take your computer out of standby, the desktop is restored exactly as it was, open files and all. Normally, you would use standby if you plan to be away from the PC for a relatively short period of time. If your system is subjected to an instantaneous loss of power, unsaved work is lost because everything is saved in volatile RAM.

When you place your PC in hibernation, it saves the current system status to hard disk and the entire computer shuts down. When you restart the system, the desktop is restored from disk to its status prior to hibernation. Typically, you would use hibernation when you plan to be away from the system for an extended period of time, perhaps all night for a desktop PC or an hour for a notebook PC running on battery power.

Windows has a variety of preset power schemes, including Home/Office Desk, Portable/Laptop, Presentation, Always On, Minimal Power Management, and Max Battery. In the Home/Office Desk scheme, the monitor is turned off after 20 minutes. In the Portable/Laptop scheme, the monitor is turned off after 15 minutes and the hard disk after 30 minutes. Also, the system is placed on standby at 20 minutes and in hibernation after three hours. I created my own power scheme, called "Larry's office," where the monitor turns off at 20 minutes and the hard disk at three hours. The system hibernates at four hours.

Software Maintenance

Software maintenance is an ongoing task that involves obtaining and installing software updates to currently installed software. It may also entail purchasing the most recent versions of installed software.

Software Updates

Invariably, errors begin to surface once a software package is released to the public, even in the most scrupulously tested software. And, invariably, software vendors see features that should have been included, but were not. To correct these oversights, vendors periodically make updates available free to registered users of their software via downloads over the Internet. You can either go to the software vendor's web site (the support/download area) or, if available, choose the Check for Updates option in the software's Help menu. Microsoft Windows operating systems and many major software packages enable updates to be downloaded automatically (see Figure 10-6).

To update the Windows operating system, choose the Windows Update feature (under Pick a Task on the Help and Support home page). When you begin the Windows Update procedure, Windows scans your system and identifies available updates. Each update is described and you are asked to choose those that you wish to install. Always install "critical" updates, as these updates may do something like plug a hole in Windows' online security.

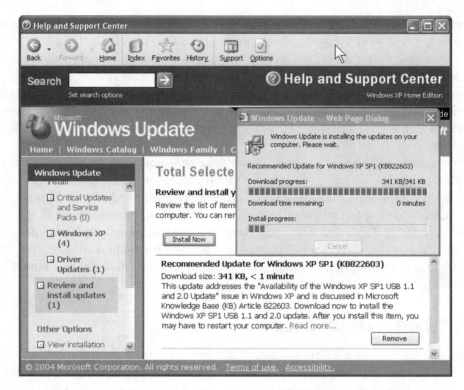

Figure 10-6   Downloading and installing Windows updates

I would recommend that you check for updates to your most frequently used programs every few months. Do the online Windows Update automatically or no less often than once a month if done manually. Windows Update options are found in the System Properties dialog box (Automatic Updates tab) in the Control Panel. If you choose Keep My Computer Up-to-Date, Windows automatically determines which updates you need and delivers them directly to your PC via the Internet.

Software Upgrades

Software vendors periodically introduce new and improved versions of their software. Versions are indicated by the numbers that follow the software title. A new version goes from one whole number to the next (version 3.3 to version 4.0). New releases of the same version, which usually reflect interim corrections to oversights in design and programming, are shown in tenths and hundredths (version 2.1, 2.13, and 2.2).

Upgrading your software to the most recent version can get expensive. For example, upgrading Microsoft Windows and the Microsoft Office suite could cost from $300 to $700. Keep in mind that the useful life of a home PC system is, on average, about four years. If your operating system, office suite, and speech recognition software are working for you and you can get by without this year's version of the encyclopedia, you can save hundreds of dollars by staying with what you have.

With vendors putting out new versions of their software every year or so, they seldom offer the dramatic changes we used to see when new versions came out less frequently. Consequently, the upgrade is becoming an increasingly harder sell. Generally, the core features, the ones you use 99.8 percent of the time, are relatively unchanged from version to version. Often, a new version will have exotic features, more clip art, or things you may not use anyway. Occasionally, there is a breakthrough in technology and the extra dollars spent on the new version can pay off, as it did for me when I upgraded my speech recognition software. The new version understands everything I say as fast as I can say it.

When you're ready to upgrade, check to see if there is an *upgrade version* of the software available. The upgrade-only versions are installed over a previous version of the software. The upgrade versions may sell for as little as a third to half that of a full version.

Upgrading Windows is major surgery for your PC. If you have a truly compelling reason to upgrade your Windows operating system and are willing to put up with several days of conversion headaches, be my guest. If not, take comfort in the fact that your existing operating system will probably do 99.2 percent of what you wish to do.

Troubleshooting

Trouble is part of the personal computing adventure, so every PC owner becomes a troubleshooter at one time or another. The typical reaction to a seemingly serious problem is panic, then anger. When trouble happens, my wife always reminds me to take a deep breath. I do and it helps me to relax. Then I remind myself that every PC owner has his or her share of PC problems and this is just one of them. This section is about demystifying the troubleshooting adventure.

It's easy to turn your anger toward your PC, Bill Gates, the manufacturers, or whoever sold you the stuff in the first place. In truth, these people are your friends. They have done a great deal to help you in time of need. There is probably a carefully documented description of your problem and what you have to do to solve it. Your challenge is to find it.

OK, so troubleshooting isn't your thing, not with the washing machine, the car, or the PC. Well, you can always mortgage your house and take your PC to a service center. However, I encourage you to try troubleshooting first, arguably the quickest and least expensive approach to fixing the vast majority of PC problems. PC problems can be frustrating, but with a little thought, research, and confidence, you can take

care of most of them. And each time you do, you get that deep-down feeling of accomplishment.

DOA and Lemons

On occasion, troubleshooting is needed the first time you flip the power-on switch. About 15 percent of PC owners are victims of DOA (dead on arrival) hardware or they encounter serious problems within the first month. One in 20 new PC systems is inoperable; at least the new owner can't get it to work. About one in 75 earns the lemon label; that is, three or more components must be replaced within the first 16 months. Of the 25 PCs I've purchased for myself, only one has been a lemon. The manufacturer eventually replaced it after a six-month ordeal.

Yes, you could have installation problems or, worse, a lemon. Installation problems usually are easily resolved with some by-the-book troubleshooting. However, a lemon can be a real problem and you might not know you have one for several months. When difficult-to-resolve problems continue to surface with some frequency, assume you have a lemon.

Manufacturers/retailers will not exchange a product for a new one until all avenues for fixing the problem have been explored, even after it becomes apparent to all that you have a lemon. I mention this because you may need to be persistent, even relentless, to get satisfaction from the manufacturer, especially if you get a lemon. Make sure that the manufacturer is aware of the problems you are having so these can be recorded in its tech support log for your system.

The Universal Solution to Most PC Problems

The number and variety of potential PC problems boggles the mind. These aggravating problems are commonplace: the PC is frozen (it has an unchanging display that is unaffected by mouse or keyboard input), the printer isn't responding, the web browser or e-mail client doesn't recognize the broadband connection, the PC is running markedly slower than normal, an application program is not responding (an hourglass appears when the pointer rolls over the application), there's no sound, and so on. Although these could be symptoms of serious problems, most of the time these and other common PC problems are simple annoyances that are easily solved with a universal troubleshooting solution. Performing this simple five-step procedure solves most PC hardware and software problems:

1. If possible, go through the normal system shutdown procedure (not restart) such that the PC is shut down and the power is off.

2. Turn off any peripheral devices that may be malfunctioning.

3. Check that all connections between system components are secure.

4. Turn on all peripheral devices.

5. Turn on the PC and reboot the system.

Vendor/Manufacturer Troubleshooting Assistance

If this universal all-purpose fix doesn't work, there's plenty of help in the form of Windows Help and Support, reference manuals, technical support web sites, and call-in technical support.

Windows Troubleshooting Support

The Windows Help and Support feature includes a number of "troubleshooters" that use interactive questioning (see Figure 10-7) to walk you through the trouble-shooting process. Available troubleshooters are listed in Table 10-1. To get to these troubleshooters, choose Fixing the Problem in Help and Support, and then find the troubleshooters in one of ten general areas of concern.

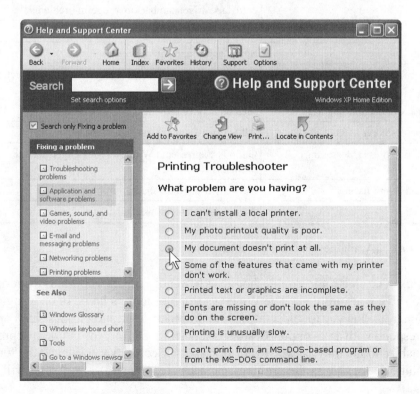

Figure 10-7   Printing Troubleshooter

Windows Troubleshooter	Problem Areas Addressed (Issues sometimes overlap between troubleshooters)
System Setup	Windows installation and setup problems
Startup/Shutdown	Startup/shutdown problems
Display	All video-related problems (graphics adapter, monitor, driver compatibility, video settings, and so)
Home Networking	Setup, Internet connection, and file/printer sharing problems
Hardware	Hardware problems: disk/disc, input devices, network adapter, USB devices, and modem
Multimedia and Games	Multimedia, gaming, USB devices, DVD, sound cards, game controllers, and related problems
Digital Video Discs (DVDs)	DVD drive and decoder problems
Input Devices	Keyboard, mouse device, camera, scanner, and infrared device problems
Drives and Network Adapters	Hard disk, floppy disk, CD-ROM/DVD drive, network card, tape drive, and backup program problems
USB	USB connector and peripheral problems
Sound	Sound and sound card problems
Modem	Modem connection, setup, configuration, and detection problems
Internet Connection Sharing	Internet service provider (ISP) problems
Internet Explorer	All Internet Explorer–related problems
Outlook Express (Messaging)	Outlook Express and Windows Messenger Service problems
File and Print Sharing	Network file/printer sharing problems
Printing	All printer-related problems

Table 10-1   Available Windows Troubleshooters

Think of an electronic troubleshooter as a friendly expert who wants to work with you to solve your problem. The Windows troubleshooters home in on a suggested solution by asking you to select the most appropriate description from several options or to respond with a yes or no to a specific question. During this interactive process, the troubleshooter may ask you to perform specific corrective actions. If the "universal solution" doesn't fix the problem, chances are, you and your partner will.

Reference Manuals

Most hardware products are accompanied by some type of hard copy reference manual. The trend with software, however, is to build manual content into the software, often within the Help facility or as a separate electronic document that can be viewed with word processing software, Adobe Reader (PDF format), or an Internet browser. These *e-manuals* become available when you install the product. Eventually all PC product manuals will be electronic, even hardware manuals.

Most reference manuals, whether hard copy or electronic, have a troubleshooting section that includes step-by-step solutions to common problems. If the troubleshooting guide does not give you the information you need to solve the problem, your next step is to go to the manufacturer for insight. You can either visit the manufacturer's technical support web site or call the manufacturer's technical support hotline (find the telephone numbers listed in product documentation). If you're comfortable fixing problems on your own, I would recommend the former. It's usually faster.

Technical Support Web Sites

It's to the advantage of the manufacturer to have a comprehensive, easy-to-use technical support web site. An hour's worth of personalized technical support can cost the company up to $100 an hour. The cost to the company of helping a customer solve a problem via an interactive tech support web site is considerably less than $1. The typical PC manufacturer has most or all of the following technical support aids:

- **A knowledge base**   In the knowledge-based tool, you simply enter keywords relating to your problem and/or enter the question directly. For example, if you're having trouble setting up a home network, you could enter "How to set up a home network?" or "Home network installation" (see Figure 10-8). Inquiries such as these normally result in a list of hyperlinks to web pages that relate to your problem and/or may lead to a solution.
- **Tutorials**   A tech support web site may offer a variety of tutorials, each designed to walk you through some facet of the operation and application of a product. Or, the site might include step-by-step tutorials on how to complete a particular procedure, such as upgrading the BIOS software.
- **Frequently asked questions**   Chances are someone else has asked your question before. Depending on the size of the tech support web site, the FAQs may be categorized and placed in a hierarchical menu so that you can easily find those that relate to your concern.

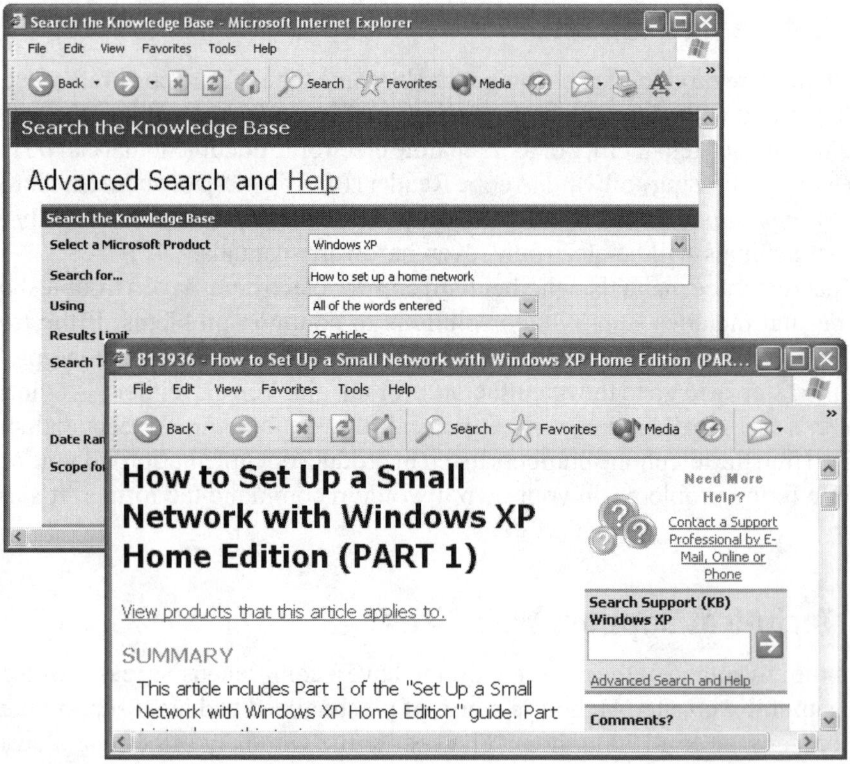

Figure 10-8   Windows Knowledge Base

- **Tips and hints**   The manufacturer may provide tips and hints to help you get the most out of your personal computing system.
- **Contacts**   This section of the online technical support web site normally allows you to submit a written description of your problem within an online form. Technical support personnel usually respond to these types of inquiries within 24–48 hours, often sooner.

Call-in Technical Support

The manufacturer would prefer that call-in technical support be your last choice, because it is the manufacturer's most expensive support service. The major PC manufacturers have thousands of technical support personnel, some of whom are good and know what they're doing. Many, however, are rookies and may not be very helpful for difficult problems.

Most of my interactions with tech support people have been positive, but some conversations are overly time consuming, sometimes expensive (not all are toll free), and of little help. Online support is so comprehensive that I seldom call tech support. To save time and possibly money, I always check the support web site first. Most of the time, I find a detailed solution to my problem within minutes.

Making the Call to Tech Support

If you have exhausted your options and feel a need to talk with a real person, be aware that there may be costs involved. Look over your warranty and/or a description of your telephone-based technical support options so that you understand the costs, if any. If you purchased a three-year warranty with 24-hour technical support, tech support usually is provided at no charge. However, if you are out of your warranty or support, a per-problem fee ($15 and up) or a per-minute fee ($1 and up) may apply. Another common approach to offering call-in technical support is to provide the user one or two free calls, just enough to get you through a successful installation. Fees apply for subsequent calls. Your product documentation or the web site details these costs.

When you call tech support, be prepared. Remember, the call might be on your dime. I would suggest that you write this information down so you can relate it clearly to the tech rep:

- A description of your personal computer (model number and/or manufacturer's ID)
- A description of the problem, noting what the system is doing now that it should not be doing and/or what the system isn't doing that it should be doing
- A description of the circumstances under which the problem occurs
- The text and number of any error messages (note whether these are Windows or application software error messages)
- What you might have done to attempt to fix the problem
- A description of any hardware or software changes you have made to your PC system just before and during the occurrence of the problem (for example, changing network preferences or the installation of a new modem)

Getting Answers

Larger companies deliver call-in technical support in levels, where the top people are consulted only after other, lower-level tech support people have failed. When you call a company's technical support hotline, you're automatically routed to level 1 technical support. These people handle a wide range of common problems. When it becomes clear that a solution at level 1 is unlikely, then, and only then, do they pass the difficult problem up to a level 2 (expert) tech support person. Unfortunately, ego sometimes drives level 1 tech support people to attempt to solve problems above

their level of expertise and training, wasting your time and theirs. When it becomes apparent that your problem is unsolvable at level 1, request level 2 technical support and don't take "no" for an answer.

System Restore: Undo System Changes

Often, a current problem is a result of a software package or driver software being installed, with or without your knowledge. When attempts to troubleshoot the problem are futile, you can use the Windows System Restore feature to return your PC to its state before the problem-causing software/driver installation. Windows automatically creates *restore points* each day and at the time of significant changes to your PC, perhaps the accidental deletion of a critical file or a virus attack. Restore points go back up to three weeks, depending on the amount of activity on your PC. You can restore your system to any of these restore points. To reset your PC to an earlier restore point, open Windows Help and Support and choose System Restore under Pick a Task.

It is important to note that the system restore process does not affect your personal data files, including Microsoft Office documents, passwords, and e-mail. The system restore process is relatively painless and can get you out of some difficult situations.

Migrating to a New PC

Eventually, troubleshooting becomes more frequent. Your system no longer does what you want it to do and, if it does, it doesn't do it fast enough. It's time for a new PC. After a PC lifetime of use, you have a lot invested in your old and slow PC. This means you have a lot to move to the new system: your user files, all of your installed software, Internet/e-mail information (including your contacts), speech recognition vocabulary, user accounts, desktop settings, and much more. The good news is that ten major companies, including IBM, Microsoft, and Intel, have agreed to work together to reduce the cost, time, and complexity of migrating to a new PC. The bad news is that they are still working on the migration standards. For the most part, you are on your own during migration.

Here is my recipe for transitioning to a new PC:

1. *Connect the old and new PC.* To do this, I put both PCs on our home network. If you don't have a network, the PCs can be linked directly with a cable (see instructions in the wizard in the next step).

2. *Use the Files and Setting Transfer Wizard.* I use the Windows Files and Setting Transfer Wizard (Accessories/System Tools program group) to move some files and settings to the new computer. This wizard transfers settings for Outlook (e-mail), Internet Explorer (browser), the desktop, dialup connections, and some other miscellaneous settings.

3. *Copy all other user files.* Copy (don't use Move) all other user files to the new system.

4. *Set up the home network connection.* See Chapter 18, "Building a Home Network," for detailed information if you have a home network.

5. *Set up the Internet connection.* If needed, use the New Connection Wizard to set up an Internet connection (Start | Control Panel | Network Connections | Create a new connection).

6. *Install software.* Install all the software packages from their original CD/DVD or downloaded files.

7. *Download and install updates to all software.* Chances are that most of your software packages will need to be updated, including your brand-new version of Windows.

8. *Set User Preferences.* With the old PC nearby, use it as your guide to work through all software packages to customize them to your personal computing needs.

9. *Remove software and user files from old system.* Uninstall any software that is not licensed for multiple-PC use and delete your user files from the old PC.

No matter how much I plan, this migration process seems to take me about a full working day. On average, the business community budgets about $300 to fund each migration.

What to Do with Old PCs

PCs usually become obsolete before they wear out. No level of maintenance, upgrading, or troubleshooting can save them. Within the next year, over 300 million computers will outlive their usefulness and have no market value. A typical PC and its peripherals contain mercury, cadmium, lead, and other toxic compounds. A CRT monitor contains several pounds of lead. These elements and compounds can have a dramatic impact on ground, water, and air quality.

Currently, only about 20 percent of PCs and peripherals are recycled, compared to 70 percent of major appliances, such as dishwashers and refrigerators. At present, there is little or no economic incentive to recycle hardware. It's only a matter of time before each of us will have "cradle-to-grave" responsibility for PCs and computer hardware.

One very real option is to give it away. However, I would recommend that you give away only systems that are no more than four or five years off the technology, fully functional (no hardware or software problems), have a good mix of software, and are Internet ready. Realistically, the rest have little or no value. Seventy percent of donated PCs are discarded.

It's possible that your city or county environmental services will be able recycle your PC for a small fee. If not, a number of private recycling companies and several major computer vendors, such as Intel and IBM, provide PC recycling services. If you can't recycle locally, you can search the Internet for a "PC recycling service" and send in your old system for proper disposal. You can expect to pay between $20 and $40 (including shipping) to recycle your PC, but, in return, you get to enjoy that feeling you get when you do the right thing.

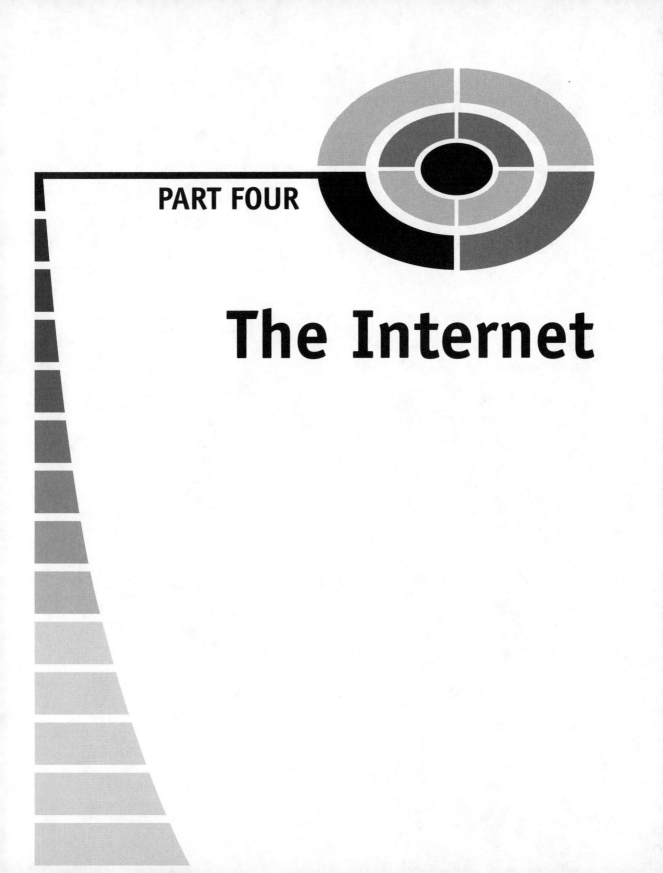

PART FOUR

The Internet

Internet Basics: Going Online

The Internet is a new door in our lives that simply was not there a decade ago. Whether you are a *newbie* (new to the Internet) or a seasoned Internet surfer, I invite you to skim this three-chapter sequence about the Internet. I've included a number of tips, hints, and suggestions that can point you in the right direction, help you open that door even wider, and, perhaps, save you some money and grief.

This first chapter of the Internet trilogy answers your question about what is needed to go online (hardware, software, and Internet services), how to go online, how to navigate between sites on the World Wide Web, and how to find information on the Internet. Chapter 12, "Internet Applications: Cruising the Internet," introduces you to the most popular Internet applications and shows you the amazing breadth of its content. Chapter 13, "Internet Security: Protecting Your PC," shows you how to recognize and cope with the shady side of the Internet.

What Is the Internet?

The *Internet* is a network that links millions of computers and computer networks in every country in the world (see Figure 11-1). The scale of the Net boggles the mind. It encompasses just about every conceivable government agency, academic institution, nonprofit entity, and, of course, every business that plans to stay in business. Each of these organizations has one or more *Internet server computers* that handle Internet traffic to and from their *web site*. Over a billion individuals like you and me subscribe to Internet service providers (ISPs) so that they can have access to the Internet and have e-mail addresses that let them send and receive e-mail to other *netizens* (citizens of the Internet).

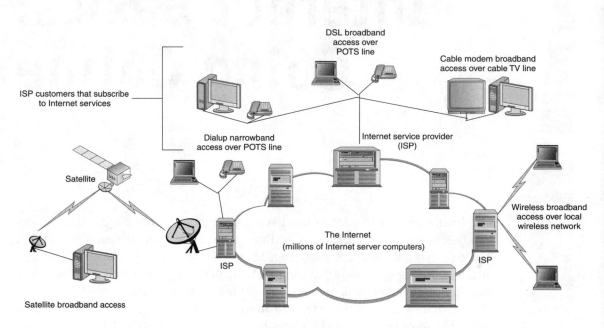

Figure 11-1   The Internet

The birth of the Internet in 1969 was overshadowed by Apollo 11's flight to the moon and even by the marathon Woodstock rock concert. In fact, hardly anyone noticed when scientists demonstrated a digital link between UCLA and Stanford University. The ARPANET, named after its government funding agency, grew to 200 government and academic sites by 1981. Over the next decade, ARPANET continued to gather momentum and evolved into the Internet.

The Internet remained a tool of scientists, primarily because of its cumbersome, text-oriented interface, until 1989, when a Swiss physicist, Tim Berners-Lee, invented an Internet application called the *World Wide Web*. The Web, as it came to be called, enabled users to view multimedia content on the Internet. However, it was not until 1993 and the introduction of the user-friendly Internet browser that the Internet was embraced by the masses. The rest is history.

Market forces now drive the Internet, along with its policies and technologies. There is no single authoritative organization that governs the Internet. It is coordinated by volunteers from around the world who serve on a variety of task groups, advisory boards, and so on. The Internet is so dynamic in its content, applications, and potential that it is continually redefining itself.

The Internet has changed our lives in so many ways—how we work, how we learn, and even how we play. Once on the Internet, you can find information on just about anything, read online newspapers in Japanese, or have videophone conversations with friends in Europe. You can send Grandma a home movie, schedule a meeting with your coworkers, pay your utility bills, listen to a live radio broadcast of your favorite sporting event, conduct research for a report, order a pizza, buy an automobile, make new friends via chat rooms, and much, much more.

What Do You Need to Go Online?

You need the following items to go online and enjoy the resources and applications of the Internet:

- **Personal computer**   Actually, you can go online with an Internet-ready PDA (personal digital assistant), cellular phone, or Internet appliance, too, but our focus is personal computing.
- **Communications software**   All the software you need for basic Internet access is built into Windows and its support programs.
- **Modem**   You need either a traditional modem for narrowband, dialup access or a cable modem, DSL modem, or satellite modem for broadband access.
- **Network interface card (NIC) or USB port**   The external broadband modem connects to your PC via an Ethernet port (NIC) or a USB port. Virtually all modern notebook PCs and most modern desktops have integrated Ethernet and USB ports (on the motherboard). However, if your broadband modem supports only Ethernet and you don't have it on your PC, you need to install an inexpensive PCI Ethernet card (see Figure 11-2).

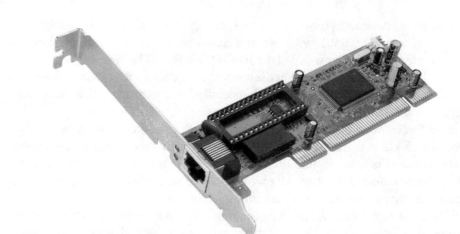

Figure 11-2   PCI Ethernet card

(Photo courtesy of U.S. Robotics)

- **Telephone or cable TV service**   You must have an installed telephone line to receive dialup or DSL Internet service. For cable-modem access, you must be a digital cable TV subscriber.
- **An account with an Internet service provider (ISP)**   You must subscribe to Internet service, dialup or broadband, through an ISP (see Chapter 9, "Supplies, Services, and Accessories").

Single-User Hardware for Internet Access

Besides the PC, the only Internet access hardware you need for a single user is a traditional modem or one of the broadband modems, and possibly an Ethernet card. Multiuser access to an Internet account is a little different and is covered in Chapter 18, "Building a Home Network." Traditional dialup modems that perform analog/digital conversions are built into notebooks and usually are included with desktops.

If the desktop you wish to buy isn't configured with a modem and you have a choice to add it, you should probably do so, even if you plan to subscribe to broadband service. An inexpensive *data/voice/fax modem* ($10 to $25) enables you to make regular telephone calls through your PC (via your headset/mike) and send faxes. Also, it provides backup narrowband Net access in case you temporarily lose your broadband—it happens. Make sure the modem you choose has the voice/fax capability.

For single-user broadband access, you need a cable, DSL, or satellite modem, either an external one or an internal PCI modem. The broadband ISP typically makes a modem available for purchase or lease. Your ISP may give you the option of buying one from a third party. If you go this route, confirm with your ISP that the modem is compatible with its network. If you purchase an external unit (see Figure 11-3), you will need a way to connect it to your PC—through either an Ethernet NIC or a USB port. Virtually all broadband modems support Ethernet, and a growing number support both Ethernet and USB.

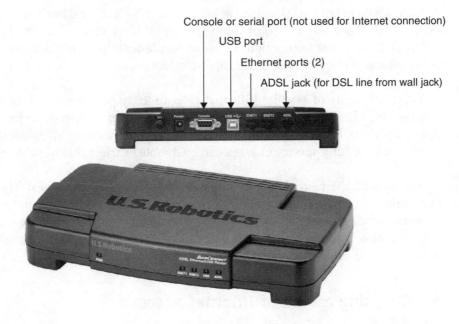

Figure 11-3   External DSL modem: Ethernet, USB, and serial ports

(Photo courtesy of U.S. Robotics)

To link any of the broadband modems to the PC, you need either *Cat 5 cabling* with *RJ-45 connectors* or a USB cable. The cabling normally is supplied with the broadband modem; if it not, it is readily available in various lengths at retail outlets. The RJ-45 connectors are slightly larger and similar in appearance and function to the familiar RJ-11 telephone connectors.

The Internet Services: ISPs

There are literally thousands of Internet service providers, most of which are local and several of which are national/international. New York City has over 100 whose name begins with the letter *A*. Our focus is on dialup and popular broadband options (cable-modem, DSL, and satellite). When you begin your search for an ISP, you may see other options listed, such as ISDN, T1, and T3. I haven't mentioned ISDN, which offers dialup service at 128 Kbps, because it is a grossly overpriced, inefficient service. I would avoid ISDN because its days are numbered. T1 and T3 are expensive, high-speed services designed for businesses.

ISP Service Options

At least 90 percent of the ISPs offer dialup service at 56 Kbps and most of them offer ISDN at 128 Kbps. About half of the ISPs offer DSL service. A few are DSL-only ISPs, but that number will continue to rise as people continue to migrate from dialup to broadband service. Your ISP for cable-modem access and your cable TV company are probably the same.

There are plenty of satellite ISPs that cater to those people who are "rural and underserved." That means you don't have access to DSL or cable-modem because, if you did, you would not be considering satellite. Although satellite offers comparable service, the monthly service charges can be double or triple that of cable-modem or DSL

Anyone with a terrestrial telephone line can subscribe to dialup access. If you live in America and have a southern exposure to the sky, you can get broadband satellite. This means that the vast majority of people will have a choice between slow and fast Internet access. Just because you have cable TV and a terrestrial telephone line doesn't mean you have cable-modem and DSL service.

Choosing a Type of Internet Access

When you are ready to subscribe to an Internet service through an ISP, your choices probably will be dialup (slow) or broadband (fast). Your choices, however, may be limited based on availability of certain types of service and your financial circumstances. You can expect to pay $X for dialup access and from $2X to $5X for broadband access. The classic Internet access decision process followed by thousands of people each day (whether they know it or not) is illustrated in Figure 11-4.

Several steps in Figure 11-4 need some explanation. In the first decision step, you are asked to choose between dialup and broadband. If you choose dialup, you are asked to respond to another question, "Can you afford broadband?" Here is an opportunity to reconsider your decision. If you can afford the extra $10 to $80 per month (average of about $40) and you expect to be a frequent user of the Internet, it is unlikely that you will be satisfied with click-and-wait dialup service. This is especially true if patience is not one of your personality traits.

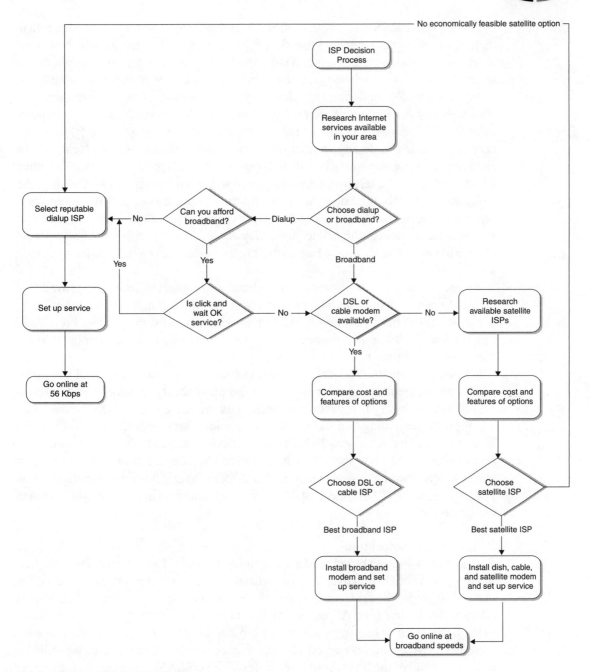

Figure 11-4   The ISP decision process

Always-on broadband access offers a completely different experience than dialup, where you must dial up the ISP each time you wish to tap into the Net. Your will to surf, to download, to send images, and to participate in real-time applications is markedly subdued when you must continually wait for web pages to build, or watch download-completion bars that seem stuck in time. Numerous studies have shown that broadband users are more willing to explore and take full advantage of cyberspace. You may pay a little more for broadband, but you get up to 50 times the access speed. If you do any work at home, the extra capacity will pay for itself in a single day of use. I'm pushing broadband because all trends point toward it as the future of Internet access: a telecom commitment to universal broadband availability, the complexity of web page design, robust Internet applications, and Internet access pricing. If you need help justifying the extra expense of broadband, just consider that you won't need an extra "data line" for dialup access. Many people with dialup access choose to have an extra phone line so their main voice line is available for incoming and outgoing calls.

Figure 11-4 shows that if you want broadband and neither DSL nor cable is available, your only choice is satellite. The problem with satellite is that it can be prohibitively expensive (possibly in excess of $1200 per year), and to some people, broadband just isn't worth that much money. This is why I have included a loop back to the dialup selection process.

Although it may not be a choice during the currency of this book, I would be remiss not to mention what appears to be the inevitability of widespread wireless broadband. Industry forecasters are telling us that wireless broadband based on a cell phone technology called *EV-DO* (Evolution-Data Optimized) will be available to most of us as early as 2006. This is different than today's very limited wireless broadband in "hot spots," such as coffee shops and airport gates. The new wireless broadband will give you broadband access at DSL/cable modem speeds on your notebook PC, PDA, or cell phone from any location in any metropolitan area in the United States.

DSL Considerations

For most of us seeking broadband access, the question is "Do I choose DSL or cable-modem?" One of DSL's advantages and disadvantages is that it is distance sensitive; that is, the longer the DSL run between the house and a telecom office or a DSLAM (Digital Subscriber Line Access Multiplexor) booster station, the less the capacity of the line. If you're lucky enough to live close to the phone company office or a remote DSLAM, the access speed you experience will be superior to those unlucky souls at the end of the line (about three miles). The DSLAM at the office or a remote facility links a number of DSL customers to a single very high-speed communications channel, usually fiber optic cable. The DSLAM for my DSL service is about 1000 feet from my home, so I routinely enjoy 1.5 Mbps speed, which is the maximum available from my ISP. If you're considering DSL, you might wish to research your location relative to the nearest DSLAM or chat with your neighbors about their bandwidth speed. A number of web sites offer a free "bandwidth speed test" service.

With DSL, you need only one telephone line for voice and data. Because they use different frequency bands, the digital DSL signal can be transmitted at the same time you are holding an analog voice conversation. When you subscribe to DSL, you will receive a certain number of line filters that are designed to eliminate "data noise" during voice conversations. If you have a lot of phones and a hissing sound on the lines without filters, you may need to purchase more of them.

Cable-Modem Considerations

Cable-modem offers a "shared neighborhood" style of connection that potentially can reach hundreds of people in a single neighborhood. Having cable-modem access is like being on a network where all people share the Internet capacity of a single cable. A digital TV cable is a "really big pipe" with an enormous transmission capacity, but it can be seriously diluted for an individual when hundreds of your neighbors choose to surf the Internet during the peak personal hours of 5:00 to 11:00 in the evening. Cable-modem is more people sensitive, so the more people on the network, the slower the transmission rate. Your best source of information regarding the level of service in your neighborhood is your neighbors. An experienced subscriber to your cable-modem ISP can give you examples of speeds that you can expect at various times during the day.

Choosing an ISP

On the scale of importance in personal computing, choosing the right ISP ranks up there with choosing the right PC. In terms of cost, this decision may top that of the PC. An ISP can be a mom-and-pop shop or a multinational conglomerate. It can offer basic Internet access and nothing else or it can offer a range of Internet access services and a laundry list of additional services. The following is a list of things you should be looking for in an ISP, with most important first:

- **Quality of the ISP**   Every company has a reputation. Pick a good one.
- **Internet access**   Unlimited service is widely available and the most desirable service. Unfortunately, high-volume users, namely those who are continually downloading/uploading movies and music, have forced some ISPs to limit the amount of information that can be transmitted per day for a given account.
- **Internet service speeds**   All dialup service is made available at 56 Kbps, but broadband ISPs can limit downstream and upstream speeds. Several web sites, such as Broadband Reports (www.dslreports.com), routinely

test the actual (versus advertised) bandwidth speeds for major ISPs and then report their findings.

- **Number of e-mail accounts**   The ISP should provide enough e-mail accounts (the main account plus subaccounts) for each person in your family to have his or her own e-mail address.
- **Support hardware**   Many ISPs will provide the hardware needed to enable broadband Net service (modem, Ethernet NIC, and so on) for free or at a substantially reduced cost. If you accept their free hardware (worth as much as $100), they probably will ask for a one-year contract.
- **Storage space**   An ISP may provide online storage space in which you can store files, photos, or whatever that can be accessed from any Internet-ready PC. This is a good way to share photos and videos with family and friends. The amount of space offered may vary from 5MB to over 100MB.
- **Personal web page**   Some ISPs will host your personal web page (size may be limited to around 10MB).
- **Technical support**   If everything goes smoothly, you can be up and running in five minutes and you may not need technical support for years. If it doesn't go smoothly, technical support is critical. Give a company that offers 24/7 support a few extra points.
- **Additional services**   The additional services that can be offered by an ISP are many and varied. For example, an ISP can offer parent controls, firewall software (Internet protection), Internet radio, an online encyclopedia, a gaming package (numerous online games), newsgroups, instant messaging, free classified ad listings, free *Consumer Reports* information, securities market research and analysis, and many other possibilities. On my personalized "home page," my ISP lists news and sports of interest to me, show times for all the local movie theaters, and the local weather.

Frequently there is a "come on" price for three months or so. Be sure to look past that price and know exactly what you will be paying upfront and each month over the term of the contract. It pays to read the small print, as telecoms are notorious for tacking on mysterious charges over and above the advertised rate. It's not unusual for these charges (not counting taxes) to be in excess of $10 a month.

Another important consideration is the number of PC users permitted on a single account by the ISP. Some ISPs are now limiting the number of PCs, often to two or three, that can tap into the Internet access for a single account. ISPs initiated this restriction because families/individuals in adjoining apartments would subscribe to broadband access, and then share the line via a wireless network. Make sure that the limit will handle your needs over the next couple of years.

American Online: AOL

Another very popular approach to gaining Internet access is to subscribe to a commercial information service, such as America Online or CompuServe. Approximately one in four Internet-ready homes subscribes to America Online. AOL is known to everyone through countless TV advertisements and its ubiquitous mailings. When you log in to AOL, you are on the AOL network, not the Internet. Once on AOL, you have a *gateway* to the Internet through its software and network. CompuServe is a subsidiary of American Online, Inc. Both offer Internet access and a variety of online services, but CompuServe may be more oriented to adults and their information and entertainment needs.

AOL is sometimes called "the Internet with training wheels." The "training wheels," however, may be AOL's greatest asset. AOL has a user-friendly proprietary interface with numerous easily accessible online services (see Figure 11-5). The many services, which include personal finance, instant messaging, news, Internet radio, travel, shopping, and many others, are easily customized for a personalized online experience. They maintain an army of technical support people who are used to working with people who are beginning their online experience.

Figure 11-5   America Online (AOL)

Virtually everything on AOL is available on the Internet in one form or another. AOL is not for everyone, but it offers a nonthreatening approach to the online experience that can be very appealing to both the novice user and the experienced user who has become comfortable within the cocoon of AOL services.

Internet Access: Setup and Installation

Once you have decided on a level of Internet service and an ISP, the rest is downhill. When you subscribe to an ISP, the ISP normally will send/give you everything you need to go online, including the broadband modem and cable and, possibly, an Ethernet NIC. The packet may or may not include an installation CD. When you run the installation CD, all of the settings necessary to establish a connection are entered automatically. Here, in its entirety, are the instructions provided to me by my ISP:

Step 1. Insert installer CD into your computer.
Follow the step-by-step instructions which will guide you through the software and hardware installation.
DO NOT INSTALL ANY EQUIPMENT UNTIL PROMPTED BY THE CD.

Step 2. Surfing.
From now on, when you want to connect to the Internet, click on the DSL icon on your desktop.

That's it, and that's typical. The installation CD includes graphics that illustrate how to connect whatever devices and cables are needed to go online. For a dialup link, this may be as basic as inserting a phone line RJ-11 jack into the "line in" socket in your PCI modem on the back of your desktop PC or somewhere on the perimeter of your notebook PC. The broadband modem is a little more involved in that you will connect a telephone line or a cable TV line to a modem and then use the supplied Ethernet Cat 5 cable to connect the modem to the PC.

If you do not receive an installation CD, your ISP will include explicit instructions regarding the hardware and you will need to run the *New Connection Wizard* (see Figure 11-6). The wizard will ask you to enter some of this ISP-provided information:

- The telephone number to call for dialup access.
- The ISP Internet address and, possibly, an IP address.
- A user name (ID) and password that you will use to log in to the Internet service.

The ISP also will provide information for setting up an e-mail account (for example, incoming and outgoing mail server information).

Figure 11-6   New Connection Wizard

Internet Basics

Internet technology at the research, development, and implementation levels is as replete with technical jargon as any other area. Fortunately, all you really need to know to be a netizen are the basics described in the following sections.

Sending/Receiving Information on the Internet: Packet Switching

The Internet is a network of networks, and your PC is one of many *nodes* (end points) on one of these networks, most likely that of your ISP. Your ISP has at least one *point of presence (POP)* on the Internet for use by its subscribers. The ISP maintains a high-speed communications link to the Internet's *backbone,* which is a system of high-level networks and communications devices that facilitate the interconnection of those computer networks with a POP on the Internet.

Data are transmitted over the Internet according to several *communications protocols,* each of which defines a set of rules that computers follow when they talk to each other. The protocols most frequently associated with the Internet are the *TCP protocol* and the *IP protocol.* You'll see references to *TCP/IP* as you work through the process of setting up and maintaining an Internet connection. The TCP (Transmission Control Protocol) and IP (Internet Protocol) protocols combine with other protocols to enable the packaging of Internet transmissions into independent *packets.* Each packet contains an *IP address* of the destination and a portion of the user data. The packets travel independently through the Internet and may actually take different paths. Once all packets associated with a particular transmission have arrived at the destination, they are reassembled as an e-mail, a colorful web page, a photo of grandmother, and so on. This communications process is called *packet switching*.

An ISP and any point on the Internet has a unique *IP address* that consists of four numbers (0 to 255) separated by periods (for example, 206.28.104.10). Typically, when you log on to an ISP, your PC is assigned a temporary IP address, called a *dynamic IP address*. Your computer has this address for as long as you are connected.

Your ISP manages your Internet traffic along with that of all other subscribers. Your ISP's server combines the packets that comprise your message with those from other end users and then transmits them together over its high-speed link to the Internet's backbone. Packets received from the backbone are distributed to the appropriate customer node.

Packet switching on the Internet permits the sharing of high-speed communications links on the Internet backbone, plus, it also lets you share your Internet service with other PCs in your home. Because messages are sent and received in packets, I can send and receive e-mail while I am downloading a file. The packets of information being sent/received by my wife and children on their PCs are interspersed with my traffic. It's all transparent to us. All we have to do is click Send Message or click on a web page hyperlink. Internet protocols and devices do the rest. Pretty amazing!

Information Organization on the Internet

The first thing an organization does to get a presence on the Internet is to register a *domain name.* You've seen them everywhere, such as on bumper stickers, TV ads, book covers, and umbrellas (some examples are www.ibm.com, www.senate.gov, and www.ou.edu). The domain name is the name or the representation of the name of an organization. Each of these domain names is assigned a four-number IP addresses. An Internet service known as the *Domain Name System (DNS)* interprets the user-entered domain names (for example, www.icann.org) into numeric IP addresses (192.0.34.65). ICANN (Internet Corporation for Assigned Names and Numbers) coordinates the assignment of Internet domain names and IP address numbers. The Domain Name System maintains one of the largest and most volatile databases in the world, yet it is transparent to us netizens. Truly astonishing!

The URL: Internet Addresses

The Uniform Resource Locator, or URL (pronounced U-R-L), designates where things on the Internet can be found, things such as Internet servers, specific documents, files, newsgroups, download sites, and so on. The elements of this Internet equivalent of the postal address are broken down and explained in Table 11-1.

http://www.mcgraw-hill.com/demystified/IT/long.html			
http:	www.mcgraw-hill.com	demystified/IT	long.html
Access method or protocol	*Domain name*	*Folder*	*Filename*
The indicator before the colon (:) specifies the access method or protocol. The *http* method is the basis for the World Wide Web. The *ftp* method is for transferring files, and *news* is for newsgroups.	The portion following the double slashes (//) is the server address or domain name. It has at least two parts separated by "dots." The domain name adheres to the rules for the domain hierarchy, with the rightmost element at the top of the hierarchy (either the country code or top-level domain [TDL] as shown in Table 11-2).	This portion contains the folder or path containing the resources for a particular topic, in this case the path for the Demystified IT series of books. Elements in the path are separated by a slash (/).	At the end of most URLs is a specific filename for the file that is to be retrieved from the server. The *html* extension indicates an HTML file. HTML is the language used to compose and present web content.

Table 11-1   Elements of an Internet Address

The domain name is an Internet host/network identifier that follows rules for a domain hierarchy, with the rightmost element at the top of the hierarchy. In every country except the United States, this is the country code. For example, the Italian State Tourist Board is www.enit.it. Other country codes include *au* (Australia), *dk* (Denmark), and *jp* (Japan). The United States country code is *us*, but it is seldom included, presumably because the Internet originated in the United States. Also at the top of the hierarchy along with the country codes are the top-level domains (TLDs). Among the most popular TLDs are *com* (commercial), *gov* (government), and *edu* (education). These and other popular TLDs are shown in Table 11-2.

U.S. Top-Level Domains	Affiliation
The 7 original TLDs:	
com	Commercial
edu	Education
gov	Government
int	International
mil	Military
net	Network resources
org	Nonprofit organizations

Table 11-2   Top-Level Domains

U.S. Top-Level Domains	Affiliation
New TLDs in 2001–2002:	
aero	Airline groups
biz	Businesses
coop	Business cooperatives
info	Purveyors of information
name	Personal web sites
museum	Museums
pro	Professional

Table 11-2 Top-Level Domains *(continued)*

The host network or host provider, which usually is the name of an organization, is at the next level of the domain name hierarchy. The *www* (www.mcgraw-hill.com) directs traffic to the host site's World Wide Web server computer.

Web Sites and Hyperlinks

Typically, when you go online, you navigate to a particular web site, perhaps that of your company or college. An Internet server computer at that web site provides on-demand distribution of information, which can be audio, video, graphics, animation, and/or interactive text. All of these various forms of information are combined and viewed in *pages*. The analogy with books, though, ends quickly in that the pages on the Internet are nonsequential, linked documents that allow you to branch in many directions from a single page. A web page can be a few sentences or it can have hundreds of lines and scores of images that can be viewed by moving the scroll bar.

When you go to a particular web site, you normally are presented with the site's *home page*. The home page contains *hyperlinks* to other areas on the site. A hyperlink may be an underlined colored word or phrase, or it may be a hot image/icon. You know when a word or object is hot because the pointer changes to a hand when it is rolled over a hyperlink. Click on the hyperlink to jump to another area of the web page, another one of the web site's pages, or to an entirely different web site.

Web Pages and HTML

Once you have an Internet connection, you have ready access to explore the Internet. To do so, you open an *Internet browser,* the most popular one being Microsoft's *Internet Explorer.* Internet browsers run on your PC, the *client computer.* The client computer interacts with a companion *server program* on an Internet *server computer.* The client and server programs work together so you can cruise the Net.

Many URLs end in *html,* indicating an HTML file. *HTML,* which stands for *Hypertext Markup Language*, enables web site designers to tell the client program on your PC how web pages are to be formatted and presented on your display. The client program interprets the HTML instructions and then works with the server program to gather all the text, graphics, and so on needed to compose the web page display. HTML documents, which are plain text, use tags to describe the formatting of the various elements on a web page. For example, this HTML statement describes the formatting for a web page title:

```
<TITLE ALIGN=CENTER>Trails in the Ozark Mountains</TITLE>
```

You don't have to be a programmer or an Internet guru to design, create, and post your own content on the Web. There are many easy-to-use web development tools you can use to create your own personal web page.

Browser Basics: Retrieving and Viewing Internet Content

We use Internet browsers, which also are called web browsers, to access Internet resources and services. The browser viewing area can be filled with documents containing any combination of text, images, animation, and video. Plus, whatever is in the viewing area can be enhanced with audio. Unlike other PC software, browsers are not intended to produce a document. Virtually all new PCs come with browser software preinstalled, usually Internet Explorer and/or Netscape Navigator. These are the main functions of browser software:

- **Retrieve and view information**   Browsers enable us to interact with web and other types of server computers on the Internet or on an intranet (a closed Internet within a particular organization). They also allow us to interact with HTML content from other sources, such as disk/disc. Many dynamic electronic documents are distributed on CD-ROM for viewing with browser software.
- **Interact with Internet servers**   Browsers enable us to purchase airline tickets, to buy and sell stocks, and to perform countless other interactive tasks.
- **Download/upload files**   Browsers give us the capability to download or upload any digital file, including video, music, images, and spreadsheet files.

Internet browsers are easy to use and intuitive in their application. Figure 11-7 shows the following basic elements of a browser, Internet Explorer, and parts of a typical web page, such as hyperlinks, search boxes, and the ever-present ads:

- **Web page**   Web site information is in *pages,* the first page being the *home page.*
- **URL bar**   The current URL is displayed in this box (http:// www.yahoo.com/). Enter a new URL to go to another web site.

- **Menu bar**   Select file options and edit options, and choose preferences.
- **Status bar**   Indicates download status, hyperlink URL, and so on.
- **Toolbar**   These buttons are common to browsers:
    - **Back**   Go to the last site visited.
    - **Forward**   Go forward in the string of visited sites.
    - **Stop**   Stop information transfer.
    - **Refresh**   Reload the current page.
    - **Home**   Go to personal default home page.
    - **Search**   Go to your default search site.
    - **Favorites**   Links to favorite web sites.
- **Hyperlinks**   Click hyperlinks to link to another place in the same page or to another web site.
- **Searching the Net**   Enter one or more keywords, such as "Grand Canyon," to search the Web.
- **Browsing the Net**   Internet portals offer menu trees for browsing.
- **Search results**   A search results in a list of hyperlinks to web sites that meet your search criteria ("Grand Canyon").
- **Click a hyperlink result**   Click a resulting hyperlink to go to a site.
- **Ads**   Advertisements are common on commercial web sites.

One of the most popular portals, Yahoo, is shown in the Internet Explorer viewing area. A *portal* is a major Internet web site that provides a variety of information and services, a menu tree of hyperlinks to other Internet sites, and a search engine that permits keyword searches for specific Internet-based content. There are many Internet portals, including Google, Excite, AltaVista, HotBot, Lycos, LookSmart, WebCrawler, AskJeeves, MSN, and Netscape (all at www.*put-portal-name-here*.com).

The services available could include but are not limited to news, sports, shopping, new/used automobile research, job search, classified ads, games, horoscopes, people search, electronic greeting cards, horoscope, white/yellow pages, stock quotes, chat rooms, television listings, map search (maps and driving instructions), personals, and more. The Internet offers hundreds of specialized portals that focus on a particular topic, such as sports (www.espn.com), news (www.usatoday.com), or personal computing (www.zdnet.com). The following Yahoo menu tree for Internet content, which is representative, is divided into these 14 categories:

- Arts & Humanities
- Business & Economy
- Computers & Internet
- Education
- Entertainment
- Government
- Health
- News & Media
- Recreation & Sports
- Reference
- Regional
- Science
- Social Science
- Society & Culture

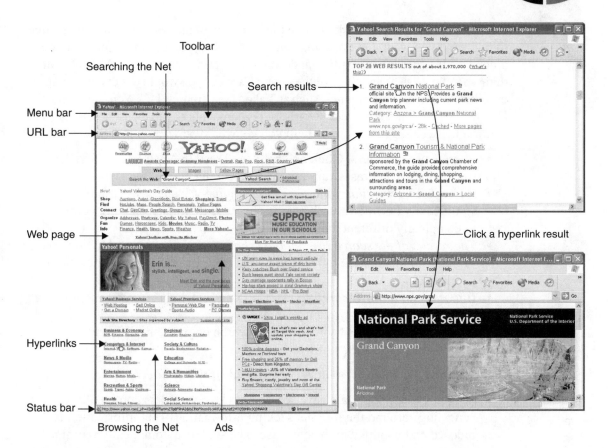

Figure 11-7   The Internet browser

Finding What You Want on the Internet

What do you want? Mark Twain's *Huckleberry Finn*? The *Congressional Record*? The starting times for local movies? The lyrics to "Come Together" by the Beatles? Job openings for teachers in your area? A video demonstration of a total hip replacement? If it can be legally digitized and it has any value, it's probably on the Net. The challenge is to find it. Of course, there's a lot that isn't legal and/or has no value that's on the Net, too. Unfortunately, Internet trash looks for and finds you.

If you know what site you wish to visit and you know its URL, just enter it in the address bar. Most of the time, however, you will not know the URL and you will need to find it. The two basic methods for finding something on the Net are *browsing* and *searching*. You can either browse through a book by leafing through its pages or search its index for specific references. It's much the same on the Internet.

Browsing is when you work through the hierarchy of menus in a portal's menu tree to find what you want. Or, browsing can also be when you use these menus to poke around the Internet with no particular destination in mind. If you are looking for something specific, such as an image of the Grand Canyon, you would use one of the many excellent Internet search engines, such as Yahoo (see Figure 11-7). You can search the Net by keying in one or more keywords, or perhaps a phrase, that best describes what you want. These suggestions may help you get what you want in less time:

- *Read the search rules.* Click on "help" and read the instructions first. The rules for search phrases vary among the search engines.
- *If you don't get results with one search engine, try another.* Results vary significantly between search engines because their databases are compiled in completely different manners.
- *The results of the search are seldom exhaustive.* You may need to go to one of the resulting sites, and then follow the hyperlinks to get the information you want.
- *Choose search words carefully.* The keywords and phrases you enter are critical to the success of your search.
- *Be persistent.* Besides trying different search engines, try different combinations and forms of words.

Most search techniques would be considered *spider* or *directory*:

- **Spider** Internet portals have search crawlers or spiders continually "crawling" around the Internet seeking information. That information is indexed and included in the database. The spiders automatically return to sites on a regular basis to update information in the database. Generally, search engines using spider technology return more results than directory searches.
- **Directories** Directories are compiled by real people rather than robotic spiders. The people at Internet portals identify web sites and pages appropriate for their audience, then include descriptions, URLs, and other information on these sites and pages in their databases. Generally, directories provide more-targeted results than searches of spider-based search engines.

Google began as a spider portal and Yahoo as a directory portal, but all portals are reluctant to pigeonhole their search methods as spider, directory, or anything else. In truth, portals typically use a combination of these methods and, perhaps, artificial intelligence and other emerging search technologies.

The typical search engine indexes and searches less than 10 percent of Internet content. Most search engines emphasize the more popular sites, that is, those with the most *hits*. A hit is when a web page is retrieved for viewing or when a page is listed in search results.

During your searches, never forget that portals with search engines are business ventures. Portals make money by selling advertising and by selling priority rights to a particular word or phrase. For example, if you enter "swimming pools" you are likely to get a long list of results with the first and most prominent being those of sponsor organizations that sell swimming pools and supplies. These may be what you want, but it's always a good idea to keep them in perspective and look at nonsponsored sites, as well.

Marking What You Find: Favorites

Rather than reentering the URL for your employer, your college, your kids' elementary school, your local newspaper, your ISP, your local weather, your favorite football team, and so on, you can add these to your *Favorites* list for easy recall at a later time. To add the current web page to an Internet Explorer Favorites list, click Favorites in the menu bar, and then click Add to Favorites. If the name of the web site is not easily recognizable, enter a more descriptive one in the Name box. In the Netscape browser, the second most popular browser, favorites are called *Bookmarks*.

The Internet is filled with informative and helpful web sites, so the length of the Favorites list tends to grow exponentially. Click Organize Favorites in the Favorites menu to display a dialog box that allows you to organize your Favorites into folders and subfolders (see Figure 11-8). To save down-the-road confusion, I would suggest you give some thought now as to how you might wish to organize your Favorites. For example, I have a "Personal" folder into which I compartmentalize my personal life into 30 subfolders. If you're like most people, you probably will be adding many new sites to your Favorites list. Eventually, you may wish to cull out those you never revisited. No problem. Just right click on the no-longer-favorite item and then click Delete.

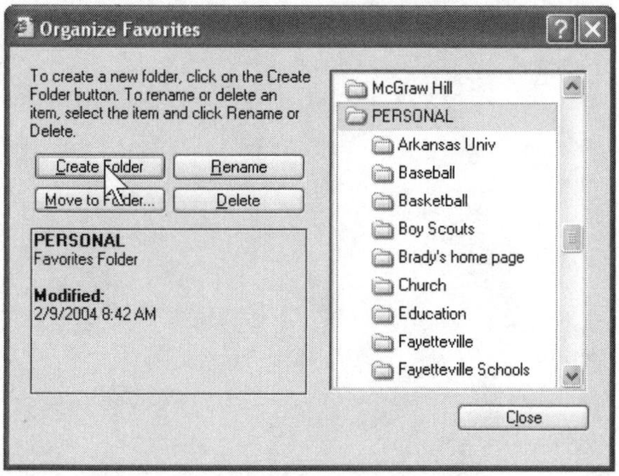

Figure 11-8   The Organize Favorites dialog box

12

Internet Applications: Cruising the Internet

Perhaps someday the term *Internet* will emerge as a new word to describe anything that is really big. Colossal, gigantic, immense, and massive simply are not adequate to describe the size and scope of the Internet. The Internet includes literally billions of constantly updated pages of information and a growing number of applications, all accessible by anyone with a PC and Internet access.

To a newbie, navigating the Internet is like trying to get around in a foreign megalopolis, like Tokyo or Budapest. Once you are able to speak a little Japanese or Hungarian, as the case may be, and know a little about the layout of the city, you can begin to explore. The more you explore, the more comfortable you become with navigating about the city and understanding its many points of interest. It's the same with the Internet. As you gain experience with this electronic behemoth, you will want to veer off the main roads and check out the side streets, as well. Table 12-1 summarizes many of the Internet's broad spectrum of applications and resources.

Internet newbies and seasoned cybernauts experience many of the same emotions each time they venture into cyberspace. It's not unusual to be shocked, overwhelmed, amazed, enlightened, and appalled during any given Internet session. This chapter is intended to give you an overview of the Internet. We'll learn more about the World Wide Web and look at a few of its many interesting destinations. Then, we will look at some of the Internet's other applications, including FTPing, e-mail, and blogging.

PERSONAL COMMUNICATIONS	
E-mail	Send/receive electronic mail.
Instant messaging	Communicate via real-time text, audio, and/or video communication.
Chat	Have virtual text-based chats among groups of people.
Internet telephony	Hold telephone conversations over the Internet.
GROUP COMMUNICATIONS	
Mailing lists	Share e-mail (all e-mail goes to all members on a distribution list).
Newsgroups	Post messages to the Internet version of a bulletin board (newsgroups are topical).
Blogs (web logs)	Create topical online journals that invite feedback.
INFORMATION	
News	Newspapers, magazines, television stations, Internet portals, and other sites provide continuously updated news.
Weather	Up-to-the-minute weather and weather forecasting is available for any city or region.
Sports	All professional leagues and teams, as well as all colleges, provide sports information and, sometimes, real-time statistics.
Research (school/job)	Billions of pages of information are available on almost any subject.
Travel information	Cities, states, resorts, hotels, national parks, and thousands more destinations offer a breadth of travel information.
Medical information	Medical data, advice, and information on virtually any condition can be found.
DOWNLOADING AND FILE SHARING	
Images and video	Still images of great variety, from NASA space shots to family photos, and brief videos, from music videos to family clips, are shared across cyberspace.
Music	Millions of songs are downloaded and shared, both legally and illegally, each day.
Movies	Commercial and private movies, both legal and illegal, are freely distributed throughout the Internet.
STREAMING MEDIA	
Video clips	News events, movie trailers, sports highlights, and so on are offered at a variety of sites.
Audio	Speeches, radio station broadcasts, and so on are streamed over the Internet.
Movies	On-demand movies may someday threaten the existence of the video store.

Table 12-1   Popular Internet Applications and Resources

ONLINE TRANSACTIONS	
Online shopping	Shop and buy almost anything on the Internet, from diamonds to airplanes.
Online auctions	Bid on any of millions of new and used items on the virtual auction block or place your own items up for auction.
Online banking	Most banking transactions can be done online.
Making reservations	All types of travel reservations, including airline, train, hotel, auto rental, and so on, can be made online.
Stock trading	Stocks can be bought and sold online.
Gambling	Visit virtual casinos and win/lose real money.
ENTERTAINMENT	
Multiplayer gaming	Play bridge or fight galactic battles with other Internet-based gamers.
Serendipitous browsing	Surf the Internet just for fun to see where it leads you.
Adult content	Adult entertainment is a major dot-com industry.
Hobbyist	All popular hobbies have sites that include information and related activities.

Table 12-1   Popular Internet Applications and Resources *(continued)*

The World Wide Web

"The Internet" and "the Web" are used interchangeably, but, actually, the World Wide Web is the Internet's dominant application for accessing information and services. The Web got its name because it is an interconnecting "web" of servers and linked multimedia documents. The beauty of the Web is that the linked relationships are independent of physical location. These are the main attributes of web sites and pages:

- They are user-friendly.
- They can contain any or all multimedia elements (graphics, audio, video, text, and animation).
- They can be interactive, enabling interactivity between users and servers.
- They are linked via hyperlinks.
- They can be composed in frames, enabling several independent sections to be displayed on a single web page.

Figure 12-1 takes you on a brief tour of the Web to show you a few of the stops along this stretch of the information highway. The operative word here is "few." These don't illustrate how you can do comparison shopping between dozens of e-tailers in seconds. They don't include the fastest-growing application on the Internet, the matching of people in pursuit of romance. For a complete tour, log on and enjoy.

Buy and sell almost anything
at an Internet auction site.

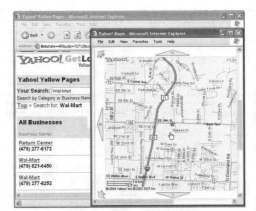

Find and get directions to any
business in the United States.

Send musical, animated, and
interactive greeting cards.

Enjoy Renoir's *La Lecture* at
the Louvre Museum in Paris.

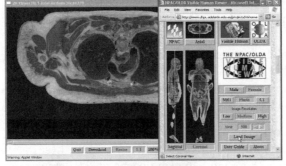

Select and view two-dimensional slices
from any part of the human body.

Search for a job with the help
of an automatic agent.

Figure 12-1   Cruising the World Wide Web

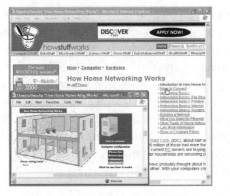

Learn how stuff works at HowStuffWorks.

Get real-time financial information.

Read and see news as it happens.

Visit pages devoted to virtually every hobby and special interest.

Scan the ultimate travel brochure to learn about points of interest and destinations throughout the world.

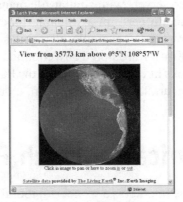

View what is happening at any of thousands of locations on earth and beyond via webcams.

Figure 12-1   Cruising the World Wide Web *(continued)*

The Internet may not become a "way of life" for you as it has for so many others, but it's not unreasonable to expect that the Web will have a significant effect on much of what you do. For those of us who have been using the Internet for a while, it's difficult to pinpoint an activity that does not in some way overlap with Internet-based information or services. For me, a good example is shopping. When I wanted to buy something in 1995, I drove from store to store until I found what I wanted. Now, I do most of my shopping online because I'm confident that I'm getting the best available price and that I will find the right shoe in my size, the exact audio/video component I need, a specific out-of-print book, and a hard-to-find part for the dishwasher. Internet sales are growing at about 40 percent a year.

File Transfer Protocol: FTP

Through the 1990s, FTPing was a popular Internet activity. *FTP (file transfer protocol)* servers on the Internet let you download and upload files in much the same way you work with files and folders on your PC. Thousands of FTP sites let netizens download music, art, games, clip art, published and unpublished books, maps, software, and anything else that can be digitized and is not copyright protected. Some FTP sites are password-protected, but most are "anonymous" so you can just enter "anonymous" for the user ID and your e-mail address for the password if prompted to do so. To find a topical FTP, just search on any portal for FTP and the topic (for example, "FTP clip art").

Much of what used to be on FTP servers has been moved to more user-friendly web servers with similar file management capabilities. However, FTP servers continue to perform a valuable function and can be accessed directly from any Net browser. For example, all the files created, revised, and prepared for this book, about 500 in all, are stored on a common password-protected FTP site. This site essentially looks like another folder on the PC to me and others around the country who do editing, art, layout, composition, indexing, printing, and project management.

Communicating with People via the Internet

The Internet is a wonderful tool for all kinds of communications, but Internet communications are different in that most of what we say over the Internet is via text and not spoken words. In this section, you learn about the more popular Internet-based methods for personal and group communications.

When we speak, our conversation is enhanced with eye contact, voice inflection, and body English—none of which is possible in a text message. Recognizing the shortcomings of text communication, ever-inventive netizens have created *emoticons* (emotion icons), often called *smileys,* to show emotion in keyed-in text and an Internet shorthand to speed text entry. Some of the more popular emoticons and keyboard shortcuts are shown in Table 12-2. As you might imagine, it was inevitable that pop art would evolve from these text glyphs. Table 12-3 shows a few of the hundreds of pieces of pop art that can be created from the characters on your keyboard.

EMOTICONS: EMOTION ICONS			
:-)	Smiling ☺	:-~)	User with a cold
(-:	Left-handed smile	(@_@)	Stunned
:-}	Mischievous smile	)-::-(	Married
:'-)	Crying (happy)	:-&	Tongue-tied
:-(	Sad ☹	:-Q	Smoker
:-((	Very sad	,':-)	A really interesting idea
:'-(	Crying (sad)	O :-)	Angel
(:-*	Kiss	;-)	Wink
:-/	Skeptical	:c)	Pigheaded
:-|	Bored ☺	8-)	Wearing sunglasses
:-D	Laughing	::-)	Wearing glasses
<:(	Dunce	#-)	Partied all night
:-o	Amazed	>:)	Little devil
:-I	Indifferent	%-6	Brain-dead
%-(	Confused	[[[***]]]	Hugs and kisses
~ :-(	Steaming mad	^5	High five
#:-o	Shocked	:-| :-|	Déjà vu
(:&	Angry	-,-	Sleepy
:-@	Screaming angry	(I	Asleep
(:-#	Wearing braces	<^O^>	Laughing loudly
(:-...	Broken heart	:-C	Unhappy; really bummed

Table 12-2 Emoticons and Keyboard Shortcuts

KEYBOARD SHORTCUTS

AFAIK	As far as I know	KUTGW	Keep up the good work
AFJ	April fool's joke	L8R	Later
AFK	Away from keyboard	LOL	Laughing out loud
BRB	Be right back	MYOB	Mind your own business
BTW	By the way...	ROTFL	Rolling on the floor laughing
CU	See you	SPST	Same place, same time
CUL (8R)	See you later	THX	Thanks, thank you
F2F	Face-to-face	TIA	Thanks in advance
FAQs	Frequently asked questions	TPTB	The powers that be
GR8	Great	TTFN	Ta-ta for now or goodbye
HAND	Have a nice day	TTYL	Talk to you later
HTH	Hope this helps	<VBG>	Very big grin
IGU	I give up	WAG	A wild guess
IMHO	In my humble opinion	Wizard	A gifted or experienced user
IRL	In real life	YKYBHTLW	You know you've been hacking too long when

Table 12-2   Emoticons and Keyboard Shortcuts *(continued)*

@–>–>–	A rose	|://	George Bush
= =):-)=	Abe Lincoln	/:-)	Gumby
~8-)	Alfalfa	=(_8^(1)	Homer Simpson
0:-)	Angel or saint	>>:-1	Klingon
~:o	Baby	)P-(	Long John Silver
q:-#	Baseball catcher	@@@@@@@@:)	Marge Simpson
]B-)	Batman	(:-(|)	Mick Jagger
*:o)	Bozo the Clown	(8-o	Mr. Bill
IIIIII8^)X	Cat in the Hat	(Z(:^P	Napoleon
=|:=)X	Charlie Chaplin	(OvO)	Owl
Q:-)	College graduate	:----}	Pinocchio

Table 12-3   Keyboard Pop Art

;-)}<////>	Corporate guy with tie	([(	Robocop
C):-)	Cowboy	7:-)	Ronald Reagan
==:-D	Don King	*<(:-{o{{{{	Santa Claus
@;^D	Elvis	*!#*!^*&:-)	Schizophrenic
[8-]	Frankenstein	(:=<	*Star Wars* stormtrooper
*<(:')	Frosty the Snowman	(-|---(: -)	The Pope

Table 12-3   Keyboard Pop Art *(continued)*

The following are some basic rules of Internet etiquette, called *netiquette,* which, if followed, will minimize the possibility of your message being misinterpreted or your recipient being offended:

- Don't send spam, the ultimate Internet faux pas.
- Use capital letters only if you wish to shout.
- Be sensitive to your recipients' values and be very selective when sending Internet content.
- Honor someone's private communication with you and keep it private.
- Be patient with newbies.
- Accept any style and say nothing. Some people may never insert a capital letter or correct a misspelling.
- Never forward a virus warning without confirming it with reliable sources, because most virus warnings are hoaxes.
- Never forward pyramid messages ("Send this to ten friends and…")
- Use antivirus software to maintain a virus-free environment, as most viruses are passed via e-mail.

E-Mail

E-mail has transformed the way we communicate with one another. We send/receive e-mail through either *e-mail client software,* such as Microsoft Outlook, or via *web-based e-mail,* such as Hotmail.com. The primary advantage of e-mail client software is that the received e-mails and their attachments are stored on your PC. Being stored locally allows the e-mail client to be more responsive to keyword searches and the e-mail application to be more easily integrated with other related applications, such as a calendar and a task list. Web-based e-mail's big advantage is that the received e-mails and their attachments are stored at the e-mail server site, so you can check your e-mail from any Internet-connected PC in the world. This type of e-mail is handled through interaction with a web site, such as Yahoo.com. Figure 12-2 illustrates an e-mail message that is received and viewed in both Microsoft Outlook and Yahoo! Mail. It also shows an Outlook reply to the e-mail.

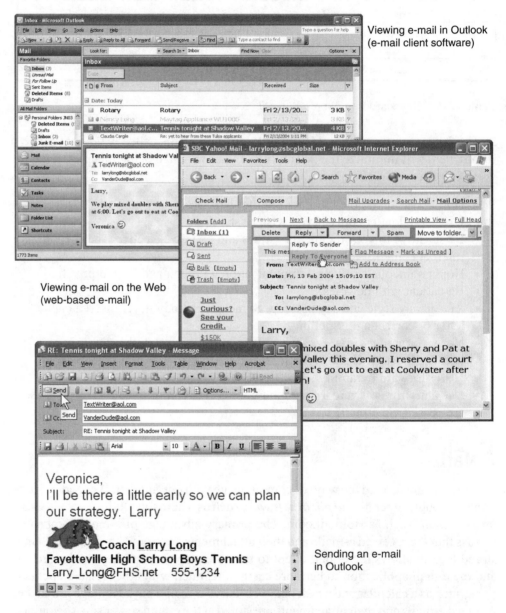

Viewing e-mail in Outlook
(e-mail client software)

Viewing e-mail on the Web
(web-based e-mail)

Sending an e-mail
in Outlook

Figure 12-2   Email: client-based and web-based

Your online identification is your e-mail address, which is in two parts separated by an @ symbol. In the e-mail address Heather_Hill@aol.com, *Heather_Hill* is the username and *aol.com* is the domain name for the Internet host/network, sometimes called the e-mail server.

If you wish, you can add graphics and use fancy formatting to enhance the appearance of your e-mails. Just click the paper clip icon to attach any type of file or files to an e-mail. The *attached file(s)* is sent with the message when you click the Send button.

Instant Messaging

Instant messaging may be the fastest-growing application on the Internet. Instant messaging differs from e-mail in that messages are sent and displayed in real time (instantly). Although most instant messaging is text-based, the Windows Messenger example in Figure 12-3 shows that it also allows voice or video conversations.

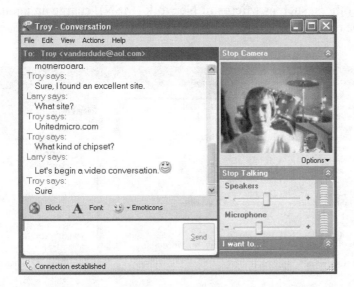

Figure 12-3   Instant Messaging: text, voice, and video

America Online popularized instant messaging and it quickly became a vehicle for casual conversations. Now, instant messaging is available from several companies, along with some very enticing services such as file sharing, simultaneous viewing of programs, *whiteboarding* (using a common workspace for drawing), and, my personal favorite, text messaging to cell phones. Instant messaging is rapidly becoming a viable and, in some companies, essential communications tool. Instant messaging eliminates the most popular corporate game, telephone tag. Telecommuters love instant messaging because it gives them the look and feel of being there.

All you have to do to begin instant messaging is sign up with one of the instant messaging services and install its client software. Then, you create a contact list with the online identities of those people you wish to track for instant messaging. When you go online, the people in your list, your "buddies" or "colleagues," are notified. People are added and deleted from your real-time list when they arrive or depart.

Chat

Thousands of topic-specific virtual *chat rooms* are filled with people talking about a broad array of subjects, from personal computers to sailboats. Figure 12-4 shows a conversation in an AOL Harley (Davidson) rider chat room. AOL has a number of organizations that sponsor chat rooms. Some chat rooms are free, such as those on Yahoo, but others, such as Microsoft Network (MSN), charge an annual fee. The people in the room "talk" to one another by keying in messages that are immediately

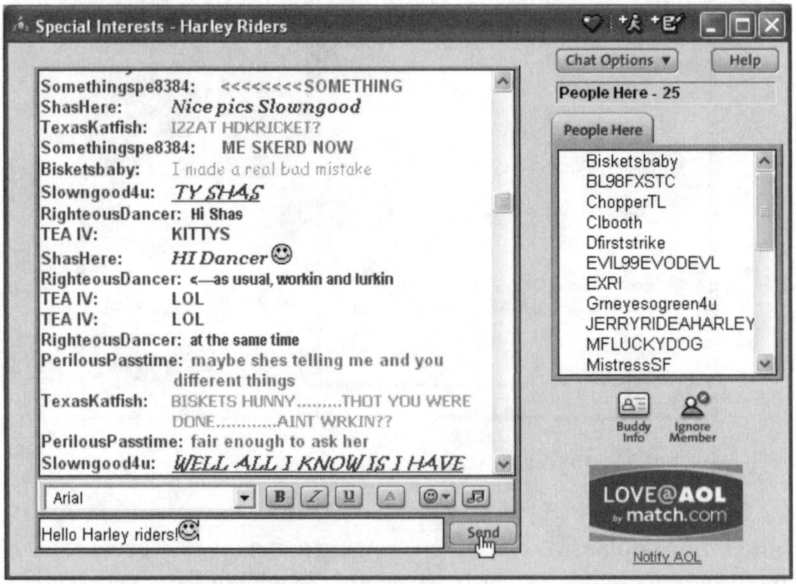

Figure 12-4 A chat room

displayed on the screens of everyone else in the room. Chatting has emerged as a favorite pastime of many cybernauts.

Chat rooms can be a great pastime if you're willing to accept that participants may not stay on topic. Actually, many chat rooms are pure drivel, no matter what the topic. The chat room shown in Figure 12-4 is typical. You may have to check out several chat rooms before you find one to join that has compatible participants and acceptable language.

Mailing Lists

I subscribe to a *mailing list,* which generates roughly half of all my e-mails. One of my volunteer Rotarian duties is to help place American exchange students to locations throughout the world. The mailing list is a very helpful tool in accomplishing these exchanges. Here is how it works. My international Rotarian counterparts and I subscribe to the Rotary youth exchange mailing list. When I or any of my fellow youth exchange leaders send an e-mail to the list, it is distributed to all mailing list subscribers. When a Rotarian in Japan sends an e-mail to the mailing list that states he has six students who would like to spend a year abroad in Western Europe, his e-mail is viewed by everyone, including those leaders in Portugal, Spain, Belgium, France, Germany, and so on. The response from a leader in France would probably be an e-mail sent directly to the Japanese leader and not through the mailing list.

This mailing list is restricted to youth exchange leaders, but there are thousands of mailing lists on myriad topics that are open to the public. If you wish, you can create one of your own, usually through your ISP's *mailing list server.* To find a topical mailing list, key in the topic and **mailing list** in any portal's search box (for example, **environment** and **mailing list**). The mailing list will have an address similar to your e-mail address (for example, RotaryYE@yahoogroups.com).

Subscribing to a mailing list can be simultaneously informative and overwhelming. Over the years I've subscribed to a number of interesting mailing lists only to unsubscribe within a short time because of the massive amount of e-mail generated by the list.

Newsgroups

The *newsgroup,* which is analogous to the hallway bulletin board, is another group communications tool. Messages are posted by individuals to a particular newsgroup on a *news server computer,* which may host thousands of newsgroups. There are tens of thousands of newsgroups on almost any imaginable topic, from Elvis Presley sightings (alt.elvis.sighting) to European politics (alt.politics.europe). Some newsgroups have a moderator who owns the newsgroup and regularly reviews postings and, if needed, deletes inappropriate messages. Others are created and have a life of their own. Newsgroups, generally, are open to whoever wants to participate. Major newsgroup topic areas include *alt* (alternative), *news, rec* (recreation), *soc* (society), *sci* (science), and *comp* (computers). For example, comp.hardware is the name of a hardware-oriented newsgroup in the computers topic area.

To read and post messages to newsgroups, you use *newsreader client software,* which is built into most Internet browser clients. Some newsgroups are maintained within the Web and newsreader software is not needed. The newsreader lets you read previous postings, respond to them, or add your own messages (see Figure 12-5). The original message and any posted replies to that message are a *thread.*

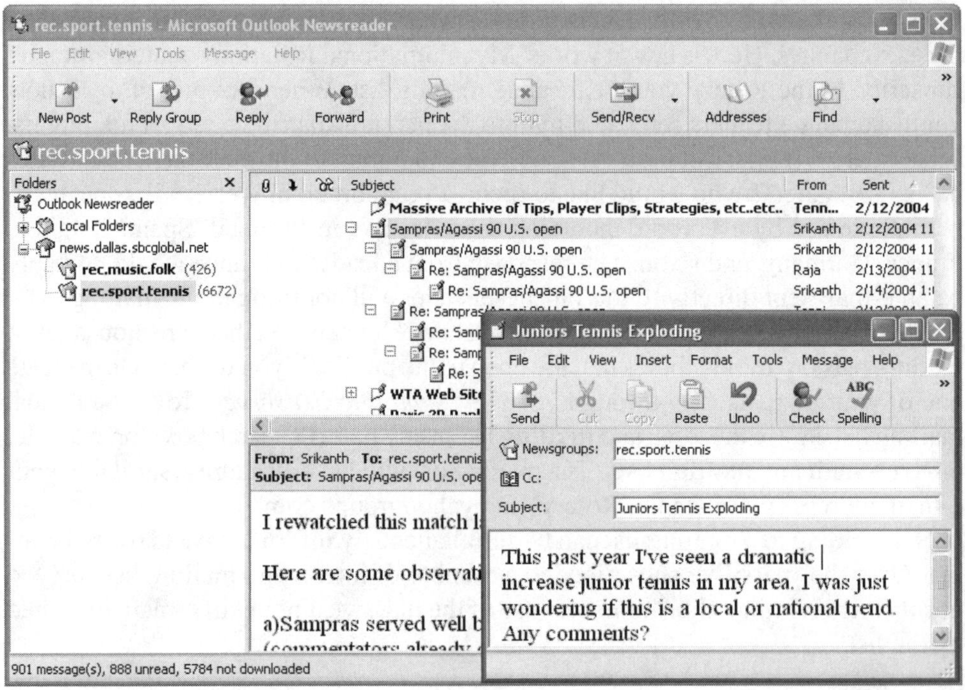

Figure 12-5   Newsgroups

Blogs and Blogging

The *blog,* short for *web log,* is one of the newest methods of Net-based communication. The blog is simply an online journal that includes the writings of a *blogger,* with the most recent entry at the top of the list. Most of the blog communication is one way, but bloggers always invite and often respond to feedback.

The focus of a blog can be anything. For example, an expectant mother might use a blog, which is simply a web site, to chronicle her thoughts and emotions during pregnancy. There are blogs on careers, education, cooking, fitness, sports, politics, and everything in between. You can find thousands of blogs on hobbies from amateur radio to winemaking. To find a topical blog, just key in the topic and **blog** in any portal's search box (for example, **health care** and **blog**).

Internet Telephony, or VoIP

Internet telephony has been around for a while. The problem is that the quality of service has not been nearly as good as that which we enjoy on public switched telephone networks that use dedicated voice circuits. Sometimes referred to as voice over IP (VoIP), Internet telephony voice transmissions are sent in the same way everything else traverses the Net—in packets. The obvious advantage to VoIP is that long-distance charges are avoided. Generally, Internet telephony requires that the parties speaking to one another be online and registered with the same directory server. There are, however, services that, for a small charge, will connect you to any phone in the world. In time, VoIP has the potential to redefine remote voice communication.

Webcasting

The Web is based on *pull technology,* where information is delivered to your PC only when you request or "pull" information from a particular site. A number of organizations use *push technology* to *webcast,* or automatically broadcast news, weather, sports, and other information in real time without being prompted by the user. For example, you can sign up to receive news on a particular topic (information technology, politics, and so on) or from a particular country, weather for your area, stock quotes for selected companies, business news for selected industries, sports news relating to a particular sport (even specific to your teams), and so on. Webcasting organizations, which include some major newspapers, The Weather Channel, sports news services, and brokerage houses, to mention a few, periodically scan available Net sources, then deliver information automatically to your PC for viewing.

The Personal Home Page

It might surprise you to find out how easy it is to create your own web page and be a part of cyberspace. A *personal home page* might include personal and family history, an ancestral tree, historical and current photos, vacation summaries (with photos, of course), a holiday newsletter, personal news and/or commentary, links to areas of personal interest, a résumé, and so on. Or, perhaps you might wish to create a presence on the Internet for your child's Boy/Girl Scout troop, the Parent Teacher Organization, or your civic service club. Some people use the Internet to showcase their artistic work (paintings, e-art, original music, and so on).

When content is placed online for public viewing via Internet browsers, the web site is said to have been *published*. Within minutes, you can publish a simple, but informative web page whose content is available to billions of people. There are two common approaches to creating and publishing a simple personal home page:

- **The "free" web site**   Most ISPs, including America Online, allow you to post a personal home page of limited size as part of your usage fee. The "free" means that you probably will have advertisements peppering your home page. All you have to do is select one of the ISP's templates and complete a user-friendly fill-in-the-blank form (see Figure 12-6).
- **The minimal fee-based web site**   A number of *web hosting services* would be delighted to host your web page and keep it free of ads, for a fee, of course. The amount charged varies significantly based on expected activity, disk space required, and quality of service needed (from as little as $5 per month). Each of these host sites will have specific instructions as to where and to whom you would send your web content for publishing.

Follow these tips and you will present yourself, your club, or whatever in an attractive, informative web page:

- Have a purpose for your web page(s).
- Keep it simple.
- Minimize download time (remember, much of your audience has slow dialup access).
- Be honest, be courteous, and, most importantly, be yourself.
- Maintain your web site (once on the Net, it's your obligation to keep your site current).

If you would prefer a more sophisticated web page, you might wish to use *web page design software,* such as Microsoft FrontPage or Adobe PageMill. Or, if you're reluc-

Figure 12-6   A "free" personal home page

tant to learn another software package, the content for a single page can be created easily with a word processing program, such as Microsoft Word, and then saved as an HTML document. Other office suite programs, such as spreadsheet and presentation software, can export directly to HTML as well. Any HTML document can be posted directly to the Net. All you need to become a player in cyberspace is a few colorful digital images, a little imagination in design, and something to say. If you have these ingredients, you're ten minutes away from a URL and virtual fame in cyberspace.

CHAPTER

13

Internet Security: Protecting Your PC

This may be the most important chapter in this book because it speaks to vulnerability—your PC's, your information's, and, yes, your own. The Internet opens the door to the wonders of global sharing, but in so doing, it also opens doors for people whose interests are scams and mindless destruction. Crackers are continually "cracking" through Internet security at the server and the PC levels to disrupt the flow of information and, generally, wreak havoc. Hate mongers, stalkers, and the like have found a home on the Internet, too. Cyberthieves will steal anything they can, including your identity. One of the most serious Internet threats is *identity theft,* which occurs when someone is able to gather enough personal information about you (without your knowledge) to assume your identity.

The Internet is a frontier that is largely without law and order. Sure, there are organizations charged with maintaining some semblance of order, and laws are being continuously proposed and enacted to protect us. Unfortunately, the cybercops are too few and ill-equipped and existing laws often are ambiguous and difficult to enforce.

Generally, it is up to you to protect yourself, your PC, and your valuable information from the continual threats and annoyances streaming over the Internet. This chapter is intended to raise your awareness of the dark side of the Internet and introduce you to the tools that can help you avoid some of these bumps along the Internet highway.

The Firewall

A large number of people and organizations are continually searching the Internet for unprotected PCs so they can hijack and use them to distribute pornography, send spam, or carry out some other illicit activity. Moreover, an estimated 5 percent of all transactions on the Internet are fraudulent or an attempt at theft. Unfortunately, we are forced by these Internet realities to build a wall around our PCs and home networks, an electronic wall called a firewall. A *firewall* is software that sets up a protective "wall" between a particular PC or network, the private side, and the rest of cyberspace, the public side. Having a firewall is a good starting point for the implementation of a personal computing plan for Internet security.

DSL, cable-modem, and satellite connections are "always on" and, therefore, pose greater risks of unauthorized access for individual PCs and home networks. Commercial firewall products, such as Symantec's Norton Internet Security Professional (see Figure 13-1) and McAfee Security's Personal Firewall Plus or Internet Security Suite, offer excellent protection from external invasion into your system. Windows XP has a built-in firewall. To enable the Windows firewall, enter **enable firewall** in the Windows Help and Support search box and follow the directions. If you have broadband, your *modem/router,* which usually is provided by the ISP, has a built-in firewall, as well. The modem/router, a communications device that sits between your PC (or your home network) and the broadband link, is discussed further in Chapter 18, "Building a Home Network." If your Internet access is through a modem/router, its built-in firewall is preferable to the Windows firewall.

A firewall is a system that enforces access control policy between your PC (or a home network) and the Internet. Firewalls differ widely in methods and levels of sophistication, but all of them have essentially two tasks, to block traffic and to permit traffic. A firewall's access control policy can be set up to screen electronic traffic in both directions such that it restricts unwanted access to a PC or home network and can block certain types of outgoing communications. Most firewalls automatically block unsolicited attempts at communication from the public side of the wall. They do this based on control policies set forth as a group of rules for access. For example, one rule might be to permit e-mail traffic and another might be to deny unauthenticated logins from the public side.

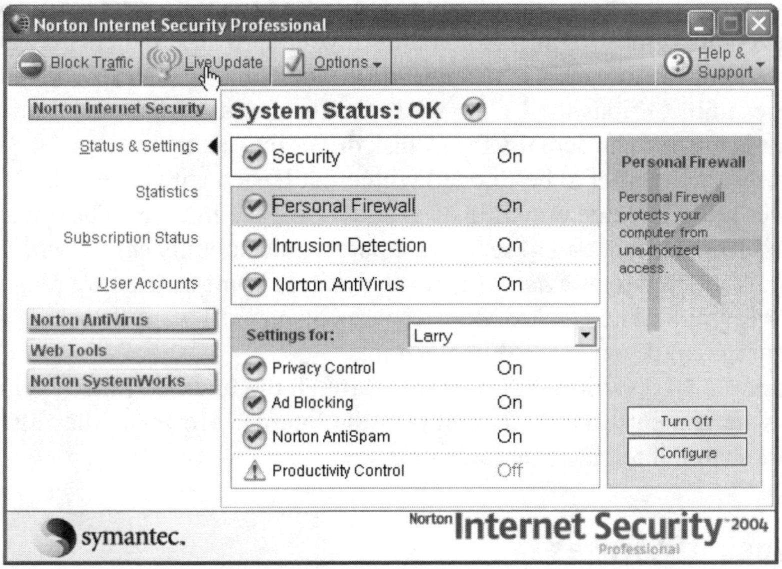

Figure 13-1   Firewall software: Norton Internet Security Professional

The screening process can be adjusted to the desired level of security. A high security setting may block all e-mail with attachments or embedded graphics. Most people choose a lower firewall setting to permit the flow of legitimate traffic. Of course, this small opening is enough for some undesirable transmissions to pierce your PC's armor. I would suggest that you choose nothing less than a medium level of security.

Internet Threats

Before the Internet, the dastardly deeds of people who do bad things were restricted by geography. The Internet has lifted that geographic constraint, enabling these seedier elements of our society to traverse the globe and reach into our PCs at electronic speeds.

Computer Viruses

The most prominent threat to Internet security is the *computer virus,* a program or portion of a program that causes something to occur in your PC, usually something bad. A virus can take over your computer and cause a range of events to occur. Some viruses act quickly, destroying the contents of your hard disk. Others may grow like a cancer, eating away at your files. Some are virtual bombs that "explode" at a preset time (for example, Friday the 13th) or when certain conditions are met. Some viruses attack hardware and can actually throw disk drives into costly spasms. One strain of virus causes the Internet to be flooded with e-mail, each with an attached program that causes more infected e-mail to be sent out over the Internet. The e-mail traffic becomes so intense that e-mail server computers must literally shut down. This type of assault is referred to as a *denial of service* attack. Some viruses are relatively benign. For example, The Cookie Monster virus displays "I want a cookie" and then locks your PC until you enter "Fig Newton."

As many as 50,000 viruses flow freely through the Internet. Mostly, viruses are spread as attachments to e-mails sent over the Internet. However, they also can be passed by shared interchangeable disks/discs.

Types of Viruses

The two main types of virus are the macro virus and the worm virus. The *macro virus* is a small program that might be embedded in an application, such as Microsoft Word or PowerPoint. This type of virus is spread via e-mail attachments. The macro program is executed when the e-mail recipient opens an infected attached file. A *worm* is a parasitic program that makes copies of itself. Worms are separate entities and don't attach themselves to programs, files, or documents.

The Trojan horse isn't actually a virus because it doesn't replicate itself. The Trojan horse appears as a seemingly useful program. For example, one Trojan horse announces that your PC is vulnerable and invites you to click OK if you want to make your system more secure. Of course, it plants a malicious program in your system. Many Trojan horses are "dialers" that use your dialup modem and phone line to make international calls or fee-based 900-number calls.

Virus Protection

Two programs combine to provide essential protection against computer viruses, the antivirus program (introduced in Chapter 9) and the firewall. Before you connect your PC to the Internet, I would highly recommend that you have both a firewall and a good antivirus program installed and running. An antivirus program protects you against all kinds of viruses by checking all material that streams into your PC from the Internet. It also checks for viruses when you open a document file and when you insert any type of removable media. The antivirus software also monitors your computer for indications that a virus may be present. Table 13-1 lists some virus protection tips.

Tip	Description
Delete suspicious e-mails.	Be suspicious of any e-mail from an unknown source, especially e-mail with an attached file.
Confirm the source of attached files.	If you're not absolutely sure that the sender and his/her attached file are legitimate, confirm the e-mail with the sender.
Be careful what you download.	Download files from the Internet only from legitimate and reputable sources—and *never* from a stranger.
Choose the option to list and not view e-mail content.	Choose the e-mail client option to see only a list of sources and subjects of received e-mail and avoid the option that includes viewing the content of the highlighted e-mail. The latter automatically opens the e-mail, which could contain a virus.
Never share your C: drive (hard disk).	Your C: hard drive normally contains the operating system and critical security information and should not be made available to external sources.
Keep antivirus software up to date.	Each month, over 500 new viruses are fed into the Internet.
Avoid common passwords.	Create passwords that are meaningless and impossible to guess (for example, "w12xutr9" instead of "wildcats").
Back up your files.	Your chances of surviving a virus attack are greatly improved if you have a backup procedure in place.
Disconnect from the Internet.	Whenever you are online, your system is vulnerable to a persistent hacker.

Table 13-1   Virus Protection Tips

The two biggest names in virus protection are the Norton AntiVirus program (Symantec Corporation), shown in Figure 13-2, and the VirusScan program (McAfee Security). Most new PCs have one of these programs installed or offer them as supplemental software. The program is used in conjunction with a virus protection subscription service that lets you download protection for the most recent viruses. The subscription services can cost from $25 to $50 a year, but they can easily pay for themselves if you are able to avoid a single fling with a virus.

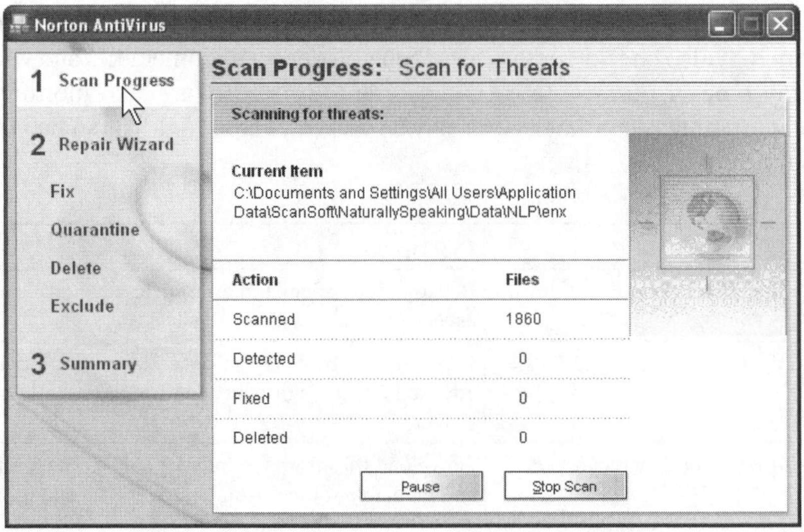

Figure 13-2   Scanning for viruses: Norton AntiVirus

Spyware

Electronic spy programs, called *spyware*, may be lurking around your PC, especially those with "always-on" Internet access. Spyware is loaded and installed on your PC without your consent. Shortly after spyware began floating around the Internet, I used a crude antispyware program to delete over a hundred clandestine programs, each of which was gathering and reporting personal information about my family.

Spyware is doubly annoying in that it steals processing and Internet capacity. If your PC is running slowly, there is a good chance that the various pieces of spyware on your PC are launching and running unwanted programs. If your Internet access is unusually slow, your spyware is probably having a conversation with its host—about you.

Once installed, spyware can monitor your Internet activity and transmit collected information back to another computer. Spyware can take on many forms. Many spyware programs monitor your web surfing habits and then report your web surfing tendencies to another computer. As you might expect, these reports trigger an avalanche of targeted e-mail spam and *pop-up ads* that stream down over the Internet and "pop up" on your desktop. One particularly malicious type of spyware plays to your fear, with Windows-looking pop-ups that announce your vulnerability to viruses and give you a web link to a corrective patch. Spyware can include *key-loggers* that secretly record and report your keystrokes, even during logins (your passwords) and when you enter your credit card numbers. Spyware can hijack your Internet browser and change the default home and your favorites such that no matter what you do you can't change them back. Some spyware programs steal your PC's computing capacity for use with a grid network of PCs.

With over 80,000 spyware programs on the loose, you must protect your PC and yourself. Ad-aware (see Figure 13-3) and Spy Sweeper are popular *antispyware* programs. The best way to protect yourself against spyware is to run antispyware on a regular basis. Spyware protection works like antivirus protection in that these programs find and remove only those programs on a spyware definitions list, so be sure to update your list before scanning for spyware.

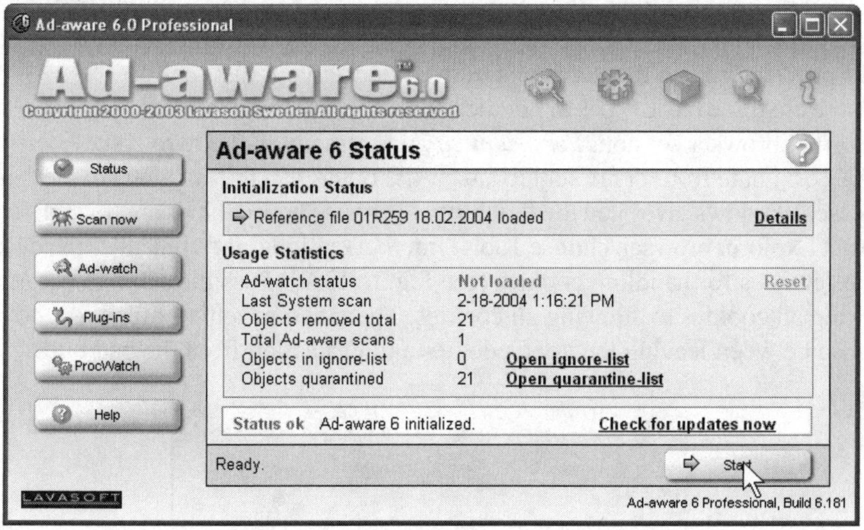

Figure 13-3   Antispyware software: Ad-aware

Adware

Some people don't distinguish adware from spyware, as they both gather and report personal information; however, most people would suggest that adware does not offer the same level of threat as spyware. *Adware* is software that prompts targeted pop-up ads to display when you surf the Web. Adware is not always bad in that it might alert you when a product or service of interest becomes available. Often, adware companies offer something you get for free, perhaps a program or an Internet service. They tell you about the adware in the fine print, but you probably missed it. Adware protection is built into antispyware software.

Cookies

As you surf the Net, you pick up cookies. The web server being accessed often will leave a *cookie* on your hard disk that describes, in some way, your interaction with the server. The cookie is a message that takes the form of a text file (.txt extension). The information in the cookie is sent back to the server each time the browser requests a page from the server. A cookie might contain your name, e-mail address, interests, and personal preferences. When you enter personal information at a web site, chances are your browser is storing it in a cookie. Cookies can personalize your interaction with a web site such that the server presents you with a customized web page, perhaps one with your name at the top of the page. A good cookie can make your interaction with an often-visited web site more efficient and effective. For example, an auction web site might provide links to the items you viewed during your last session.

There are three basic types of cookies. *Temporary cookies* are deleted at the end of the current browser session. *Persistent cookies* remain on the hard disk. *Third-party cookies* originate from or are sent to a web site other than the one you are viewing. In any case, Windows gives you the flexibility to choose how cookies are treated. In your Internet Explorer browser, choose Tools | Internet Options, and click the Privacy tab to set preferences for handling cookies (see Figure 13-4). Possible settings range from blocking all cookies to allowing all cookies. The medium setting offers a good compromise between leaving the good cookies and protection from the bad ones.

Figure 13-4   Setting preferences for handling cookies

To view and delete cookies, choose Tools | Internet Options, click the General tab, click Settings, and then click View Files. You may need to scroll through the files to the filenames that begin with "cookie." I routinely cull cookies from my system, but I leave those from the trustworthy web sites I visit often so I won't have to reenter information. If I don't recognize the site associated with a cookie, I delete it. These probably are third-party cookies generated by companies that want as much information as possible about my computer settings, web surfing habits, preferences, and anything else they can get.

Spam and Spim

The cyberworld's version of junk mail, called *spam,* is among the most annoying of all annoyances. Spam is unsolicited e-mail that bombards us with advertising for mostly worthless, deceptive, and/or fraudulent products or services. "Quit your day job," "Is your health important?," "Loose that weight while you are still alive," and "Want to play," comprise a typical mix of spam. Occasionally, a spam will provide information on legitimate services, but most are scams.

It's virtually impossible to avoid the spammers' lists. Many web sites and spammers sell their "hit list," the e-mails of the people who visit their sites. Especially prized are the response lists, the e-mails of those who actually respond to spam. Often, spammers will give you the opportunity to "opt out" of receiving further messages, but as any veteran cybernaut can attest, clicking "opt out" simply confirms that the spammer has a valid e-mail address. Some spammers ask you to call them to opt out—at $2 a minute! My personal strategy is to tap the DELETE key on any spam-looking e-mails that make it through my spam filter, typically from one to five a day.

Each day, over two billion spam messages are sent to our electronic mailboxes—without our consent or invitation. In contrast, the instant messaging (IM) version of spam, called *spim,* arrives at the rate of around two million spim messages a day. Most forecasters are predicting that spim will spin out of control as soon as spimmers find a way to abscond with large numbers of IM screen names, which are not as readily available as e-mail addresses.

To me, spam and spim are particularly irritating because they invade my personal cyberspace, wasting my time and my resources. So how do you get rid of them? Well, you don't. You control them, primarily by practicing responsible Internet surfing habits and by the judicious use of *spam filters* that filter out obvious spam.

The typical e-mail client software, such as Microsoft Outlook, has filters that do a pretty good job of detecting and isolating junk e-mail, especially pornography-related spam. Keep the Outlook filter up to date by periodically choosing Help | Check for Updates. The client filters send spam to a junk e-mail folder if certain keywords or phrases are found in the subject or message ("100%," "guaranteed," "Viagra," "best mortgage," "refinance," "FREE," "!!!," and so on). Commercial antispam software programs, often called *spam blockers,* have more-sophisticated, continuously updated filters that do a much better job. Norton AntiSpam (Symantec), shown in integration with Microsoft Outlook in Figure 13-5, does an excellent job, as does SpamKiller (McAfee Security).

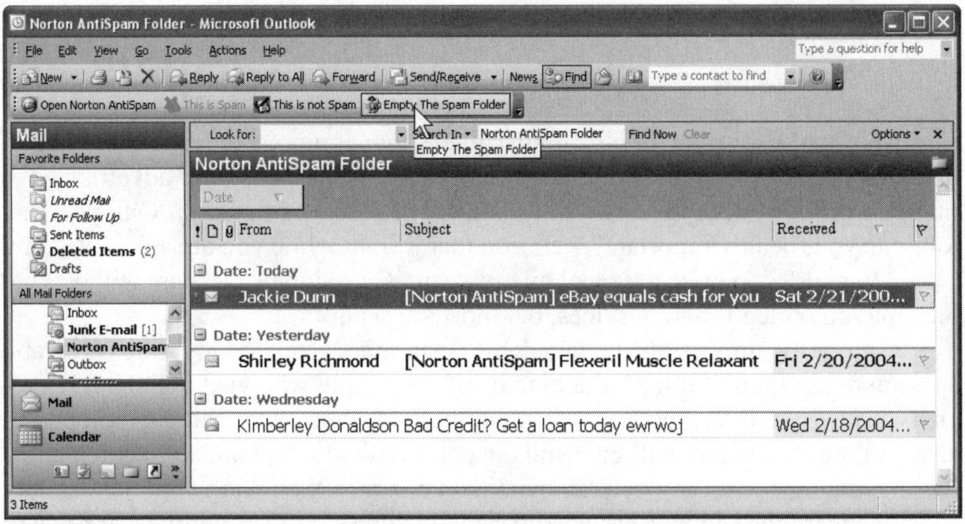

Figure 13-5   Norton AntiSpam integrated with Microsoft Outlook

Transaction Security on the Internet

Most of the bits that travel the Net are unsecured and vulnerable to being intercepted en route between computers. This is a concern, especially for financial transactions and those that involve personal data. A byproduct of an explosion in electronic commerce (e-commerce) is that Internet security is maturing and is better prepared to handle these transactions. Web site security may not be perfectly secure, but I'm a lot more comfortable entering my credit card number for an online transaction than I am handing my credit card to a waiter in a restaurant.

Secure web sites use the *Secure Sockets Layer (SSL)* protocol and encryption technology to encrypt data that are transferred over SSL links. Reputable e-commerce sites use this protocol to ensure secure transmission of sensitive information, such as credit card numbers, between web client (your PC) and web server computers. You'll know it's a secure site if the "http" in the browser's URL address bar changes to "https" (the added "s" for secure) and/or a padlock icon appears in the status bar at the bottom of the browser (see Figure 13-6).

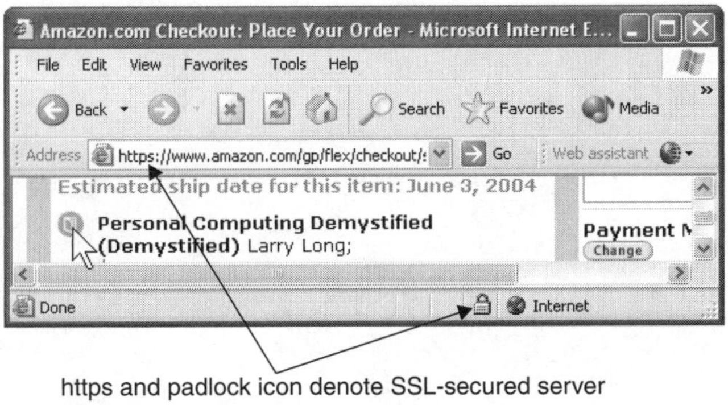

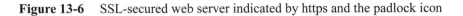

https and padlock icon denote SSL-secured server

Figure 13-6   SSL-secured web server indicated by https and the padlock icon

Although our PCs sit safely in the confines of our homes and offices, their online links to the Internet expose them to the unsavory elements of the virtual world. The Internet community is employing SSL and other tools to ensure Internet security, but all their security measures go for naught if we netizens don't do our part, too. This chapter identifies points of vulnerability and presents specific approaches that can be implemented to create a secure personal computing environment. The threats are real, so I encourage you to adopt these suggestions and build an envelope of security around your personal computer and its stored information.

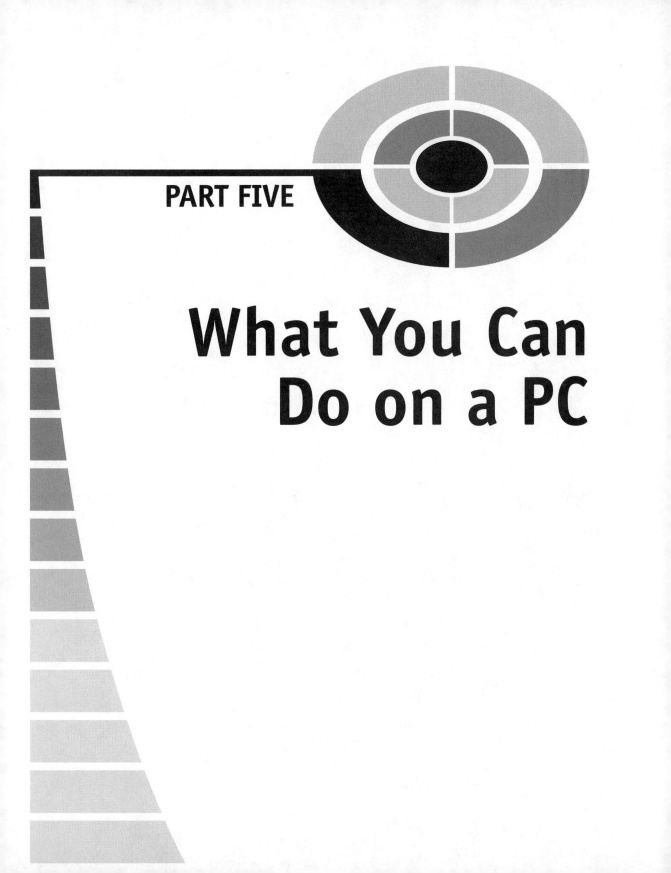

PART FIVE

What You Can Do on a PC

14

Building a Software Portfolio

A PC is a virtual university, providing interactive instruction and testing. It's an entertainment center with singleplayer and multiplayer games. It's a canvas for a painter. It's a video telephone. It's a CD player or a DVD player. It's a home library. It's the biggest marketplace in the world. It's a print shop. It's a recorder. It's an alarm clock that can remind you of appointments. It's an expert partner that can help you perform hundreds of functions that require specialized skills, such as preparing taxes, drafting legal documents, building a shed, and much more. However, to offer these applications, the PC must have the right software.

This chapter begins a four-chapter sequence devoted to demystifying PC software. This overview chapter introduces you to the world of PC software and to the concept of building a personal software portfolio. The next three chapters are intended to expose you to the breadth and scope of PC applications, with multimedia and graphics applications and gaming applications being covered in the last two chapters.

PC Software in Perspective

Let's put software in perspective. Software is the instructions that tell the computer what to do. An office suite application, such as Microsoft Word, can have millions of instructions that do your bidding when you enter or select a command.

Imperfect PC Software

With millions of instructions compiled in a complex labyrinth of syntax, you would think that a few programming errors might make it to the retail shelves. Well, they do. Microsoft, Corel, IBM, and other major software vendors create amazing software, but my four-decade search for error-free software continues.

The propensity to rush a product to market is, has been, and will always be common in the software industry. Today, I tacitly expect minor glitches, and, sure enough, one of my programs will "freeze," not permit interaction, several times a week. On rare occasions, my entire system freezes and I must restart my PC. The good news is that we have the Internet and the Check for Updates option in the Help menu. Mostly, these periodic updates provide patches to programming oversights.

PC Software Trends

Several trends are apparent in personal computing software, all of which ultimately impact our bank accounts. One trend is *unbundling,* the separation of software from the cost of the hardware. When I began a career in computers, IBM, Univac, Honeywell, and other major hardware manufacturers sold the hardware and provided the software as a service, free of charge. IBM unbundled its software from the cost of its corporate mainframe computers in 1969 and, almost overnight, the software industry was born.

Until relatively recently, new PCs were sold with the operating system and a nice complement of applications software. Now, the trend to unbundling is repeating itself in the PC market. If you have shopped for PCs recently, you've probably noticed that the price of PCs has dropped to as low as $499. Much of this reduction in cost can be attributed to the fact that software that used to come preinstalled on the system is now sold separately. For example, if you wish to include the de facto office suite, Microsoft Office, and essential Internet security software, that $499 PC might cost in excess of $1000. For the past quarter-century, hardware has been the big-ticket item in personal computing. In the future, I would expect most of the cost of personal computing to be associated with software and software-related services.

Another trend that has been ongoing for several decades is the consolidation of software into relatively few much larger companies. We have only to look at Microsoft to see how the larger companies can use their clout and marketing wisdom to make their products de facto standards. At one time, Netscape's browser was the rage of the industry. WordPerfect dominated in word processing. Lotus 1-2-3 was the killer application that legitimized the PC for use in business. Now, Internet Explorer, Word, and Excel are the de facto standards for the industry. This consolidation of literally hundreds of software companies is continuing in all areas of personal computing, including gaming and home computing applications.

One positive aspect of consolidation is the potential for integration of applications. For example, all of the office suite applications for Microsoft and Corel, the major players in office suite software, work together seamlessly, such that you can insert a spreadsheet into a word processing program, import a contacts list into a database, and so on.

Software Choices

There are tens of thousands of software packages, each of which can be classified as one of the following:

- **Commercial software**   Commercial software has a price tag and can be purchased off the shelf or ordered from an e-tailer. General product support is built into the price of the software.
- **Shareware**   This is copyright software for which the author requests a small fee for its use. It can be downloaded for free, but its use is based on an honor system where users pay a small fee to the author(s) for using it. As an incentive to pay the fee, some shareware programs will continually nag you to pay up. Launching a commercial software product can be very expensive. Shareware and the Internet offer a way for small companies and home office operations to get their products to market. Some shareware is excellent. Some of it is a waste of Internet download capacity.
- **Freeware**   This copyright software can be downloaded and used free of charge. Some freeware, especially that made available by commercial software vendors, is much used and appreciated. However, mostly, you get what you pay for.

- **Public-domain software**   This software is not copyrighted and can be downloaded and used without restriction.
- **Open-source software**   This is software for which the actual source programming code (the instructions) is made available free of charge to users for use, review, and modification. Open-source software is the result of a collaborative effort by programmers who want to improve the code and share their ideas with the online community.

Retail outlets, such as Home Depot, Barnes & Noble, and Wal-Mart, and online e-tailers, such as TigerDirect and CDW, mainly sell popular commercial software packages, which number in the hundreds. You won't see the many thousands of special-purpose commercial software packages unless you know where to look. For example, if you are a screen writer, there is a good chance that the Screen Writers Guild's web site will feature support software, such as Screenwriter. If your hobby is astronomy, you can enter "astronomy software" into any search engine and find over 100 astronomy applications.

There is personal computing support for just about any application and the boldest imagination. In Figure 14-1, I've listed eight broad software categories into which most personal computing software can be grouped. The list is less than exhaustive, as I assumed you didn't want to wade through a ten-page outline. This abbreviated set of categories, however, should give you some insight into the breadth of available PC software and applications. The focus of the list is personal computing, so it does not list business software (for example, payroll, order entry, and billing), professional software (for veterinarians, attorneys, and electricians), or workgroup computing software (for example, brainstorming and forms/surveying). Gaming genres are discussed in detail in Chapter 17.

The list in Figure 14-1 identifies general software functions that may be embodied in a single software package or suite. For example, an e-mail client may offer newsgroups and personal information management. A graphics suite might provide paint, draw, and animation software.

Your Software Portfolio

Early in life, most of us begin a humble securities portfolio with a few carefully selected stocks and bonds. Over time, the portfolio grows with our experience, wealth, and financial needs and the mix of securities changes constantly to meet evolving investment objectives. Your securities portfolio is important and demands your scrutiny and attention. So does your *software portfolio,* that mix of software you have on your PC.

SYSTEM

- **Operating systems**
- **Home networking**
- **Device drivers and utilities**
- **Utilities:**
  Disk organization
  File management
  Performance enhancement and measurement
  Screen savers
  Screen capture and image conversion

INTERNET/WEB

- **Personal communications:**
  E-mail
  Instant messaging
  Chat
  Videoconferencing
  Fax
- **Internet security:**
  Firewall
  Antivirus
  Antispyware
- **PC remote access**
- **File sharing**
- **Web site development**
- **Electronic document**

GENERAL PRODUCTIVITY (Office Suite)

- **Word processing**
- **Spreadsheet**
- **Data management**
- **Speech recognition**
- **Desktop publishing**

HOME APPLICATIONS

- **Home:**
  Accounting and tax preparation
  Investment management and financial planning
  Cards and banners
  Diet, nutrition, and recipes
  Health care reference and advice
  Home/interior/landscape design
  Legal document preparation
  Travel planning
  Application-specific database (genealogy,
  audio library, recipe, Boy Scout troop, and so on)

HOME APPLICATION (cont.)

- **Personal:**
  Personal information management (calendar, to do lists, journals)
  Hobbies (gardening, sewing, knitting, and so on)
  Resume and job search
  Self-improvement (personality analysis, biorhythms,
  memory improvement, and so on)
- **Entertainment:**
  Gaming (see Chapter 17)
  Edutainment (games that are education based)
  Audio/video
- **Student (college):**
  College selection
  Financial aid
- **Student (K through 12, all subjects)**

EDUCATION AND TRAINING

- **Education** (anatomy, foreign languages, algebra, and so on)
- **Training** (personal computing, keyboarding, guitar, and so on)

REFERENCE

- **Dictionaries and other general reference**
- **Encyclopedias**
- **Geographic information system (GIS)/travel**
- **Health/medical**
- **Language translation**
- **Religion**
- **Magazines**
- **Pop culture** (movies, *Guinness*, world facts, and so on)

GRAPHICS

- **Paint and draw**
- **Image editing**
- **Drag-and-drop**
- **Clip art**
- **Computer-aided design**
- **Image viewer and management**
- **Scanning (images and OCR)**

MULTIMEDIA

- **Presentation**
- **Authoring**
- **Animation**
- **Music/MIDI (sequencing and composition)**
- **Sound capture and editing**
- **Video capture and editing**

Figure 14-1　Categories of software for personal computing

Windows, a basic office suite, antivirus software, and, perhaps, a few other software packages might be preinstalled on your computer at the time of purchase. This software forms the foundation for your software portfolio. As you gain confidence and experience in personal computing, you will need to grow your software portfolio to keep pace with your expanding personal computing needs and goals. It is your software portfolio that allows you to explore the potential of your PC.

The investment you make in a software portfolio can easily exceed that of your hardware investment. There is a reason why Bill Gates, of Microsoft, is the richest man in the world. It makes good economic sense for you to familiarize yourself with the software options. With a little software knowledge, you are better prepared to plan and build a cost-effective software portfolio, now and as you mature in personal computing.

I would suggest that you conceptualize the growth of your software portfolio in three tiers (see Figure 14-2). The Tier 1 portfolio has a software mix for novice PC users. The Tier 2 portfolio is for experienced users, and the Tier 3 portfolio is for advanced users. Of course, there are no hard and fast rules that say you must master all Tier 1 software before progressing to Tier 2. In practice, there may be some overlap between the tiers. The tiers are essentially suggestions for your consideration as to how you might grow your software portfolio.

The Tier 1 Software Portfolio

There is an amazing cornucopia of applications software that you can add to your software portfolio to make you more productive at work, save you time, make life easier at home, and give you many hours of enjoyment during leisure time. However, in most PC homes, the "big 5" are the main applications: word processing, Internet communications (e-mail/instant messaging), surfing the Web via browsers, the Internet security group, and gaming. Word processing takes care of all the text-based tasks, and they are many (homework reports, letters, to do lists, signs, newsletters, soccer team rosters, PTA procedures, and so on). E-mail and instant messaging are now part of what we do and the basis for much of our personal and business communications. The typical netizen will surf the Web with intent and/or serendipitously from four to ten hours a week. Essential Internet security software includes firewall, antivirus, and antispyware software. Typically, gaming can be one of the most often-used applications on a PC. In some homes, gaming is a minor element of the personal computing mix, so, in these homes, it's the "big 4."

New computer systems come with most of the Tier 1 software portfolio preinstalled, basically a "starter kit." After that, additions and changes to the software portfolio become your responsibility. You may need to purchase at least one or all of the Internet security programs separately. Although Windows comes with several games, including solitaire, minesweeper, checkers, and pinball, a true gamer will want to purchase a few popular commercial games, too.

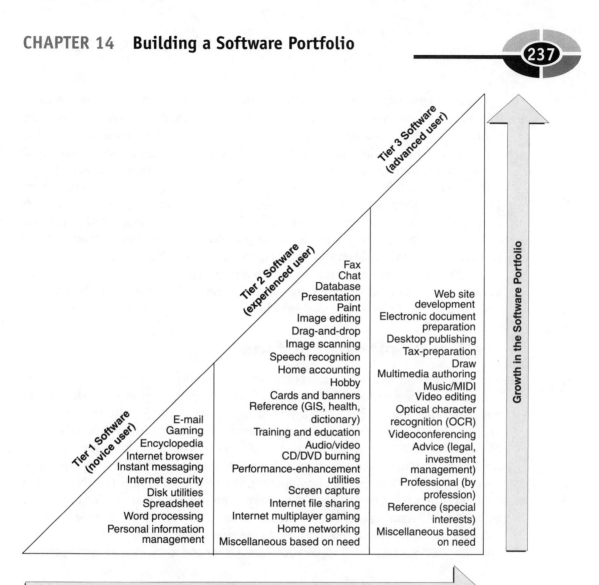

Figure 14-2 The three-tier software portfolio

The Tier 2 Software Portfolio

Today's powerful personal computers generally are underused, both at home and at work. This is because many PC users don't know how to build their software portfolio. You could become a happy PC user and never venture far from the capabilities of the high-use Tier 1 applications. However, there is a lot more to personal computing than Tier 1 applications.

Once you gain a little experience and become comfortable with your PC and personal computing, it's time to expand your applications horizons and, therefore, your software portfolio. A high percentage of PC users never grow their software portfolio past Tier 1, but because you are reading this book, my bet is that you will begin expanding into Tier 2 applications within the first year (see Figure 14-2). For example, Tier 2 encompasses software in one of the hottest areas of personal computing, graphics and multimedia. This growth has been spurred by the availability of inexpensive support hardware, such as digital cameras and image scanners. In Tier 2, we begin to embrace the PC as a new approach to learning for keyboarding, Spanish, guitar, and so on. You may begin creating your own calendars, greeting cards, and banners at your PC. You might like to use travel software, which works in conjunction with global positioning system (GPS) hardware, to show you the best route to your destination and the best stops along the way. The next three chapters give you a good sampling of Tier 2 software.

The Tier 3 Software Portfolio

The advanced user will continue to build a software portfolio that includes some of the Tier 3 software in Figure 14-2. Actually, anyone who is familiar with the elements of personal computing and has a willingness to learn can use Tier 3 software. Software at the Tier 3 level may require some training or serious self-study. For example, this tier includes software for web site development and video editing. It's quite possible that you can find a continuing-education course devoted to these and other Tier 3 applications.

At this top level of personal computing, it's likely that you'll be tapping your computer for advice on investment management and legal matters. You might be authoring self-running multimedia presentations. People with sophisticated Tier 3 software portfolios might routinely hold videoconferences with neighbors, friends, or colleagues. Several Tier 3 applications are introduced in the next three chapters.

Tips for Growing Your Software Portfolio

Here are a few tips that might prove helpful as you build your software portfolio:

- *Do* grow your software portfolio at a pace that's comfortable for you.
- *Do* test-drive software, whenever possible. Test software at a store or friend's house. Or, download demonstration software from the vendor's web site and try it out.
- *Do* shop around for the best deal. Check price ranges at an Internet comparison-shopping web site (CNET Shopper.com, BizRate, or Pricegrabber.com). Software prices can vary substantially (up to 40 percent).

- *Do* read software reviews. Software is widely reviewed in the print and online media (search "*name of software* review"). You also can read customer reviews at e-tail sites and in newsgroups.
- *Do* use common sense when purchasing software. For example, if the price is too good to be true, it probably is.
- *Don't* buy software if your PC does not meet its minimum system requirements (for example, not enough RAM). Requirements are on the box and the web sites.
- *Don't* purchase popular commercial software unless it is in the original retail packaging. "White box" software may be fine, but, for a few dollars more, why take a chance.
- *Don't* believe the money-back guarantee, unless it is from a reputable mainline vendor.
- *Don't* purchase software via direct download from a third-party vendor. Software sales scams are commonplace on the Internet. You may get worthless bits while someone gets your money.

The important "what to purchase" and "where to purchase" questions are addressed in detail in Chapter 8.

Software Licensing and Activation

The same federal copyright law that protects intellectual property, such as books and audio recordings, automatically protects software. When you click "I agree" (with the license terms and agreements) during the software installation process, you enter into a contract with the software vendor. Unless specifically stated otherwise in the license agreement, you can install the software to only one computer.

The growth of home networking has prompted software vendors to consider offering *site license* agreements to home users, as they do to businesses. Within the near future, I expect to see home site licenses that permit the use of a software package by a specific number of PCs. During the next few years, I believe that software vendors will become very creative with their licensing options. For example, should a person who uses two PCs (a portable and a desktop) pay the same for software as two people who use two different PCs? The drive behind this trend toward more licensing options is rampant *software piracy*. Software vendors estimate that for every software product they sell, two more are copied illegally.

In an effort to thwart software piracy, software vendors are asking their customers to *activate* their software upon installation. Basically, the activation process "unlocks" the software for long-term use. This process requires that you contact the vendor and provide it with a valid product serial number. The vendor gives you a key (a number) that you enter to activate the software. If you have Internet access during installation, this process is automatic. If not, you may be asked to call a toll-free number.

The amount of computing capacity in the world is doubling every two years. The number and sophistication of personal computing applications are growing at a similar pace. You can bet that next year there will be applications that are unheard of today.

CHAPTER **15**

Personal Computing Applications Galore

The next three chapters expose you to a variety of useful applications and illustrate uses for popular software packages in each of the eight broad software categories presented in Chapter 14. This chapter covers six of these categories—*system, Internet/web, general productivity, home applications, education and training,* and *reference.* The emphasis in Chapter 16 is on the concepts and software associated with *graphics* and *multimedia* software. Chapter 17 is devoted to a significant subset of home applications software, *gaming* software, its many genres, and the issues

associated with gaming. The applications discussed and illustrated in these chapters are intended to show you just a few of the many points of light in the personal computing spectrum. Just be aware that there are many, many more.

System Software

Generally, we classify software as either *system software* or *applications software.* The operating system and utility programs are system software. The primary function of the operating system (for example, Windows) and of most system software is to manage system resources and enable the running of applications software. Some types of system software exist to complement the personal computing activity. For example, *screensavers,* programs that cause dynamic designs to appear on your display after a period of inactivity, are utility programs. In contrast to system software's overview function, applications software normally addresses a specific user task. Windows, the centerpiece for system software, is covered in some detail in Chapters 5 and 6.

A variety of *utility programs* help you keep your PC running at peak performance and assist you with the day-to-day chores associated with personal computing. Windows has several handy utility programs, such as the disk maintenance utilities covered in Chapter 10 (Disk Cleanup, Check Disk, and Disk Defragmenter). Figure 15-1 presents a sampling of common utility programs you might use to enhance your personal computing environment.

Internet/Web Software

Software for the Internet and the Web is growing as fast as the Internet. Much of the end-user Internet software is introduced in Part Four, "The Internet." We interact with the World Wide Web via an Internet browser (Chapter 11) and we communicate via e-mail, instant messaging, chat, and newsgroups (Chapter 12). We protect our PCs and valuable information from hackers with Internet security software that includes firewall, antivirus, and antispyware software (Chapter 13).

Clearly, there is trend toward increased use of the *electronic document.* Electronic documents are easily created from any type of file and can be distributed to one or many people via the Net and then viewed on an Internet browser. Plus, they

Temperature and power monitor for alerting
the user when temperature or power is out of
acceptable range (Intel Active Monitor)

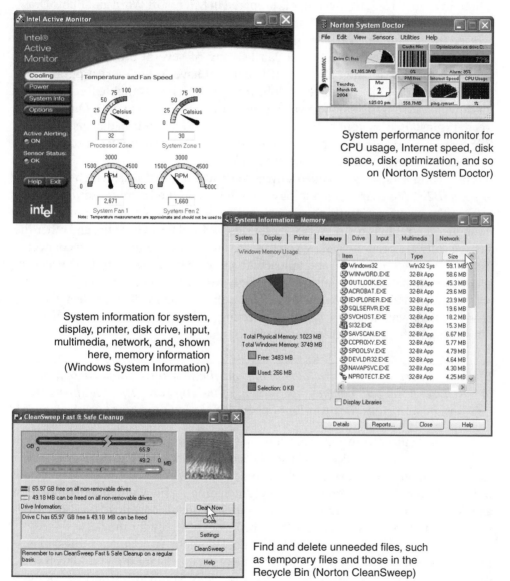

System performance monitor for
CPU usage, Internet speed, disk
space, disk optimization, and so
on (Norton System Doctor)

System information for system,
display, printer, disk drive, input,
multimedia, network, and, shown
here, memory information
(Windows System Information)

Find and delete unneeded files, such
as temporary files and those in the
Recycle Bin (Norton CleanSweep)

Figure 15-1   Utility software

have the added advantage of being searchable. The de facto standard for electronic documents is the *Portable Document Format (PDF)* file created by Adobe Corporation. In Figure 15-2, a newsletter is prepared in Microsoft Word and PhotoDraw, and then Adobe Acrobat converts and combines the two files into a highly compressed (made smaller) PDF file that can be posted to a web page or distributed in other ways over the Internet. You can use any of several programs, including Adobe Acrobat, to create PDF files. If you do not have one of these programs and wish to read a PDF file, you need Adobe Reader, which is available free of charge for download from the Adobe Systems web site (www.adobe.com). Once Adobe Reader is installed on your system, it becomes a browser plug-in that enables PDF files to be viewed within your browser. A *plug-in* is a complementary program that enhances the functionality of a piece of software.

The "world's most downloaded software application" is Kazaa, which uses *peer-to-peer (P2P)* file sharing technology. Individuals on the Internet use file sharing software to connect directly to one another, peer-to-peer, without the need to go through a central Internet server. Kazaa, iMesh, Morpheus, Gnutella, and other file sharing software programs allow you to search for and share files among connected users via Internet download and upload. At any give time, over a million users are sharing over a half trillion music files (mainly MP3 files). Peer-to-peer file sharing software also enables the sharing of images, software, and videos and lets you play or view the downloads, as well. Many aspiring authors, musicians, and artists use file sharing technology to distribute their original work.

CAUTION   If you wish to participate in Internet file sharing, I would encourage you to purchase a "no ad" commercial version of the software. The free downloaded versions are notorious for installing spyware along with the file sharing software.

Companies that create copyright content for the commercial market are less than enthusiastic about the widespread use of peer-to-peer file sharing, especially that of music and movies. It is against the law to share or download copyright intellectual property of any kind. Several companies, including Apple Computer Corporation and Wal-Mart, offer a service that lets you purchase music downloads at about a dollar a song. In time, similar services will be made available for movies.

Although most commercial web site development is done by professionals, many intermediate-level PC users with little or no formal training build web sites, too. User-friendly web development tools, such as Microsoft FrontPage, let you create web documents. Simply enter text in text boxes, then drag-and-drop images and other elements as needed into the WYSIWYG (what you see is what you get) display.

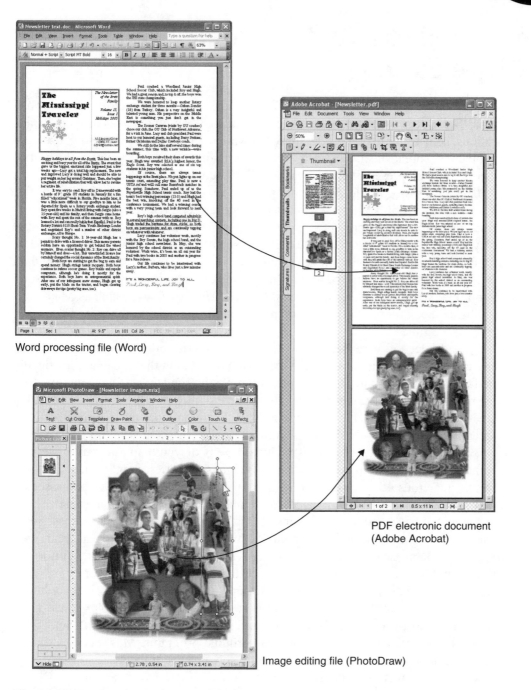

Word processing file (Word)

PDF electronic document
(Adobe Acrobat)

Image editing file (PhotoDraw)

Figure 15-2   Creating a PDF portable document (Adobe Acrobat)

General Productivity Software: The Office Suite

Office suites, such as Microsoft Office, Corel WordPerfect Office, and Lotus SmartSuite, are composed of several complementary applications. The main applications, sometimes called productivity software, include word processing, desktop publishing, spreadsheet, database, and presentation software. The latter, the multimedia-oriented presentation software, is discussed in Chapter 16.

Word processing is one of those often-used "big five" applications. Popular packages, such as Word (see Figure 15-3) and WordPerfect, give you the tools to create, edit, and format documents in preparation for output. The output can be printed, displayed, e-mailed, posted to the Internet, and so on. Word processing is all you need for most document-generation tasks; however, if you are preparing a document that is to be professionally printed, such as a brochure, flyer, restaurant menu, and so on, you might wish to consider using *desktop publishing software,* such as Microsoft Publisher (see Figure 15-3). Desktop publishing is included with the professional-level office suites.

Spreadsheet software (see Figure 15-3) is just a grid for entering data into rows and columns. The grid, however, is somewhat magical in that it can automatically perform a variety of math (for example, column totals) and logic (for example, select the most or least in a category) operations. From the spreadsheet data, it's easy to create all kinds of bar, pie, and line graphs. There are countless applications for spreadsheet software—basically, anything that has rows and columns of data. My personal spreadsheet applications include dozens of youth sports team rosters, a complete room-by-room home inventory, budget summaries, family financial statements, numerous schedules and itineraries, expense reports, neighborhood association data, school booster club finances log, tennis coaching drills grid, and many more.

Often, the basic and home versions of office suites do not include database software, which is more business oriented. With database software you can create and maintain a database and use a variety of tools to make inquiries and extract information from the database. You can also sort the information and generate reports. Basically, database software gives you all that you need to create a business or home information system. Database software is considerably more complex to use than spreadsheet software, which is relatively intuitive, and will take a significant effort to learn, especially if you plan to include original programs. Most personal/home data-oriented tasks can be handled by either spreadsheet or database software. My recommendation is to try the spreadsheet approach first.

The software suite programs give you plenty of help in getting started. You don't have to start from scratch to create a document. As you might imagine, it's all been

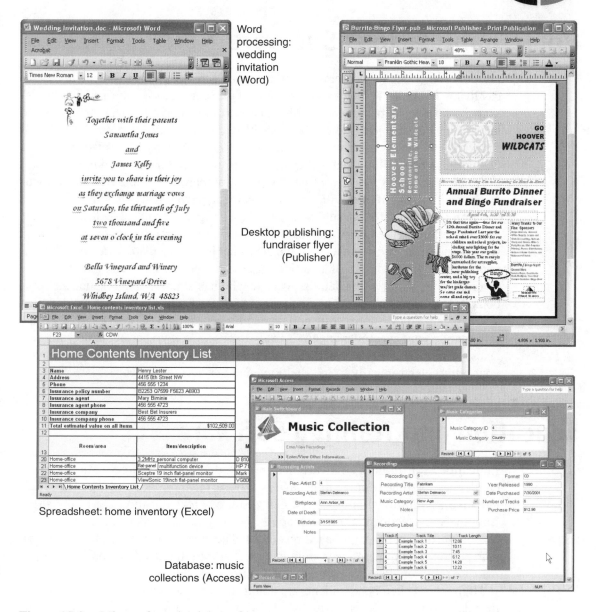

Word processing: wedding invitation (Word)

Desktop publishing: fundraiser flyer (Publisher)

Spreadsheet: home inventory (Excel)

Database: music collections (Access)

Figure 15-3   Microsoft productivity software

done before, whether it's an expense report, a fax form, or a recipe database. Each software vendor offers a variety of *templates,* which are simply documents that have been designed and formatted for a particular task, such as the wedding invitation and home inventory spreadsheet templates in Figure 15-3.

Home Applications Software

Personal computing is becoming one of the many activities we associate with day-to-day living. Figure 15-4 shows you just a few of the scores of software applications designed to help you to better accomplish the chores of life. For example, I credit personal information management (PIM) software, with its *contact database, calendar,* and *to do list,* with elevating my life from total disarray to organized chaos. PIM software, such as Outlook, can be synchronized with similar software on cell phones and PDAs.

Home legal advisor software can help you prepare most common legal documents such as a bill of sale, will, license agreement, power of attorney, and so on. It's much less expensive to "consult" with a PC-based expert than to talk with an attorney. My whole family uses *print projects software* to create greeting cards, certificates, signs, banners, iron-on transfers, and many other jobs. I used *home design software* to prepare a general design of an office annex to my home, and then I gave the plans to an architect to fill in the details. Anyone who has attempted to balance a checkbook, pay bills, or prepare a budget will appreciate *home finance software,* which also can help you with investing and managing your money. Come tax time, all the information your accountant needs is ready to print. Or, if you prefer to do your own taxes, you can feed the information to a tax preparation program, which can transmit your return electronically to Internal Revenue Service computers.

Education and Training Software

Education and training software may not be the solution to education's many challenges, as some people might have us believe, but it provides one very viable alternative to traditional approaches. Our resources for education are in transition from the static, sequential presentation of books and manuals to dynamic, linked, and interactive technology-based resources. The current generation has grown up with personal computers and is embracing technology-based education. Those of us who are traditionalists are coming around, although slowly.

High school chemistry students are doing lab exercises with bits and bytes rather than dangerous chemicals. Virtually all keyboarding training revolves around interactive software. I learned Spanish in the old school and am improving my skills with the help of some imaginative software, which even evaluates my pronunciation. Technology-based education and training software, which is available for everything from astronomy to zoology, can be very effective at all age groups. Figure 15-5 provides a sampling of education and training software.

Legal advisor: college trust (Family Lawyer)

Personal information management (PIM): calendar (Outlook)

Print projects: awards (The Print Shop)

Home design: floor plan, model, elevation (Home Architect)

Home finance: accounting and check writing (Quicken)

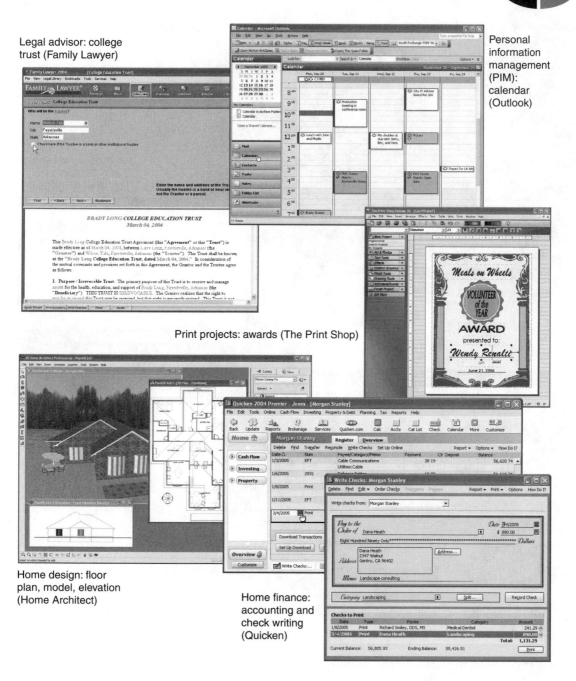

Figure 15-4   Home software

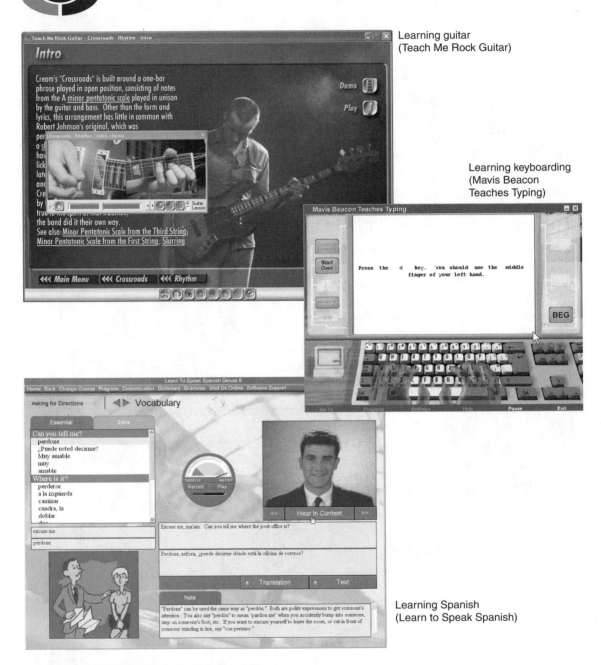

Learning guitar
(Teach Me Rock Guitar)

Learning keyboarding
(Mavis Beacon
Teaches Typing)

Learning Spanish
(Learn to Speak Spanish)

Figure 15-5   Education and training software

Reference Software

The Internet and high-capacity CD/DVD technologies are rapidly transforming the manner in which we maintain and view reference materials. For a number of years, a 20-plus volume, 200-pound encyclopedia was the standard for family reference. Today, it's a one-ounce CD-ROM/DVD-ROM multimedia encyclopedia (see Figure 15-6). That same trend, from paper to electronic, is evident in all reference materials. Those law books you see lining the shelves of an attorney's office are mostly for show. Generally, lawyers subscribe to legal reference services, which provide continuously updated, easily searchable materials in CD/DVD format or via the Internet. A wide range of reference materials is available to home users in the form of software packages. For example, you can purchase software that provides medical advice and information, entrance requirements and contact information for thousands of colleges, multilingual dictionaries, every conceivable type of map, and many other areas of reference.

Computer-based reference materials go far past a simple textual/static image presentation. Electronic encyclopedias not only talk about geographic destinations throughout the world, they give you a 360-degree panoramic visual and a video along with hyperlinked text. Rapid keyword searches make it easy to find what we want.

If you do much traveling to unfamiliar places, the GPS (global positioning system)/street map software combo can be invaluable. Street map software is used in conjunction with a GPS receiver, which plugs into a notebook PC's USB port. Once the GPS receiver establishes a satellite fix, an arrow tracks your exact location on a seamless street map of the entire country (see Figure 15-6). Once my son and I hit rush-hour traffic in Dallas about 12 miles from our destination, a soccer field in north Dallas. Troy had the notebook open and a "fix" established, so he requested that the software suggest alternate routing. We took the first exit and began to navigate through the back roads and neighborhoods of Dallas until we arrived at the fields. Two other teammates were mired in the same traffic jam, but they did not arrive until the beginning of the second half—an hour after we got there!

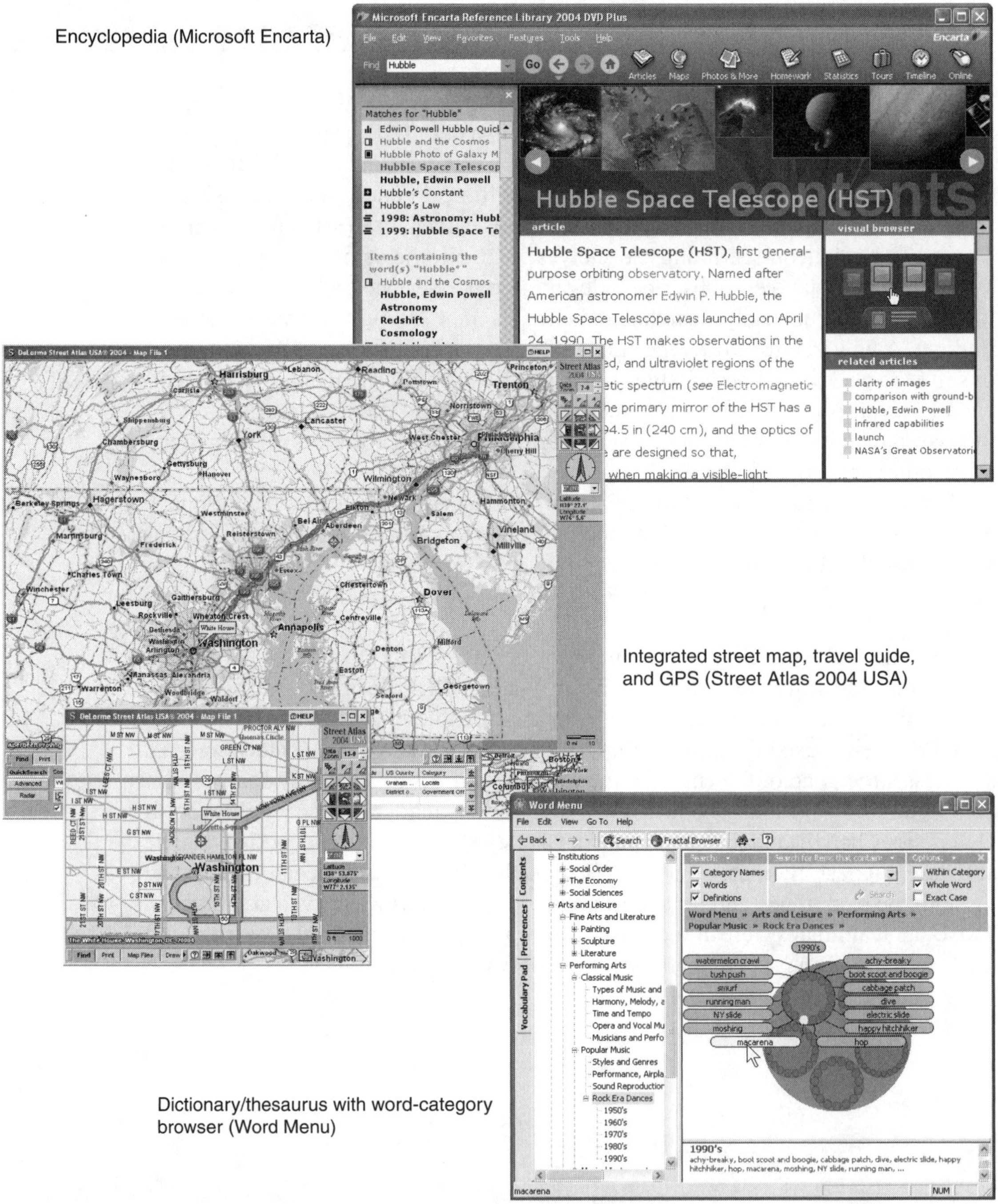

Encyclopedia (Microsoft Encarta)

Integrated street map, travel guide, and GPS (Street Atlas 2004 USA)

Dictionary/thesaurus with word-category browser (Word Menu)

Figure 15-6   Reference software

16

Working with Digital Media

During the early personal computing era, bits and bytes were displayed as letters, numbers, and character-size shapes. PC sounds were beep-like tones from a tinny little speaker. That was it, but times have changed. Today's PCs are multimedia entertainment centers with a full complement of digital media accessories, such as digital cameras, scanners, and MIDI music devices. A wide range of software has been created to help us capture audio, video, and graphics, and then do amazing things with these files.

The Multimedia Experience

This chapter is about demystifying the audio/video element of personal computing so that you can add some pizzazz to your multimedia experience. The term *multimedia* describes the PC's ability to integrate text, images, videos, animation, and/or sound.

Every modern off-the-shelf PC can play, show, or print multimedia content found in DVD movies, audio CDs, web sites, encyclopedias, and your PC-based photo album. To get the most of your multimedia experience, including creating your own content, you may need to invest in some additional hardware and/or software, such as the following:

- **Digital camera**   A digital camera captures digital images.
- **Video camera**   The video camera (digital or analog) lets you capture motion video.
- **Television**   The TV provides an alternative, large-screen monitor.
- **Synthesizer keyboard**   A piano-style synthesizer allows you to reproduce a variety of special effects and sounds, including those of almost any musical instrument.
- **Video capture card**   This expansion card lets you capture and digitize full-motion color video with audio from an analog video camera or TV signal.
- **Scanner**   A scanner lets you capture high-resolution images from hard copy source material.
- **CD-RW or DVD±RW**   Multimedia applications, which generally have huge storage requirements, can be easily burned to CD/DVD disc media.
- **Multimedia software**   If you wish to move past simply playing and viewing multimedia applications to creating them, you may need to upgrade your software portfolio to include graphics and multimedia software.
- **PC source library**   Multimedia applications generally are an integration of original and source library material that might include digitized "clips" of art (*clip art*), video, and audio to be used as needed.

Capturing the Elements of Multimedia: Images and Sound

Before you can produce original multimedia content, you may need to create your own images and sounds.

Digital Cameras: Digital Photography

At one time in my life I considered myself a camera buff, one of those people who carried a large leather carrying case filled with at least one 35mm SLR (single-lens reflex) camera and a full complement of lenses, filters, and accessories. I even developed my own black-and-white film and made my own prints. I mothballed that equipment in the mid-1990s, shortly after I bought my first digital camera.

It costs nothing to take and view a picture with a digital camera. Also, you can upload all the images directly from the camera to your PC-based photo album in seconds, and then view them on your large-screen monitor at your leisure.

Typically, I take five to ten times more pictures than I did on my SLR, and then select the best ones to keep and, possibly, print. SLR purists will argue that they have greater artistic flexibility and can achieve greater clarity in prints. On the other hand, people like me who are sold on digital photography can cite the advantages of convenience, cost, and the ability to manipulate and enhance images with image editing software.

Megapixel cameras, which start at around $100, are capable of producing an image with over a million addressable "dots" or points of color. The high-end nonprofessional digital camera sells for $500 to $1000 and can offer resolutions up to eight megapixels. At one time, the megapixel designation meant quality in a digital camera. Now, the multimegapixel camera is commonplace. You pay extra for features such as greater resolution, more zoom (4X, 6X, or 8X), the quality of the lens, more image storage format options, exposure control, and so on. Once you own a digital camera, the cost of photography plummets because the costly, time-consuming developing processing is eliminated.

When you take a picture with a digital camera, a digitized image goes straight to an onboard *flash memory card*. Several technologies are used for these cards, including memory stick, CF, and SD technology. Once stored in a memory card, the images can be uploaded to a PC and manipulated (viewed, printed, modified, and so on) in the same ways as other graphic images.

To upload images to your PC, use the USB cable that came with the camera to establish a link with the PC. If your PC has a built-in photo card slot, you have an alternative method for transferring images. Simply remove your camera's flash memory card and insert it into your PC's universal memory card slot. In either case, whether you use USB or the memory card, your PC should immediately recognize your camera's memory as a storage device as soon as you set your camera to "connect" or insert its card. From there, you can move, copy, and delete the images with Windows Explorer just as you would any files on a disk drive. Unless specified otherwise, your uploaded images are named with consecutive numbers. To rename these numbered images after they are copied to hard disk, highlight them (CTRL+A highlights all files in a folder), then choose Rename from the File menu or the right-click menu. All of the files are renamed in sequence with the new name—Kim 7th birthday (1).jpg, Kim 7th birthday (2).jpg, and so on.

Some printers have built-in photo card slots that allow you to print directly from the camera's flash memory card, thus bypassing the PC. Some of these printers have small viewers so that you can select what you want to print. Anything that can be done with a stand-alone offline printer can be done more quickly and better with an online printer, so I question whether these features are worth the extra cost ($25 to $75).

Digital Camcorders

Having a *digital camcorder* ($500 to $1000) is a big plus if you want to create innovative multimedia content. You can use a digital camcorder to capture high-quality video and sound on digital tape and then upload the video to a PC hard disk via a 1394/FireWire cable for video editing. Once on a hard disk, video information can be edited; that is, the content can be selectively organized and integrated with text, graphics, special effects, and other forms of presentation.

You can also capture digital video with a standard *analog camcorder* or VCR in conjunction with a *video capture card*. To capture video and convert it to digital format, simply plug the standard cable from the video camera or VCR into the video capture card and play the video. Some *all-in-one AGP graphics cards* include video capture card functionality, eliminating the need for a separate video capture card.

If you are in the market for a digital camcorder, you may not need to spend the extra money for a separate digital camera for still photography. Most modern digital camcorders function well as multimegapixel cameras for still images, too. Still images, as well as small amounts of video, are stored on the camera's flash memory card and uploaded via a USB cable or a PC's built-in photo card slot.

Scanners

The scanner, discussed in Chapter 3, gives us the flexibility to scan photo images, any hardcopy document, and small three-dimensional items, such as jewelry, into digital images. Scan software, which comes with all scanners, is easy to use. Just scan the image, and then use your mouse to highlight the area to be scanned and saved to disk as a digital image (see Figure 16-1). If your personal computing plans call for working with digital media, I would highly recommend that you invest in a relatively inexpensive scanner or an all-in-one multifunction device with an integrated scanner.

The Microphone

Your PC can be a simple sound-recording device that allows you to capture sound via your microphone (select Start | All Programs | Accessories | Entertainment | Sound Recorder). Or, it can be a sophisticated recording studio that will allow you to lay down your own multitrack recordings from external sources. To do this, you'll need some extra hardware and software, namely a high-end sound card, quality microphones, and *digital audio sequencing* software (see Figure 16-2).

Figure 16-1 Scanner software (HP PrecisionScan Pro)

Figure 16-2 Digital audio sequencing software (Record Producer Deluxe)

Sound files are of two types, *waveform* and *nonwaveform*. Recording via the Windows Sound Recorder results in a waveform or wave file, like the ones we listen to over the radio and via audio CDs. The primary Windows waveform file is identified with the *.wav* extension (soundfile.wav). When you use a synthesizer keyboard in conjunction with software like Record Producer, the result is a nonwaveform file that contains instructions as to how to create the sound, rather than a digitized version of the actual sound. The MIDI file is the most common nonwaveform file, which is identified with an *.mid* extension (for example, musicfile.mid). MIDI stands for Musical Instrument Digital Interface. MIDI files, which are compact and small, are easily converted to Windows WAV files, which can be much larger, for play on traditional audio devices.

Graphics Software: Creating and Working with Images

We use graphics software to create, manipulate, and manage digital still images. With graphics software we can create line drawings, blueprints, flowcharts, colorful art, or any other imaginable image. Most digital images are stored in either of the following formats:

- **Bitmap**   This type of image is composed of patterns of dots called picture elements, or *pixels*.
- **Vector**   This type of image is composed of patterns of lines, points, and other geometric shapes.

You can't tell by looking at a particular image whether it is one format or another, but there are significant differences when it comes to manipulating the images with graphics software. Also, there is a considerable difference in the size of these files. Bitmap files define colors for each pixel and can be very large. Vector files are more efficient in the way they store images and, therefore, take up less storage space than bitmap files.

Paint and Draw Software

The Windows Paint program is *paint software*; that is, the result is bitmapped such that the image is "mapped" on to the display in rows and columns of pixels. Select Start | All Programs | Accessories | Paint to use the Windows graphics program, which is shown in Figure 16-3. Think of paint software as an electronic canvas. Whatever you draw becomes a part of that canvas, so you must erase or draw over any part with which you are dissatisfied. Digital cameras and scanners produce bitmap images.

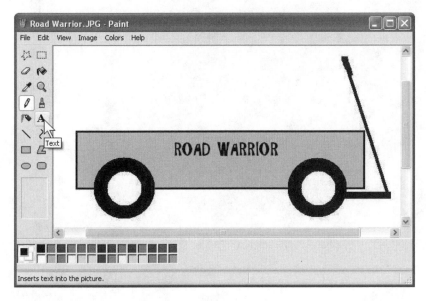

Figure 16-3   Paint software (Windows Paint)

Images are stored according to a particular file format, and there are many formats. Common types of bitmap graphics files are identified by their filename extensions: *JPG* (web pages and digital photography), *BMP* (common Windows format), *GIF* (patented format for web pages), *TIF* (print publishing), and *PNG* (patent-free alternative to GIF).

Draw software, also called *illustration software,* employs vector graphics, so you can work with objects. Virtually all art and professional illustration is done with draw software, such as shown in Figure 16-4. With draw software, any object can be moved, copied, deleted, rotated, tilted, flipped, stretched, and squeezed without affecting other parts of the drawing. Several of the many objects that were individually created to make up the drawing in Figure 16-4 are moved to demonstrate the composition of a vector graphics drawing. Popular vector graphics file formats include *EPS, CGM,* and *CDR. WMF* is a popular metafile format that is used to exchange graphics between Windows applications. Popular draw software includes CorelDRAW (Figure 16-4), Adobe Illustrator, and Macromedia Freehand.

Figure 16-4   Draw software (CorelDRAW)

Image Editing

Image editing software lets you do just about anything to digitized images, such as photographs, scanned images, digital paintings, and so on. You can fine-tune or dramatically alter the appearance of an image by retouching it or applying special effects to it. For example, image editing software was used to alter the scanned image in Figure 16-1 to create the image in Figure 16-5. The image was cropped, made brighter, given a different hue with a tint adjustment, and sharpened (for better focus). To give the image an artistic touch, a neon filter was applied and the edges were softened. Popular image editing software, such as Microsoft Digital Image Pro (Figure 16-5), Adobe Photoshop, and Corel Photo-Paint, serves a dual function in that it allows you to create (paint software) and edit bitmap images.

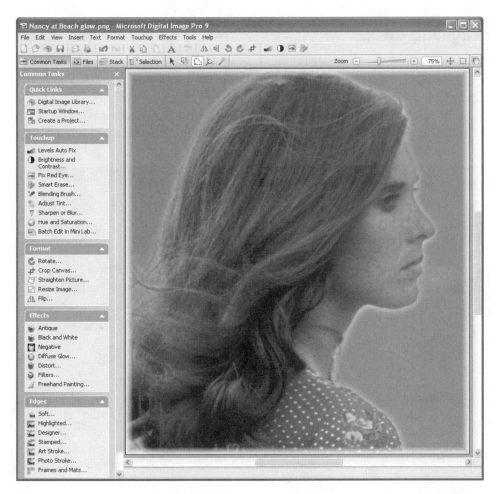

Figure 16-5   Image editing software (Microsoft Digital Image Pro)

With image editing software you can eliminate flaws in the photography or the subject matter and achieve stunning special effects. For example, you can easily eliminate red eye resulting from flash photography, whiten dark teeth, smooth facial blemishes, and straighten photos with the horizon. Also, you have a number of special effects at your disposal that allow you to diffuse and distort the image. You can use this software to create an antique, black-and-white, or negative version of the image. If needed, you have the capability to do freehand painting, too. A selection tool lets you make changes to one area of the image without affecting other areas. When you are through, you can frame the image with any of scores of designer frames or apply an artistic edge treatment.

Drag-and-Drop

Drag-and-drop software is for the vast majority of us who are not graphics specialist but, on occasion, need to create drawings and diagrams. The illustration in Figure 16-6 is my rough drawing for a figure in Chapter 11. You create drawings and diagrams by dragging ready-made shapes from application-specific stencils to a position on the drawing area. You can select from a wide variety of stencils to create flowcharts, orga-

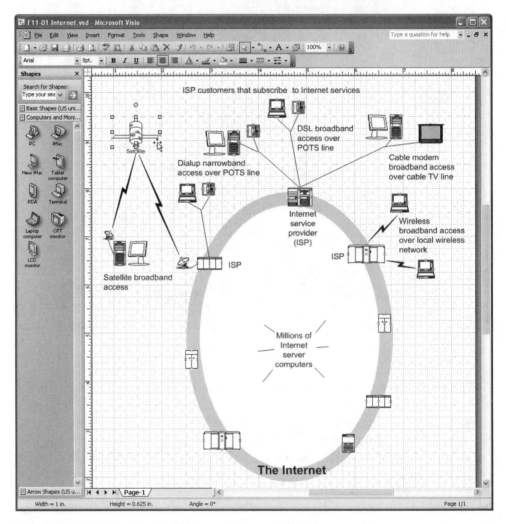

Figure 16-6   Drag-and-drop software (Microsoft Visio)

nizational charts, landscaping schematics, maps, plant or office layouts, bath and kitchen plans, network diagrams, project management charts, business graphics, and much more. The shapes are "intelligent"; that is, they take on different forms, proportions, colors, and other properties depending on how they are used. If you drag a linked object, the connecting arrow is changed accordingly.

Image Viewer and Management

As the family photo album moves from print to digital, you will need an intuitive, easy-to-use interface for organizing, finding, and viewing your photos. *Image viewer and management software,* such as Broderbund's MediaManager and Microsoft Digital Image Library (see Figure 16-7), simplify the task of organizing images and enhance your viewing pleasure. They also give you the flexibility to print images in standard sizes, multiples (for example, 12 to a sheet), or contact sheets (thumbnails). If you don't have image management software, you can use the Photo Printing Wizard to accomplish the same print tasks (choose Print Pictures in the Windows Explorer Picture Tasks pane for the My Pictures folder).

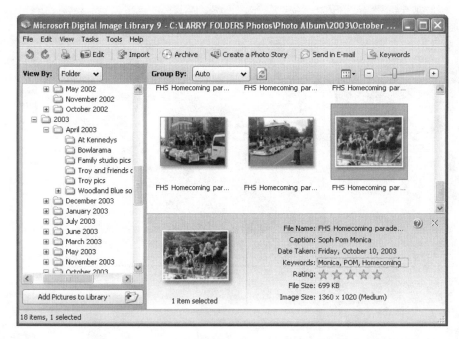

Figure 16-7   Image viewer and management software (Microsoft Digital Image Library)

Multimedia Software

To integrate your sight and sound resource materials, you can choose to use any one of a variety of multimedia software packages. Microsoft PowerPoint, which is *presentation software* that comes with most versions of Microsoft Office, is a popular multimedia software package for creating slide-show presentations. *Video editing software,* such as Windows Movie Maker, gives you everything you need to capture and edit video.

Presentation

Presentation software, such as PowerPoint, lets you create highly stylized images for group presentations. A good presentation might include some or all of the following: photo images, charts and graphs, original drawings, clip art, audio clips, full-motion video, and animation (see Figure 16-8). Chances are that the presentations you see in the classroom, at trade shows, during office meetings, and in many

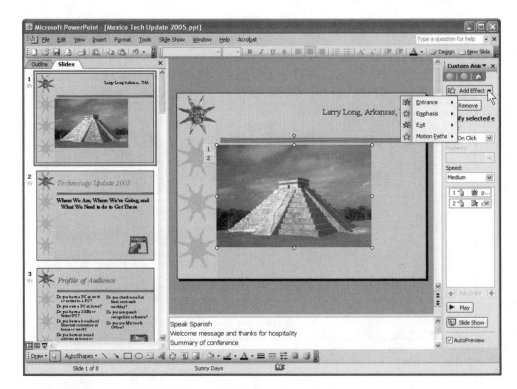

Figure 16-8   Presentation software (Microsoft PowerPoint)

other settings are created with PowerPoint. Presentation software makes it easy for you to give your audience a little candy for the eyes and ears with the judicious use of a variety of special effects. For example, you can fade out an image or play canned applause to make a point. You can animate text and objects to "fly" in from the perimeter of the screen.

Video Editing

A few years ago, video editing software and hardware were way too expensive for home use. Now, any modern PC has the power to push a relatively inexpensive consumer-oriented video editing package, such as Windows Movie Maker or Pinnacle Studio. Video editing software adds another dimension to what you can do with your digital camcorder. With this software, you can perform sophisticated video and audio editing on your video to create amazing results. Besides cutting and splicing, you can mix and dub sounds and apply a variety of special effects, such as slow-motion video and geometric scene transitions (see Figure 16-9).

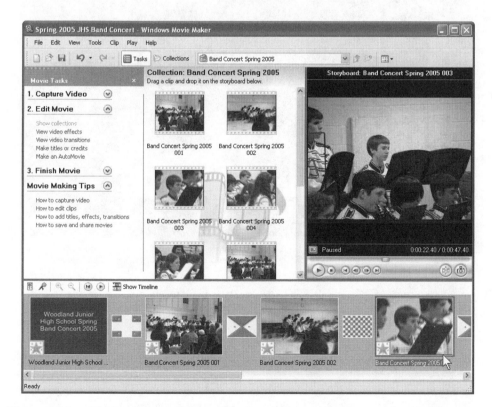

Figure 16-9   Video editing software (Windows Movie Maker)

Viewing and Playing Digital Media

To view or play multimedia content on your PC or content streaming down over the Net, you need *digital media player software.* Windows Media Player comes with Windows (see Figure 16-10), but you can use other programs, including RealPlayer, QuickTime, Roxio Player, and a half-dozen more. Generally, they will play whatever is in your music or video library on your hard disk or CD/DVD and any multimedia content from the Internet. This might include music, video, and pictures in a variety of formats, and DVD movies, CD audio, as well as mixed content. Most of the players offer easy access to downloadable music/video and Internet radio stations. Figure 16-10 shows a video of Astronaut Neil Armstrong taking the first step onto the Moon in 1969.

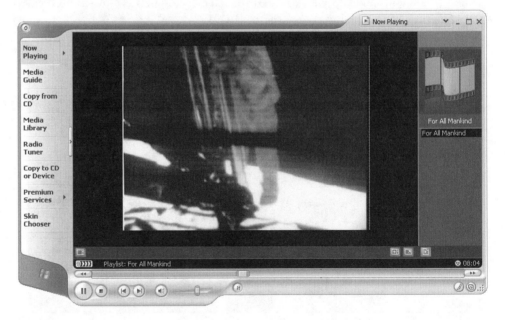

Figure 16-10   Digital media player software (Windows Media Player)

Burning Your Own CDs and DVDs

With their propensity to consume vast amounts of storage, multimedia projects are made to order for high-capacity CD/DVD media. This section is about using CD/DVD burners to create inexpensive CDs and DVDs that contain your personally created content, such as the video in Figure 16-9, the family photo album, and legal copies of intellectual material. Songs can be purchased from a number of Net sources, such as iTunes, for about a dollar apiece. Of course, high-capacity CD/DVD writeable and rewritable media work well for archiving and backup, too.

The typical modern PC has the capability to *burn* audio CDs and DVD movies. The term "burn" is derived from the fact that lasers record bits by darkening or "burning" the disc coating to encode a 0 bit or leaving the coating translucent to encode a 1. This ability to burn personal CDs and DVDs, combined with widespread broadband access and Internet file sharing, has prompted the music and film industries to proclaim that we have an international crisis in the theft of intellectual property. Hopefully, the illegal sharing of copyright content will subside as lawmakers, industry magnates, and personal computing enthusiasts work out the details for the legal Internet distribution of copyright products. In the interim, CD/DVD burners have many legal applications, too.

There are as many programs for burning CD/DVDs as there are for playing/viewing the various types of multimedia files. In any case, it is a three-step process:

1. Insert a blank CD-R or DVD-R into the appropriate disc drive. Windows should detect the blank disk and present you with several options, including Open Writable CD Folder Using Windows Explorer and, possibly, Windows Media Player. You may have other choices, as well, such as Roxio Easy CD and DVD Creator, Apple iTunes, or MusicMatch.

2. Select the files to be copied. If you are working with Windows Explorer, use the procedures described in Chapter 6, "Working with Files." For explicit instructions for burning a CD/DVD using Windows Explorer, search for **copy files to CD** in Windows Help and Support.

3. Copy/move the selected files to burn them to CD/DVD. What you do here can vary depending on the software you use. You may need to choose the "copy" or "burn" option to transfer the files to the disc. For some programs, burning a disc is as easy as dragging the selected files from Windows Explorer to the "burn" icon on the desktop.

Many people build and burn custom audio CDs by assembling songs from their personal CD library. According to the music industry, this is OK as long as the songs are for your personal use. In Figure 16-11, songs from a Peter, Paul, and Mary album are being burned to a custom CD with Windows Media Player.

Figure 16-11   Burning an audio CD (Windows Media Player)

No matter what program you use to burn CD/DVDs, the procedure usually is no more complicated than selecting the files and copying them to the disc media. However, a little caution should make the burning process run more smoothly. Make sure that you're using the proper media for your disc device. Check your disc to ensure that it has enough disc space for the selected files. Plan your burn projects during a period (a few minutes to 20 minutes) when you can close other applications and dedicate the PC to burning the disc. The latter is not an absolute requirement, but the more processor capacity you have available for the CD/DVD burn project, the better.

CHAPTER

17

PC-Based Gaming

Jettisoned into the air out of a newly formed crater by an unexpected blast, your character lands within the enemy camp. Dodging fire from all directions, your character continues to press onward into the opponent's territory. He hears the footsteps of an approaching foe from his rear right, giving him warning and enough time to hide and reload. Shots surround him as he grabs the flag and then runs through the portal to score for his team. Voices emerge from the speakers, carrying calls of congratulations and relief as a new game begins to load.

Gaming is not just a hobby or activity to gaming enthusiasts, it is an experience. And that's why gaming is the dominant application in many homes.

Introduction to Gaming

Do you play an occasional game of solitaire on your PC or are you an all-out gaming fanatic? It's not unusual to see more retail shelf space devoted to gaming software than to all other software combined. To fully understand gaming, consider what drives a person to game or not to game.

The Upside of Gaming

Why do people spend hours each week and, for some, each day at gaming? The obvious reason, of course, would be that it is "fun." It's fun and exciting to be able to snowboard down a mountain, work in teams to defeat an enemy, or cross increasingly difficult levels to solve a puzzle. Sometimes you are a winner and sometimes you aren't, but, as with any other game, the number of victories you have depends on your level of skill and experience.

Gaming software is designed so that gamers become immersed in a virtual reality that lets their imagination take control. This ability to escape from reality for a while is a big draw to the gaming community. Gaming lets you do what you want and be what you want. For example, you can become anything from a WWII flying ace to a shape-shifting cockroach.

The Downside of Gaming

Gaming can become a circle of activity. The more you game, the better you get and the more you want to play. Opponents of gaming claim that valuable time is wasted on gaming. Gaming proponents say that if you weigh the pros and cons, time spent on gaming can be positive, as long as it is done in moderation.

The hardware notwithstanding, the cost of the games themselves can be a significant expense. Games cost from $10 to $70 and accessories can add to the cost. It's not unreasonable for gamers to justify this expense by viewing gaming as an alternative to other hobbies (piano, tennis, snowboarding, astronomy, and so on).

The gaming community and Hollywood are giving people what they feel people want—sex and violence. More and more games are rated "Mature" (ratings are discussed later in this chapter). The idea of exposing children to uncontrolled violence is a serious concern to parents and to society in general.

Some people claim that gamers can develop a dependency on gaming that can lead them to seclusion from the outside world and cause them to lose their ability to cope with reality.

PC-Based Gaming vs. Console-Based Gaming

The most fundamental decision in gaming is whether to pursue *PC-based gaming* or *console-based gaming.* Let's look first at the pros and cons for PC-based gaming. The PC can be faster and offer better graphics and sound than console-based games. PCs offer greater variety in controllers, which is useful for people who like to use different control sets for their games. Game updates are easily downloaded on the Internet. On the con side, PCs are considerably more expensive, but, of course, they are multifunction devices that can do more than just gaming. Also, the PC market is more volatile, so the constantly changing technical specifications can make controllers obsolete more quickly.

The technical specs for console-based hardware, such as Xbox, GameCube, or Playstation 2, remain constant, making hardware and software obsolescence a trivial issue until a new console is released. The display for console hardware is the television, which does not offer near the resolution of a PC monitor. Generally, games for consoles are more expensive than PC-based games. Overall, PC-based gaming leads to more open-ended choices for gamers.

Gaming Genres

For the first decade of PC gaming, games could be easily classified into the eight *gaming genres* (categories) described in this section. This is still true for most games; however, the trend is to combine several genres in a single game. This makes it difficult to peg a game to a specific gaming genre. For example, in the James Bond 007 series of games, you'll find several genres represented, including action, adventure, racing, and simulation.

Action

Action games consist of intense encounters and rapid movement. This niche of gaming is characterized by *first person shooters (FPS),* where the view is of the character's line of sight. The character usually has a weapon of some sort and is involved in objective-based fighting. Quick reflexes and good keyboard, mouse, and console skills are required to excel in this category. Battlefield Vietnam by EA Sports is an example of an action game (see Figure 17-1). Choices in this game include type of soldier, weapons, and location maps, all related to the Vietnam conflict. Fighting games and games based on cartoon-type characters and movie franchises usually are in this action genre.

Figure 17-1   Action genre: Battlefield Vietnam™

Adventure

Adventure games usually overlap into other categories. Games are classified as "adventure" when the character must explore and travel over different worlds. In this genre, a character, controlled by the gamer, will have to run, leap, and climb to find entryways that allow progress to the next level. Along the way, they unlock mysteries so they can continue their journey and overcome evil obstacles to reach an objective. The novel-like story line plays an important role in adventure games, such as in the Indiana Jones series of games.

Strategy

More commonly referred to as *real-time strategy (RTS)* games, these games are for people who favor thoughtful finesse over raw mouse-clicking skills. In an RTS game, a base usually is established, and a civilization, an army, or an encampment emerges from the base. Objectives, such as "destroy the enemy base," are common for this gaming genre. Having a keen memory and a good multitasking brain is helpful in strategy games because the player often controls up to 50 game characters, called *units*. Figure 17-2 shows a scene from Warcraft III: The Frozen Throne, another chapter in the Warcraft saga by Blizzard Entertainment. In this game, players become leaders who must collect and use their resources wisely to overcome their opponent, sometimes alien invaders.

Figure 17-2   Strategy genre: The Frozen Throne™

Role Playing Game

The *role playing game (RPG)* allows the gamer to take on the role of a character that is at the epicenter of a fantasy that may involve war, betrayal, and faith. The gamer controls the actions and fate of the character. Generally, there is greater story line and character depth in these games. Usually, the character grows, learns, and/or improves throughout the game. This is the case in the Star Wars series of games.

RPG, action, adventure, and strategy games can be challenging. At times, it becomes very difficult to figure out how to complete a tricky maneuver or find the clue that opens the door to the next level. Gaming companies do provide assistance in the form of *strategy guides*, which can cost from $10 to $20. In addition, the Internet is a source for *cheat codes* (ways to enter "codes" to alter the game), tips, tricks, and other information about the various games.

Simulation

In simulation games, the gamer takes the role of someone or something else, for example a pilot in a simulated environment (see Figure 17-3). For example, in Flight Simulator 2004: A Century of Flight, you fly in an interactive 3-D "virtual" cockpit. You can view the scenery throughout the world from aloft and can even land at true-to-life airports. The Sims, developed by Electronic Arts, is another popular simulation game series that lets players micromanage the lives of the characters they create as they live and learn in a simulated city.

Figure 17-3   Simulation genre: Flight Simulator 2004: A Century of Flight

Sports

If the game's focus is on playing a sport, it's in the sport genre. Players become batters, quarterbacks, fishermen, and so on and swing the bat, throw the ball, or cast a line. In FIFA Soccer 2004 by EA Games, shown in Figure 17-4, you become one of the players and can play against other friends or against the computer. There is an amazingly realistic game for every popular sport, including tennis, golf, hockey, baseball, football, and so on.

Figure 17-4   Sports genre: FIFA Soccer 2004

Racing

In racing games, the gamer normally drives some kind of vehicle, including NASCAR autos, snowmobiles, motorcycles, spaceships, and just about anything else that can race. Driving with an attitude adds to the excitement in racing games.

Puzzle

In puzzle games, gamers rely more on their mind than their manual dexterity to overcome the challenges of the game. Want to play bridge but no one else is around? Try Sierra Entertainment's Hoyle® Card Games and have an instant partner and opponent (Figure 17-5). Many card games, such as bridge and hearts, and many traditional board games, such as chess, checkers, and Monopoly™, are now available as electronic games.

Figure 17-5   Puzzle genre: Hoyle® Card Games

Game Ratings

Computer games are rated by the Entertainment Software Rating Board (www.esrb.org). As described in the following table, ESRB ratings have two parts: *rating symbols* (on the front of the game box), which suggest age appropriateness for the game, and *content descriptors* (on the back of the game box), which indicate elements in a game that may have triggered a particular rating and/or may be of interest or concern.

	EC, Early Childhood	The content is suitable for persons ages 3 and older. Titles in this category contain no material that parents would find inappropriate.
	E, Everyone	The content is suitable for persons ages 6 and older. Titles in this category may contain minimal violence, some comic mischief, and/or mild language.
	T, Teen	The content is suitable for persons ages 13 and older. Titles in this category may contain violent content, mild or strong language, and/or suggestive themes.
	M, Mature	The content is suitable for persons ages 17 and older. Titles in this category may contain mature sexual themes, more intense violence, and/or strong language.
	AO, Adults Only	The content is suitable only for adults. Titles in this category may include graphic depictions of sex and/or violence. Adults Only products are not intended for persons under the age of 18.
	RP, Rating Pending	This indicates that the title has been submitted to the ESRB and is awaiting final rating.

Buying Gaming Software

The rules that apply to software in general don't always apply to gaming software. This section includes hints that will help you get the right games at a good price.

Check It Out First

Gamers aren't impulse buyers. Most tap the experiences of those who have used a particular game and, if possible, try it out, too. Reading reviews is the first step to making a good decision about investing in a game. Game reviews are pasted all over the Net at game-oriented sites, at e-tail sites, and in online forums (just search for "review *name of game*"). Reviews also are available in PC and gaming magazines and even at the retail stores. Gaming reviews are surprisingly consistent. The prevailing mood of the reviewers usually reflects the quality of the game.

If the reviews are positive, look at the trailers available at the gaming software vendor's web site. Often, you can download a demo version of the game or you can order it on CD. The demo, which lets you play a portion of the game, usually is the most important consideration in a gamer's decision.

System Requirements

Gaming software places a heavy demand on system resources, so you must take a game's system requirements seriously. The system requirements are on the box and are posted at the game's web site. These requirements usually reflect the bare minimum for enabling the game to run, which means that it will run with low-resolution graphics and minimal sound features. These system requirements for Flight Simulator 2004: A Century of Flight are representative:

- Windows PC platform: 2000/XP with 128MB RAM, 98/Me with 64MB RAM
- 450 MHz processor, minimum
- Available hard drive space of 1.8GB
- Video card: 8MB/3-D with DirectX 7.0 or later drivers
- Other: mouse, joystick/yoke, sound card, speakers/headphones
- Online/multiplayer: 56 Kbps modem or LAN

As a rule of thumb, if you wish to have the gaming experience intended by the designers, you need a PC with at least double the minimum RAM and processor requirements. The DirectX mentioned in the preceding requirements refers to Microsoft technology that enables high-performance graphics and sound for gaming and multimedia applications.

Finding and Purchasing Games

You can purchase gaming software at the usual places, retail stores and online. If you just can't wait for your game, the local retail store is the place to go. However, if you're not in a hurry, you will find a larger selection and, usually, better prices if you shop online.

Software Updates, Mods, and Expansions

After a game is released, fixes and new software add-ons are created to give the gamer a smoother and better gaming experience. Initial updates are *patches* that fix minor problems within the game. *Mods,* or *modifiers,* come next. The mods change the game to resemble something similar, but with different variables than the original game. For example, an online shooting game mod might give the shooter a no-gravity option. Finally, the game's creator releases *expansions.* Expansions usually are separately purchased software packages that "expand" the original game, often making it longer and/or more complex.

Gaming Hardware and Hardware Considerations

Gaming software is unique in that it has its own family of support hardware. Also, the complexity of the software places unusual demands on PC hardware resources.

Gaming Controllers

Having good support hardware can make a big difference in the quality of the gaming experience. If you're not a gamer, you might be surprised to learn that the mouse and the keyboard are among the mainline *gaming controllers.* The mouse can take on many functions, but often gamers use it to look around and select views. Gamers use the keyboard arrow keys to move objects in any direction and to speed up or slow down their movement. The keys on the keyboard can have a variety of functions based on how the gamer configures the game.

Other popular types of game controllers include the joystick, game pad, steering wheel, and flight yoke (see Figure 17-6). *Joysticks* can be used for anything from controlling third-person characters to flying a jet. Their versatility makes them a good pick for beginners. The *game pad,* which is similar to those of console gaming systems, doesn't offer the precision of joysticks, so some players may opt to use the keyboard rather than investing in a game pad. *Steering wheels* and *flight yokes* are for driving and flying games, respectively.

You can pay a little more and purchase any game controllers with *force feedback* capabilities. This means that they shake, push, and pull at your hand based on what is happening in the game. This tactile link lets you feel the bumps, the collision, and the blows, so you really are part of the action.

Gamepads are relatively inexpensive and can interface with any game. You don't have to have a joystick or flight yoke, but they do add realism to flying games, especially if they have force feedback. Flight yokes and pedals give you that realistic feel of switching on the engine, adjusting the flaps, and more. The same is true of steering wheels and driving games. A good strategy is to let your enjoyment of a particular game or gaming genre drive the need for controllers (and not the other way around).

The most widely accepted connection for game controllers is USB 2.0. USB 2.0 is much faster than the old game port, plus, it offers plug-and-play capabilities. *Plug-and-play* lets gamers switch, add, or remove controllers without shutting down the PC.

Joystick

Gamepad

Steering wheel and pedals

Flight yoke with quad engine controls

Figure 17-6 Game controllers

(Photos courtesy of Logitech and of CH Products [flight yoke])

Critical Hardware Components for Gaming

The basic PC components that have the greatest impact on the quality of the gaming experience are RAM, the video card, the processor, the sound card, and the speakers. In all cases, the bigger the numbers, the better the experience. These components are discussed in detail in Part One of the book and in this section as they relate to gaming.

Games are resource hogs and require a lot of RAM. If you are short on RAM, play can be halting and jerky. Different RAM technologies offer different speeds, but the quantity of RAM is what really matters. Table 17-1 shows the quality of the gaming experience relative to various PC tasks for common amounts of RAM. If you think more RAM would help, it's a relatively inexpensive and easy upgrade. Just make sure you purchase a type of RAM that is compatible with your motherboard.

General Capability	Amount of RAM	Gaming Experience
Windows and little else	128MB	Minimal
Standard individual applications such as word processing or Net browser	128–256MB	Substandard
Multiple open applications	256–384MB	OK
Light gaming and multimedia applications	384–512MB	Good
Heavy-duty gaming and multimedia applications	512MB or greater	WOW!

Table 17-1   RAM and the Gaming Experience

The video card is critical to having smooth-building graphics and good gaming. Onboard video, where the video function is built into the motherboard, is not nearly as effective as an AGP video card. A quality video (graphics) card allows the display of flawless detail and fluid motions. Graphics cards come with built-in RAM, usually 64MB, 128MB, or 256MB. If you are serious about gaming, get one with at least the 128MB.

Gamers assess processors relative to their FSB and speed. The *FSB*, or *front side bus*, is the speed between the processor and the motherboard. For modern gaming, 533 MHz FSB is acceptable, but 800 MHz FSB is better. Any processor speed around 2 GHz is acceptable, but 2.5 GHz or more is better.

The chopping of the helicopters, the roar of the NASCAR engines, and the clash of the swords—these are the sounds of gaming. Having a quality sound card that supports EAX® Advanced HD, a standard for high-performance audio, can add greater audio realism. For example, the sound of the helicopter follows its movement as it traverses the landscape. The better sound cards support 4.1, 5.1, and 6.1 surround sound. High-end cards support 7.1. The point one (.1) denotes subwoofer support and the larger number refers to the number of satellite speakers supported.

If you want to actually feel a shell exploding as you scramble up Omaha Beach, you'll want a quality set of speakers, at least 4.1. The satellite speakers add to the direction effect of the game. For example, with 2.1 speakers, a bullet coming from the front right traveling to the back right would sound only in the right speaker. In contrast, with 6.1 speakers, you can hear the bullet travel from the front to the rear.

Playing the Game

Gaming can be you against the computer, you against others on a local network, or you against others on the Internet, whether it is across town or on the other side of the world.

Singleplayer Locally Installed Games

Nearly all locally installed games, meaning those games installed on your PC, have a *singleplayer* feature. This is where you play against or with the computer. Singleplayer games generally have more in-depth missions than multiplayer games.

Multiplayer Locally Installed Games

In *multiplayer games,* the gamer plays with or against other players. These games span the spectrum from classical card games to action-packed shooters. They resemble singleplayer games, but may have less detail because of the limits of the connection speeds. Too much detail in a game can cause latency in response time or, as gamers call it, *lag.* Lag is not good when you're trying to block an opponent's blow to your head with a sword.

The two main ways players are linked when playing multiplayer games are via a PC network and via the Internet. Lag can be a problem when games are played over the Internet at dialup speeds. However, lag is never a problem when games are played over a network with direct high-speed connections between the PCs. Connections in a network are faster, but each person must have a computer in close proximity. Sometimes gamers have "LAN parties," where players bring their PCs to one location so they can enjoy higher connection speeds and personal camaraderie.

Most multiplayer gamers choose to game from their own home over the Internet. In Internet games, you can join a game, host a game, or just play on your own with the information on the Internet. For example, after installing Warcraft, you are given the choice to play locally or go to Battlenet.com on the Internet where you can join thousands of others playing the game.

Browser-Based Games on the Internet

An Internet browser allows you to access and play games that do not need to be installed on your system. To play these *browser-based games,* go to a web site, such as Shockwave.com, Yahoo.com, or MSN.com, and you'll be able to choose from a variety of singleplayer or multiplayer games. Although these can be insanely fun and addictive, they are not nearly as intricate or visually appealing as locally installed games. Browser-based games span the gaming genre with a variety that is mind boggling.

Gaming in Perspective

Many people are of the mindset that computer games are bad for children and adults. We won't resolve this argument anytime soon, but I invite skeptics to open their minds to a world that can stretch the imagination in so many ways. To be successful, gamers must develop winning strategies, play roles, compete with tenacity, remember everything, and understand the social dynamics of fellow gamers and entire societies. Of course, games are a proven parental ploy for getting their kids excited about computers. They do, however, have a way of mesmerizing, so, in the end, moderation and selective exposure are needed to keep gaming in perspective.

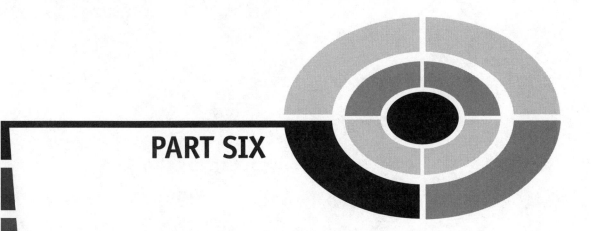

PART SIX

At Home: Networking and Telecommuting

Building a Home Network

Until a few years ago, networks of any kind were for businesses that could afford expensive communications gear and a salary for a network administrator. These expenses and the required technical expertise made home networks prohibitive—until now. The term "networking" may be a bit threatening to some users, but creating a home network is surprisingly easy to do. The moderate cost of home networking is easily justified with the savings you realize in resource sharing. This chapter demystifies the home network by showing you what it can do, introducing you to the options, and explaining how to set one up in your home.

Homes with more than one PC are becoming increasingly common. They may have one or more kids' PCs, a parents' PC, and, perhaps, a parent's notebook PC from the office. This spread of PCs throughout the house has prompted an explosion in home networking.

Networks and Networking

Whether in a business environment or in the home, a network is about sharing and communications between endpoints on the network, called *nodes.* The PCs in a home network and network printers are nodes that are linked physically by wires or by a wireless link.

Generally, networks are classified by their size and scope. A home network is a *local area network,* or *LAN,* which connects nodes in close proximity. The Internet is a *wide area network,* or *WAN,* which connects nodes in widely dispersed geographical areas. One of the primary reasons people install home networks is to share broadband Internet access among all PCs in the home. This means creating a link between the home LAN and the Internet WAN.

Personal computers can be linked in a number of ways to create a LAN, but the approach used most often for home networking is called *peer to peer,* or *P2P.* In a peer-to-peer network, the PCs are peers, or equals. On a network, only one PC or node can transfer information at any given time, so others must wait their turn, but only a few microseconds. The transfer of information between nodes is controlled by a *network access method* that is built into the logic of a *network adapter,* which is also called a *network interface card (NIC).* In the most widely used access method, *Ethernet,* each node must compete with the others for the right to send a message. The message is distributed over the entire network, but only the addressee node recognizes and accepts the message. Ethernet transmits messages at 10 Mbps, 100 Mbps (Fast Ethernet), or 1 Gbps (Gigabit Ethernet).

Although the Ethernet is the most common network access method for local area networking, both in the home and at the office, there are other ways to link PCs in a home network. PCs can even be linked directly with a USB cable.

What Can You Do with Home Networking?

With a home network, sister can print a document from a PC in the upstairs bedroom to a printer in the downstairs den—without leaving her chair. Dad can check stock quotes on the Internet while brother searches the Net for homework projects. Mom can take her notebook and work under a shade tree in the backyard and still be able to recall files from the desktop in the den and interface with her company's customer database. There are many good reasons to create a network in multi-PC homes, but these are the ones most often cited:

- *Share broadband Internet access.* Every PC on a home network can share a single always-on broadband link to the Internet. Users in a home network setting seldom access the Internet at exactly the same time, so more often than not, users can enjoy the full capacity of the broadband line.

- *Share files among PCs on the network.* At our house, files are continually passing between PCs. All of us use each other's PCs to back up our important files. One PC has a second hard drive that serves as a music and image server, so we all have ready access to our family's growing music collection and the ever-changing family photo album.
- *Enhance PC and network security.* The communications hardware associated with a home network provides another layer of protection from hackers, viruses, and cyberthieves.
- *Share printer and fax.* One printer or any all-in-one multifunction device (printer and fax) should be able to handle the printing needs for most families. My family has an all-in-one in the house, which is more than adequate for the printing needs of three heavy PC users. I have a printer in my office, but only because my home office is in an outbuilding 300 feet from the house.
- *Play multiplayer games.* At any given time, thousands of games are being played on the Internet…and you are invited to join. Or, you can have a gaming party in your house.
- *Share other resources.* You can share other resources, too, but you might have to move files and yourself between PCs in your home network. For example, you can scan images at one PC, and then transfer the resulting files to your PC. Or, if your PC does not have a CD burner, you can transfer the files to one that does.

Home Networking Technologies

Because home networking has a smorgasbord of options, home networks are like snowflakes—no two are alike. Your home, your personal computing hardware, and your personal preferences are unique, so it stands to reason that your home network will be one of a kind.

Connectivity: The Transmission Media

Your primary home networking decision centers on whether you want a wired network, a wireless network, or a network with a combination of these connectivity alternatives. Home network technologies, including connectivity options, are summarized in Table 18-1 and explained in the sections that follow.

	WIRED NETWORKS			WIRELESS NETWORKS
	Ethernet	**HomePNA**	**HomePlug**	**Wireless-B and -G**
Maximum speed (decreases as transmission distance increases)	10/100/1000 Mbps	10 Mbps (HPNA 2.0) 128 Mbps to 240 Mbps (HPNA 3.0)	14 Mbps	11 Mbps for Wireless-B 54 Mbps for Wireless-G
Operational speed	4 Mbps 55 Mbps 500–600 Mbps	5 Mbps 60–100 Mbps	6 Mbps	4–6 Mbps 15–20 Mbps
Effective range	328 feet	1000 feet	1000 feet	100–300 feet (indoors) Up to 1300 feet (outdoors)
Residential/home gateway	Includes a router for broadband Internet access and any or all of these features: cable/DSL modem, firewall, 2- to 6-port Ethernet switch, print server, and/or wireless access point (AP): $40–$250			
Network adapters: cost per PC (NICs for USB, PCI, and PC card)	A standard feature on most modern PCs: $15–$35	HPNA 2.0: $20–$50 HPNA 3.0: $40–$60	About $60–$100	About $50–$70
Other network hardware (if not built into home gateway)	Ethernet hub (half duplex) or Ethernet switch (full duplex): $40–$100			Access point (AP): $100–$150
Cost of hardware	Least expensive	Moderately priced	Moderately priced	Most expensive
Transmission media	Cat 5 or Cat 5e cabling with RJ-45 connectors	Standard telephone lines with RJ-11 connectors	AC electrical power lines	Wireless-B (802.11b) and Wireless-G (802.11g)
Cost of transmission media	Most expensive Cost: About $100 for Cat 5 for a typical three-PC network	Minimal (if existing telephone lines used)	Minimal (if existing power lines used)	Least expensive (no wires)
Cost of transmission media installation	Most expensive (new wiring)	Minimal (if existing telephone lines used)	Minimal (if existing power lines used)	Least expensive (no wires)

Table 18-1   Home Networking Technologies

	WIRED NETWORKS			WIRELESS NETWORKS
	Ethernet	HomePNA	HomePlug	Wireless-B and -G
Pros	High-speed, low-cost, reliable, and proven hardware technology; de facto standard in office LANs	Offers excellent balance among cost, ease of installation, and speed	Offers excellent balance among cost, ease of installation, and speed; multiple AC outlets in every room	Flexibility in location of nodes; notebook PCs have network portability; easy to install (no cables to buy and run); de facto standard in office wireless LANs
Cons	Running cables between rooms/floors can be cumbersome and expensive	Requires a telephone jack near each PC	Security (vulnerable to unauthorized access from immediate neighbors)	Signal speed affected by location and obstructions; possible interference from devices on same frequency band (Bluetooth devices, portable phones, etc.); security (vulnerable to unauthorized access)

Table 18-1   Home Networking Technologies *(continued)*

Wired Networking Technologies

If you choose to link the PCs in your home network with wires, the popular technologies are *Ethernet, HomePNA,* and *HomePlug.* The primary difference among these alternatives is that you will need to install cabling for Ethernet links, but existing telephone wires and electrical wiring provide the wiring structure for HomePNA and HomePlug connectivity, respectively. Each of these proven technologies has its advantages and disadvantages, which are summarized in Table 18-1.

Most modern PCs and home networking communications gear are set to handle Ethernet. The greatest challenge associated with installing Ethernet links is the installation of the wiring. The amount of effort and expense involved in the installation of Cat 5 (Category 5), Cat 5e, or Cat 6 cabling depends on where you place your PCs and the structure of your home. All of these cables have four twisted-pair wires within a common jacket terminated by Registered Jack–45 (RJ-45) connectors. The RJ-45 connectors are similar to and slightly larger than the RJ-11 connectors used with telephones, which have only two twisted pairs. The difference among the categories is performance, with performance and cost increasing from Cat 5 to Cat 5e to Cat 6. Most current wiring structures for Ethernet-based home networks are built with Cat 5 cable, which works well for 10 Mbps or 100 Mbps networks. However, an increasing number of home networks are using high-performance Cat 5e and Cat 6 cables that enable gigabit networks (1000 Mbps or 1 Gbps). The cost of the Cat 5 cabling for a representative three-PC home would be in the range of $50 to $150. Add a little extra for Cat 5e or Cat 6. Cat 5, Cat 5e, and Cat 6 cabling can be purchased in bulk or in a variety of premade lengths, with RJ-45 connectors on each end. You can save a little money if you purchase Cat 5 in bulk, but you will need a special crimping tool and some electrical savvy to attach the RJ-45 connectors to the cable.

If the installation of cabling takes place during new construction along with telephone and electrical wiring, a qualified electrician can install the cabling that terminates at RJ-45 wall jacks for about $50 a room. However, if the wires are to be installed in an existing house, the cost can be two to five times that amount per room, depending on how unobtrusive you wish to make the wiring and jacks. If all you wish to do is run a cable between adjacent rooms, you simply need to install and connect RJ-45 wall jacks on either side of the wall. However, if you plan widely dispersed PCs throughout the house, that's an entirely different and more complicated project.

Over the last 25 years my family and I have strung several thousand feet of cabling in two existing homes for our security system, phone/intercom system, home theater, and home network. We spent many hours contemplating how to get cables from one room to the next and sometimes just across the room. We used attics, narrow crawl spaces, soffits, windows, and external eves. We have run wires up and down walls, within ceiling rafters, and across cabinet shelves. The wiring process can be time-consuming and, frequently, difficult, even if you have some expertise in carpentry and electrical wiring. We chose to do all the wiring ourselves for two reasons. First, the cost of hiring a contractor was prohibitive. Second, finding a qualified contractor willing to do a "small" wiring job on a timely basis can be difficult.

If you don't mind the added expense and effort required to string Cat 5 wire between the nodes, Ethernet may be the best solution. Ethernet is relatively inexpensive and offers speeds at 10 Mbps and 100 Mbps, normally the latter, which is faster than the current HomePNA and HomePlug technologies. If you wish to plan for the future and higher speeds, you can upgrade to gigabit Ethernet cards that support Gigabit Ethernet at 1000 Mbps. With the trend toward Gigabit Ethernet, many new PCs already have integrated 10/100/1000 Ethernet cards.

The HomePNA (HPNA) technology enables home phoneline networking, where PCs are linked and communicate over the home's existing telephone wiring at speeds up to 10 Mbps. If the next generation of HomePNA, called HPNA 3.0, lives up to its promise of reliable speeds of 128 to 240 Mbps, the decision between Ethernet and home phoneline networking will be made more complex. The typical home is peppered with RJ-11 jacks and already has the wiring structure for an HPNA-based home network.

The HomePlug technology uses the AC power lines throughout the house as the transmission media in the network. HomePlug has a rated line capacity of 14 Mbps. Power outlets are everywhere in the typical house—in every room, the garage, and, often, at points outside the house—so the wiring structure for a HomePlug network already is intact.

Wireless Networking Technologies

Not too long ago, wireless was too slow and way too expensive for home networks. Not anymore. Wireless is emerging as a viable, if not the preferred, networking technology for all or a part of home networks. Wireless options let you position your desktop PCs in any room and give you the added flexibility of being able to take your notebooks anywhere in and around the house—to poolside, the deck, in bed, or anywhere within the range of the wireless link (see Table 18-1).

The most popular connectivity standards used for short-range wireless networking are the IEEE 802.11 communications standards. The *IEEE 802.11b* standard (*Wireless-B*) permits wireless transmission at 11 Mbps up to about 300 feet from an access point (up to 1300 feet outdoors). The *IEEE 802.11a* standard (*Wireless-A*) permits a transmission rate of 54 Mbps, but because the effective range can be less than 25 feet in a house, this standard is not a player in home networking. The *IEEE 802.11g* standard (*Wireless-G*) offers Wireless-A speeds with Wireless-B distances. The speeds and effective ranges of wireless alternatives are summarized in Table 18-1. The actual range of wireless transmission may vary markedly, depending on the quality of the wireless hardware and whether or not the point-to-point transmission is impeded with obstructions. The wood and wallboard construction in the typical home has relatively little impact on wireless transmission speeds. Water and metal, however, cause problems for wireless transmission.

Connectivity: The Hardware

In the business world, professional network administrators use a variety of communications devices, including routers, bridge routers (brouters), switches, hubs, concentrators, bridges, access points, network adapters, and other communications devices, to link PCs in local area networks. The LAN in the home, however, is on a smaller scale and is not nearly so complex. Home networking is vastly simplified because the good people who sell communications equipment have wrapped much of the necessary LAN functionality into a single unit called a *residential gateway* or *home gateway.*

Home networks are created by connecting the network adapters in the PCs via some type of data transmission medium, either wired or wireless. There are two viable ways to do this and enjoy shared Internet access. One approach is to designate one of the PCs as the *host PC*. In this network design, the host becomes the central point in the home network and handles the communications duties between the networked PCs and the Internet. For a number of reasons, one of which is that the host PC must be on and running to enable Internet Connection Sharing (ICS), I would highly recommend that you consider the second approach, which uses a multifunctional residential gateway. There is no comparison when it comes to convenience and overall network functionality. Using a residential gateway wins easily over the "computer as gateway" solution. For example, the residential gateway's firewall offers a greater degree of protection because the gateway has no files or folders and, therefore, can't be hacked to manipulate network PCs.

In the late 1990s, I chose and installed a host-based home network that used ICS. At that time, the necessary communications gear cost $1000 or more. Today, I can purchase the convenience and flexibility of a residential gateway for under $100. In my opinion, this relatively small investment for a residential gateway has one of the best, if not the best, paybacks in personal computing.

The advantage of not having to buy a residential gateway for a host-PC network is more than offset by the overwhelming advantages of building a network around a relatively inexpensive residential gateway. Moreover, it's likely that your DSL or cable broadband ISP is promoting the use of residential gateways for delivering Internet access to home networks. Indeed, the argument for residential gateways is so compelling that this approach is assumed throughout the remainder of the chapter. Those who currently have host-PC networks will likely switch to home gateways.

The Network Adapter

To set up a home network, you need a network adapter (an NIC) installed on each PC. The network adapter can be installed internally as a PCI card on desktop PCs and as a PC card on notebooks. Or, it can be an external unit connected via a USB cable. An *Ethernet adapter* is built in to most modern desktops and all notebooks. Other popular types of home network NICs are the *HomePlug powerline adapter,* the *HomePNA phoneline adapter,* and the *wireless adapter.* Table 18-1 provides a summary of costs, speeds, and advantages of these technologies, all of which can be mixed in a single home network.

The HomePlug adapter is usually an external or wallmount unit that links to the PC via an Ethernet or USB cable. In either case, you plug the unit into a normal AC power outlet just as you would any other appliance. Both electricity and data flow to the adapter.

The HomePNA adapter usually is a PCI card in a desktop or a USB external unit. In either case, a regular telephone wire with RJ-11 connectors links the adapter and the telephone wall jack. The phoneline adapters link PCs via the regular phone lines that run throughout the house. The phoneline home network adapters work on a different frequency than your voice conversations and your DSL broadband signal (which also is delivered over telephone lines), so you can use your telephone while data flows between your computers and over the Internet.

The other option is the wireless home networking adapter. Again, these can be internal or external devices. The internal wireless network adapter is a PCI card in desktops and a PC card on notebooks (see Figure 18-1). The wireless adapters, which link to an access point, eliminate the need for extra wiring and give you flexibility to move about and around the house if you're operating from a notebook PC. The transmission speeds for wireless home networking are comparable with HomePNA and HomePlug (see Table 18-1).

Figure 18-1   Wireless PCI adapter and wireless PC card

(Photo courtesy of U.S. Robotics)

Often, the residential gateway will have a USB port. If this is the case and two of the PCs to be networked are in the same room as the gateway, then one of them can be linked with a USB cable, thus eliminating the need for any special network adapters.

The Access Point

If you design a home network with at least one wireless link, you will need an *access point* or *AP*. The AP is a communications hub that enables the transceivers embedded in the wireless network adapters to link to the home network via short-range radio waves, like those used by cordless telephones. The AP can be a stand-alone unit or integrated into a residential gateway (see Figure 18-2). Under normal circumstances, a single AP is all that is needed to link the PCs in a home network.

Figure 18-2   Wireless-G cable modem residential gateway

(Photo courtesy of Cisco Systems, Inc.)

Having an AP is highly recommended for home networks with wireless communication, but the AP is not essential. PCs with wireless NICs can also communicate with each other in *ad hoc mode,* where devices communicate directly in a peer-to-peer manner. Mostly, ad hoc mode is used to form spontaneous networks. For example, any group of people with wireless NIC-equipped PCs can easily form an impromptu LAN using ad hoc mode.

Here are a few tips that can help you optimize the performance of your wireless connections:

- To minimize the possibility of eavesdropping, position the AP near the center of the network.
- Keep line-of-sight obstructions to a minimum.
- Avoid placing wireless components next to large objects, such as refrigerators or fireplaces.
- To minimize radio wave interference, position wireless components away from radios, TVs, microwave ovens, and cordless telephones.

The Residential/Home Gateway

The central component in a home network is a residential gateway, also called a home gateway. The residential gateway doesn't have a specific function; instead, it embodies a variety of functions needed to control a home network and interface with the Internet. Most home gateways include these features:

- **Router**   The router provides a link between the home network (a LAN) and the Internet (a WAN) such that the entire home network can share a single high-speed Internet connection. Sometimes the connectors on routers are labeled LAN and WAN.
- **Cable and/or DSL modem**   Although some home gateways may have both, most have either a cable modem or a DSL modem for broadband Internet access. Some home gateway products are designed to connect to the modem provided by your ISP.
- **Access point**   The AP works with wireless network adapters to enable wireless communications over the network. Gateways with wireless access normally have two, and possibly three, antennas. Most wireless gateways include a data encryption feature that protects transmissions within the network. Without encryption, wireless signals on the network are vulnerable to external interception. For example, someone could park in front of your house and tap into the Internet through your broadband access.
- **Ethernet switch**   The typical home gateway has a four-port Ethernet switch (four RJ-45 jacks) into which four Ethernet cables can be connected. Essentially, the switch enables the connection of PCs in a network. The switch interprets the destination address, perhaps the PC in the upstairs bedroom, and then forwards the information to the appropriate port. If you need more jacks, you can expand the network by connecting any Ethernet cable to an *Ethernet hub,* which provides more RJ-45 jacks (usually 4, 8, or 16). These inexpensive hubs can be daisy-chained at any point in the network to create as many Ethernet ports as you need. There is a four-hub limit for 10 Mbps networks. The limit is two and one for 100 Mbps and 1000 Mbps, respectively. You can pay a little more and get an intelligent *switching hub* that can expedite the flow of information through the network.
- **Firewall**   The convenience of always-on Internet comes with a price—the ever-present threat of Internet intruders. A built-in firewall keeps Net intruders and attackers out of your home network. Firewalls are described in Chapter 13, "Internet Security: Protecting Your PC."
- **USB port**   Residential gateways often have a USB port for connecting another PC to the network without the need for a network adapter.

The home gateway may include these optional features, as well:

- **Print server** This feature allows you to connect a USB printer directly to the network, thus eliminating the need for a PC to perform printer server duties. In a network without a print server, the PC that shares a printer must be on all of the time. The print server function is built into some high-end printers and all-in-one devices.
- **Modem** Some home gateways have a traditional dialup modem embedded into the unit. This feature is designed to provide backup Internet access if the broadband signal fails.
- **Parental control** This handy feature gives parents peace of mind by blocking Internet transmissions that contain selected keywords and by enforcing Internet access time limits.

The all-in-one residential gateway shown in Figure 18-2 is representative. It includes a cable modem, a router, a Wireless-G access point, a four-port Ethernet switch, a firewall, and a parental control feature. In casual conversation, people often refer to a multifunctional home gateway as a "router." The router, however, is just one of its functions.

Making Home Networking Decisions

Before you make any decisions about which network technologies to use in your home network, consider the following:

- *Your budget.* Each increment in convenience, speed, and flexibility has a cost.
- *Location and number of PCs.* Identify where you wish to place current and future PCs on the network. Wireless access must be part of your planning if you wish your notebook(s) to be portable and networked.
- *Your networking expertise.* Installing a home network is relatively straightforward; however, some solutions are more challenging than others. My advice is to keep it simple for your initial effort, and just keep the possibility of expansion in your mind during the planning days. Home networks are easily expanded to meet growing needs. If you choose the wired Ethernet option, carpentry and electrician skills may come in handy.
- *Expected growth.* Networks seem to have a life of their own, so think ahead. For example, you may wish to integrate your home entertainment system into the network and, perhaps, add a few internal and external security cameras.

After you have made the decision regarding nodes and technologies, you are ready to draw a schematic of your home network, noting all hardware and wiring.

The home diagramed in Figure 18-3 employs several network technologies and links a variety of devices. At the center of the home network is an all-in-one residential gateway with wired and wireless capabilities. The gateway accepts either DSL or cable Internet access. Two PCs have a wired Ethernet link directly to the residential gateway's Ethernet ports. A HomePNA bridge enables a phoneline link to any computer with a HomePNA network adapter (one in the example). An all-in-one multifunction device with print/fax capabilities is networked via a *wireless print server* so that it can be located any place in or around the house. RJ-45 wall jacks in the two downstairs rooms are connected with a Cat 5 Ethernet cable. An Ethernet cable connects one jack with the residential gateway and another cable connects to an Ethernet hub in the adjacent room. The hub provides expansion ports that can be used as needed, perhaps for a multiple-PC gaming session. A wireless game adapter permits Internet access for an Ethernet-ready game console. A wireless PDA is networked and online anywhere in and around the house. A notebook PC with a wireless PC card is linked and portable within the range of the home gateway and its access point. The upstairs printer is shared and available whenever its PC is turned on. The

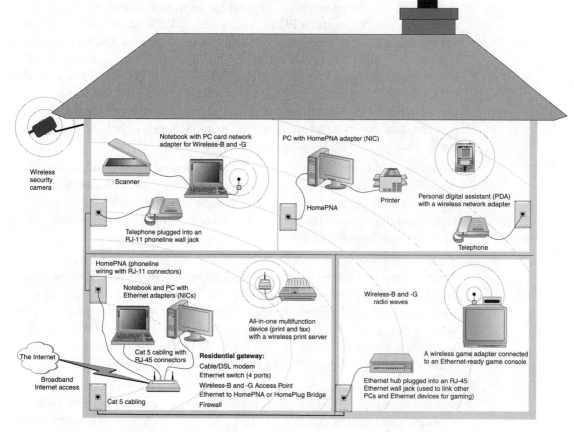

Figure 18-3   Home networking example

wireless security camera can be controlled and its images viewed from any networked PC. Figure 18-3 is an example of a mature home network; however, millions of home networks are growing rapidly to the level of this example and beyond.

Steps to Installing a Home Network

Once you have designed your home network for now and the foreseeable future and you have made the important decisions regarding what communications technologies and hardware to use in the network, you have completed the difficult work. The actual installation is the easy part. Follow these steps to create your own home network:

1. *Install the necessary wiring.* If any part of your network design involves running Ethernet Cat 5 or other types of wiring, do this first.

2. *Install network adapters (NICs).* Install the appropriate network adapters, either internal PCI cards or PC cards or external USB adapters. Follow the network adapter manufacturers' explicit instructions for installing the hardware and the adapters' driver software. The driver software enables the NIC to communicate with Windows. When you start your PC, Windows should detect the NIC and install the NIC driver software automatically. If it doesn't, the New Hardware Wizard will pop up and lead you through the installation process. You may need to insert an NIC manufacturer's CD-ROM containing the software or, possibly, your original Windows CD-ROM.

3. *Set up the residential gateway.* Set up the residential gateway according to manufacturer's instructions and link it to the first PC in the network. This will involve installing the software that came with the gateway. The software should guide you through the process of configuring the gateway, its firewall, and the first PC.

4. *Establish an Internet connection.* The residential gateway, with its broadband modem and router functions, provides the gateway to the Internet and enables Internet access sharing. The router function handles processing duties, so any PC on the network can be turned off or on without affecting Net sharing or the network. Your ISP will provide instructions on how to configure your system for Internet access. Some ISPs provide software that automatically configures your PC for Internet access and sharing.

5. *Set up other communications hardware.* Depending on your network design and the features built into the residential gateway, you may need to install other communication devices according to their manufacturers' instructions (Ethernet hubs/switches, wireless access points, and so on).

6. *Physically connect the PCs to the network.* This is where you plug in all of the cables to the residential gateway, PCs, network adapters, jacks, and switches/hubs.

7. *Set up network software.* When you turn on a networked PC for the first time as a network node, the Windows Network Setup Wizard should pop up and lead you through the setup procedure. To start this wizard, select Start | Control Panel | Network Connections | Network Setup Wizard (under Common Tasks). Do this for each PC. During this step you will give each PC a name (for example, office, den, and so on) and a description (for example, home office 4 GHz desktop) and configure the PC to run on the network and share the Internet.

8. *Share printer(s).* To share a printer that is connected to a PC on a home network, select Start | Control Panel | Printers and Faxes, and then right-click on the printer you wish to share. On the Sharing tab, click Share This Printer and give it a name. If other PCs are running different versions of Windows, you may need to click the Additional Drivers button and install other drivers. Some printers have built-in printer servers and can be connected directly to the network via an Ethernet or USB cable.

9. *Share disks and/or folders.* To share a disk with other networked PCs, click My Computer on the desktop of the PC you wish to share. Right-click on the disk you wish to share and choose Security and Sharing. On the Sharing tab, check Share This Folder on the Network and give it a name. Check Allow Network Users to Change My Files if you wish to allow others to save to this disk and modify its files. If you prefer not to share the entire disk, you can follow this same procedure to share a specific folder and its subfolders. Shared disks and folders are displayed under My Network Places in Windows Explorer.

For the price of an average printer and with a little effort, you can set up an efficient, time-saving, and money-saving LAN in your home. If you already have one, you might wish to consider upgrading to a higher speed and/or one with wireless capabilities. Over the next decade, our home networks will grow in scope and functionality. For example, our telephones, PDAs, MP3 players, automobile PCs, entertainment systems, home theaters, internal/external security cameras, and many other devices will ultimately fall under the home networking umbrella. This is just the ground floor of home networking.

19

Working @ Home

An increasing number of knowledge workers are asking themselves this question: "Why should I travel to the office when I can telecommute and be more productive?" Businesses are asking a related question: "How can I find and retain quality employees who want more flexibility in their lives?" Millions of knowledge workers have already answered this popular question: "Why don't I just work for myself—at home?" Working at home has emerged as one of the fastest growing and important applications for personal computing.

The Trend Toward Working at Home

One of the byproducts of the personal computing revolution is a clear trend toward more and more people working at home. A number of surveys confirm that the United States is experiencing a dramatic increase in the number of knowledge workers,

possibly as much as 40 percent of all workers, who work at home or telecommute at least part time.

People who work for a company but may "commute" to work via data communications are said to *telecommute* to work. For millions, like me, our home office is where we work so we aren't officially telecommuting. However, we routinely communicate and share ideas, reports, and so on over the Internet. The umbrella term used for teleworkers and self-employed people who use the tools of personal computing and the Internet to accomplish their jobs is *telework*.

I have been self-employed and working at home for almost 25 years, so I've seen all phases of the telework era. At the beginning of my work-at-home career, when I wasn't doing consulting, giving a speech, or teaching my once-a-week class at the university, I was in my home office at my computer preparing for outside work or writing a book. The only telework, though, was between my office and my wife's in the adjacent room. During the late 1970s and early 1980s, PCs were crude and limited, so we actually had a business minicomputer and several workstations on a network. All results of our work, including that which was electronic, were sent and received via air courier until the early 1990s. I was on a first-name basis with all the drivers, even the weekend subs.

Although I went online at the beginning of the Internet's public era, it offered relatively little value because so few people were connected and, if they were, the communication was at 12 Kbps on a good day (about 1 percent the speed of a typical broadband link). By the mid-1990s, the telework community was cruising along the Net at 56 Kbps and most companies had Internet access and, often, an Internet presence (a web site). The World Wide Web and user-friendly e-mail began the modern Internet era and, with it, a new era in the way people work and where they work.

Today, a typical telework day for me involves communication and sharing with colleagues in at least three different locations in the United States and, often, with people in other countries. Most of my personal communication and all of the results of my work are electronic.

Today's Internet/personal computing environment is very accommodating for telework. Millions of people already work at home or telecommute full time: writers, stockbrokers, financial planners, programmers, buyers, and graphic artists, to mention a few. A larger group is working at home at least one day a week, including physicians, engineers, certified public accountants, company presidents, lawyers, mayors, and plant managers. Even if the soothsayers are half right, the telework movement is on course to turn office tradition upside down.

Today's PCs can run circles around a 1960s mainframe computer that did all the processing for a large bank. Broadband Internet access to the worldwide Internet is universally available. Home networking is becoming commonplace. These and other factors, such as concerns about the environment, are fueling the growth of telework and *cottage industries,* where people work exclusively from their home offices.

Arguments for Working at Home

If you wish to be a teleworker but haven't approached the boss for fear of being thought of as less committed or being left out at promotion time, think again. There are plenty of good reasons for you to do telework and for your company to encourage it:

- *Increased productivity.* A stream of studies have shown that teleworkers are more productive at home than at the office, often by as much as 40 percent. Also, they work more hours, about two hours longer a day on average. For example, teleworkers at American Express handled 26 percent more calls and produced 43 percent more business than their office-based counterparts.
- *Better retention of employees.* Having the telework option attracts and helps to retain top talent. Now, literally millions of teleworkers are migrating to wherever their lifestyle criteria takes them—to smaller towns, warmer weather, their roots, nearer water, or the Rocky Mountains.
- *Improve employee morale.* Teleworkers cite improved morale and job satisfaction. AT&T encourages its employees to do telework on Tuesdays in an effort to support the lifestyle workers want.
- *Money savings on office space.* Various studies show that on average a teleworker saves the company about $6000 in annual facilities costs.
- *Money savings on commuting expenses.* Employees can save from $25 to $250 a week in fares, tolls, parking, gasoline, and automobile wear-and-tear costs.
- *Improved relations with family.* Teleworkers spend more time with or around their family. Employees can optimize the scheduling of their personal and work activities to achieve better balance at home. Telework demands a lot of planning and dialog between all family members, especially regarding childcare. Generally, attempting simultaneous telework and childcare is difficult, at best.
- *No commute.* The average commuter in a major metropolitan area spends the equivalent of one working day a week traveling to and from work, about ten work-weeks a year!
- *Less pollution.* In pilot programs in several metropolitan areas, the United States Department of Transportation (DOT) is offering significant incentives to encourage telecommuting to reduce traffic and pollution.

- *More comfortable and less expensive clothes.* Men willingly trade ties for T-shirts and women often prefer sneakers to heels.
- *Reduction of sick time.* Because teleworkers miss fewer days of work as a result of sickness, the company benefits in two ways—greater worker productivity and lower overall health-care-related costs. Generally, the telework environment is less stressful, and stress-related illnesses often are the reasons for missed work.
- *Impact of company disasters is less.* The telework community kept many companies afloat after the 9/11 crisis.

Arguments Against Working at Home

Telework is not the answer for all workers or companies. Many managers see telework as a win-win situation, but others feel that it causes resentment among office-bound colleagues and weakens corporate loyalty. The following are some arguments against working at home:

- *Office routine missing in telework.* There are knowledge workers who thrive on the office routine and prefer ready access to management. The office environment is their fuel for achievement.
- *Telework counter to some company philosophies.* The culture, function, and/or tradition at some companies just don't jive with telework.
- *Some jobs not appropriate for telework.* Bank tellers, elementary school teachers, and others whose job requirements demand daily face-to-face interaction must "go to work."
- *Limited personal interaction.* Telework does not permit "pressing of the flesh" and important nonverbal cues. Clearly, on-site work offers a level of personal interaction that simply is not possible with telework.
- *Can cause morale problems.* What about those at the office who, for whatever reason, do not have the option for telework?
- *Can complicate security issues.* Cyber and physical security are more manageable when people work at a central site.
- *Telework more difficult to manage.* Managers are forced to manage remotely and, often, must also prepare and enforce a different set of guidelines and policies for teleworkers.

Is Telework for You?

Working at home takes a special type of personality. The successful teleworker will have, at varying degrees, these personality characteristics:

- Self-motivated and does not require day-to-day management feedback
- Willing to work alone and does not require the company of colleagues to produce
- Able to maintain focus while thinking through, planning, and solving problems
- Able and willing to work out family conflicts with scheduling
- Self-disciplined and able to ignore the distractions of home
- Able to set work priorities and then honor them
- Able to adopt new approaches to communication with clients, bosses, and coworkers
- Able and willing to perform tasks that may be done by specialists in an office setting (for example, troubleshooting a PC)

The Workplace

First, you need a good location for your home office. These are the primary considerations for choosing a home office location: having a sufficient amount of space, having a separation between the office and the living areas, having a space that is physically secure, having ready access to the Internet and a telephone line, and having an ample number of electrical outlets and circuits. Some teleworkers share space in a seldom-used room, such as a guest bedroom. This will work, but telework is not compatible with the more popular rooms in the house.

The beauty of having a home office is that it can be custom-designed to fit your personality and work habits. In that regard, you may as well choose and/or create an aesthetically pleasing location, perhaps near a window with a view. Remember, this is the place where you will spend about a third of every working day.

To enjoy the full benefits of telework, I would suggest that you create an ergonomically designed workspace. An ergonomic workspace is one that employs the principles of human-factors engineering to ensure that your office is comfortable and gives you the best opportunity to be effective and efficient in your work. Here are

a few ergonomic hints regarding the chair, desk, and monitor that can help you avoid some of the health concerns often associated with long periods of personal computing:

- **Chair**   Select a chair with a lot of flexibility, one that can be adjusted to the size and contour of your body, including the lumbar area.
- **Desk**   Wraparound desks work well with PCs because both hardware and office materials can be positioned within arm's reach. An adjustable keyboard/mouse tray is a plus because your objective should be to maintain a 90-degree angle at the elbow with the forearm parallel to the floor.
- **Monitor**   Position the monitor at arm's length with its top at forehand level. To avoid glare, place the monitor to the side of any windows.

Companies that support telework recognize that teleworkers will occasionally need to spend a day at the company's office building. To meet this need, many organizations have implemented hoteling, an office space management concept. In *hoteling,* a pool of fully equipped offices is set aside for teleworkers and mobile workers. These offices are reserved by remote workers by the hour or day.

The Tools of Telework

The essential tools in a teleworker's toolkit include a middle- to high-end PC, a full range of peripheral devices, a good mix of software, and Internet access.

- **PC**   If you plan to bring your work home, bring home a quality PC. The unproductive wait periods resulting from slow processing can easily accumulate to in excess of an hour a day.
- **I/O devices**   A good all-in-one multifunction peripheral (print, scan, fax, and copy) should suffice for most home office settings. If you have unusually high-volume output requirements, you may need to purchase separate devices. Depending on the type of work you do, other peripheral devices may be required to meet specific needs.
- **Software**   In most situations, teleworkers should spend the extra money and get Windows XP Professional (versus the Home Edition). The expanded security and networking features will facilitate interaction with corporate server computers. Also, the typical teleworker can easily justify the extra expense associated with Microsoft Office 2003 Professional because it offers a full complement of productivity software. Of course, the Internet security software discussed in Chapter 13 is considered must-have software for a home office. These are the essentials, but your home office software portfolio would probably include other software to meet specific work requirements.

- **Internet access**   Broadband Internet access is desirable in a home office because a high-speed link can significantly reduce wait time. Less wait time means increased productivity.
- **Telephone**   Both the telephone and the fax in their present form may be obsolete in a few years, but for now, they remain integral elements for telework.

Backup and Recovery

If you wish to survive and thrive as a teleworker, you will need to adhere to rigorous system backup and recovery procedures (see Chapter 10, "Installation, Maintenance, and Troubleshooting," for more on system backup). Any modern PC will have the necessary hardware for creating backup for off-site storage—a CD-RW or a DVD±RW drive.

As an alternative or supplement to disc-based backup, I would recommend that you back up your files to another computer. If you have a home network, you can maintain backups of your files on other networked PCs. If you work for a company, the best approach is to upload backup files to your corporate server computer. If you are self-employed, you can take advantage of the personal storage space made available to you by your ISP, usually 5MB to 30MB.

Working Smart

The personal computer is the centerpiece of the home office, but it can be a serious diversion, too. If you plan to be a teleworker, you may need to visualize yourself in a controlled office setting, on occasion, lest you fall prey to a plethora of mostly PC-related diversions. For example, as a teleworker you might wish to adopt the e-mail policies of your company—basically, keep personal e-mail to a minimum. The sending and receiving of frivolous e-mail can eat up a work day in a hurry. A self-imposed limit on personal e-mail, instant messaging, and telephone calls is a central theme to successful telework.

The Internet stands in front of every teleworker with an intoxicating array of diversions: the latest movie reviews, the book value of your old car, the stats from last night's game, the latest MTV video, and much, much more. As a teleworker, you may not wish to impose a zero-tolerance policy on yourself, but you need to be ever-sensitive to the fact that nonbusiness cybersurfing is a productivity killer.

Some diversions are positive, such as the periodic minibreak. These minibreaks should involve looking away from your monitor and/or generally altering your body orientation for a few seconds. Just do whatever helps you to reenergize and refresh: make a fist, turn your head from side to side, twirl your arms, roll your shoulders, walk around your desk, wiggle your toes, or wrinkle your nose.

Perhaps the greatest challenge confronting the teleworker has nothing to do with personal computing or technology. It stands about six feet tall and weighs around 300 pounds—the refrigerator. The beckoning call of the fridge is one of the most frequently cited reasons teleworkers choose to return to the traditional office setting. As any teleworker will attest, it's tough to work within a few feet of all the goodies in the kitchen. If the lure of the food is unrelenting, you may as well give in, but only with healthy snacks and in moderation. The key to mind-over-fridge is good planning and a commitment to a healthy lifestyle, at least during your telework day. It's unrealistic to think you can maintain a kitchen devoid of less-than-healthy food, especially if you have kids, but you can keep your kitchen stocked with a variety of easily prepared, nutritionally balanced, and tasty snacks. In the end, hardware, software, and the Internet have less to do with having a successful and satisfying telework career than healthy eating. Bon appétit.

INDEX

INTERNATIONAL CONTACT INFORMATION

AUSTRALIA
McGraw-Hill Book Company
Australia Pty. Ltd.
TEL +61-2-9900-1800
FAX +61-2-9878-8881
http://www.mcgraw-hill.com.au
books-it_sydney@mcgraw-hill.com

CANADA
McGraw-Hill Ryerson Ltd.
TEL +905-430-5000
FAX +905-430-5020
http://www.mcgraw-hill.ca

**GREECE, MIDDLE EAST, & AFRICA
(Excluding South Africa)**
McGraw-Hill Hellas
TEL +30-210-6560-990
TEL +30-210-6560-993
TEL +30-210-6560-994
FAX +30-210-6545-525

MEXICO (Also serving Latin America)
McGraw-Hill Interamericana Editores
S.A. de C.V.
TEL +525-1500-5108
FAX +525-117-1589
http://www.mcgraw-hill.com.mx
carlos_ruiz@mcgraw-hill.com

SINGAPORE (Serving Asia)
McGraw-Hill Book Company
TEL +65-6863-1580
FAX +65-6862-3354
http://www.mcgraw-hill.com.sg
mghasia@mcgraw-hill.com

SOUTH AFRICA
McGraw-Hill South Africa
TEL +27-11-622-7512
FAX +27-11-622-9045
robyn_swanepoel@mcgraw-hill.com

SPAIN
McGraw-Hill/
Interamericana de España, S.A.U.
TEL +34-91-180-3000
FAX +34-91-372-8513
http://www.mcgraw-hill.es
professional@mcgraw-hill.es

**UNITED KINGDOM, NORTHERN,
EASTERN, & CENTRAL EUROPE**
McGraw-Hill Education Europe
TEL +44-1-628-502500
FAX +44-1-628-770224
http://www.mcgraw-hill.co.uk
emea_queries@mcgraw-hill.com

ALL OTHER INQUIRIES Contact:
McGraw-Hill/Osborne
TEL +1-510-420-7700
FAX +1-510-420-7703
http://www.osborne.com
omg_international@mcgraw-hill.com

Sound Off!

Visit us at **www.osborne.com/bookregistration** and let us know what you thought of this book. While you're online you'll have the opportunity to register for newsletters and special offers from McGraw-Hill/Osborne.

We want to hear from you!

Sneak Peek

Visit us today at **www.betabooks.com** and see what's coming from McGraw-Hill/Osborne tomorrow!

Based on the successful software paradigm, Bet@Books™ allows computing professionals to view partial and sometimes complete text versions of selected titles online. Bet@Books™ viewing is free, invites comments and feedback, and allows you to "test drive" books in progress on the subjects that interest you the most.